MENAGERIES IN BRITAIN
1100–2000

by

Christine E. Jackson

Pompey

The Old Lion who died in the Tower
Nov. 10. 1758. See the list of Deaths.

Menagery is a Place where they keep Animals
of several kinds for Curiosity
(Le Blond, *Gardening*)

Menageries: A collection of wild animals in cages or
enclosures especially one kept for exhibition as in
zoological gardens or a travelling show. Also the
place or building where they are kept.
(*Oxford English Dictionary*)

Aviary: A large cage, house or inclosure, in which
birds are kept.
(Mrs Delany, 1757)

Volary: A little place with the face of it wire.
(Margaret Calderwood, 1756)

Zoë —

Happy Christmas!
Here are a few more animals to
keep you company during the year!

With my love,

David

THE RAY SOCIETY

INSTITUTED 1844

This volume is 175 of the series.

LONDON

2014

ISBN 978-0-903874-45-8

Published 2014 by the Ray Society c/o The Natural History Museum, Cromwell Road, London, SW7 5BD, U.K.

Registered Charity Number: 208082

Sold by: Scion Publishing Ltd, Bloxham Mill, Barford Road, Bloxham, Oxfordshire, OX15 4FF, U.K.

Designed, typeset and printed by Henry Ling Ltd, The Dorset Press, 23 High East Street, Dorchester, DT1 1HD, U.K.

CONTENTS

Frontispiece: *A group of leopards* by Jacques-Laurent Agasse who painted them in Polito's menagerie in 1808. He listed them in his *Record book* on 5 November as 'life, size, canvas 5ft by 4ft'. The painting was bought by his friend and patron Lord Rivers. Sold in 1988, private collection.

INTRODUCTION

Lions, tigers, ostriches mammoths, leopards, leviathans, cockatrices, animals both fabulous and real, were just names and words to most Britons for centuries before one was seen in real life in this country. The nation was brought up on the Bible and spoke the language of the Bible. Consequently, they heard about these exotics from distant lands when they attended divine service. They learned that all these animals originally lived in harmony with man until this idyllic state became part of a lost paradise. The story of Noah and the animals going into the ark two by two, created a vivid mental picture of the animals, still peacefully coexisting, being rescued to populate the world after the flood. Stained glass windows and costly hand-painted bestiaries supplied the earliest glimpses of these rare species.

The sheer excitement and sense of wonder generated by the first view such people had of an elephant, a lion, or an ostrich, can hardly be imagined by us today. For centuries only kings could indulge such luxurious pleasures and even then, because of the expense, kings only owned one or two specimens which they might, or might not, share with their subjects. British royalty had a monopoly on captive foreign animals, frequently sent as presents from other kings and emperors, until the 17th century when their wealthiest subjects began to import them.

'Curiosities' were brought home by sailors and sold at the docks in London from the 1600s onwards. They were purchased by innkeepers and exhibited as an additional attraction and source of income. There anyone could go and gaze in wonder and experience a frisson of pleasure and fright in equal measure. It was not until the 18th century that travelling menageries, small at first and then increasing in size, began to show a mixed group of animals in the towns and villages across the country. These became large touring caravans in the 19th century and it was only then that the Biblical names of many animals took a physical shape, and others, not previously seen in Europe, stimulated the curiosity of scientists and the general public alike.

When science took a hand, the zoological gardens and parks were established and the travelling menageries died out. In the 20th century, they lingered on as side-shows when the circuses allowed the public to view the animals between performances. Gradually, the old idea of keeping animals purely for entertainment became unacceptable. Educational, scientific and finally conservation motives became the only admissible reason for retaining animals in captivity. Then, at the end of the 20th century, the aristocracy turned the purpose of keeping animals in their safari parks full circle back to entertainment for visitors, while claiming an additional educational intent. These changes in attitude, including attempts at acclimatisation of foreign animals, are followed as the story of keeping foreign species in Britain unfolds.

Whatever the method of showing animals used by kings, aristocrats, dealers and travelling showmen, it was the animals themselves, in their infinite variety and beauty, that were the source of deep pleasure and excitement for those who went to see them. They rarely failed to delight, surprise and amuse both their owners and visitors. Through their records of such visits, diaries and letters, in journals and books, we can share in their enjoyment.

Here we trace the presence of rare and strange animals in Britain from the beginning of the 12th century to the end of the 20th century. Over nine centuries, mammals and birds have added greatly to the sum of human happiness in this nation of 'animal-lovers'.

ROYAL MENAGERIES

Chapter 1

'We bid you find necessaries for our Lion'
1100–1603

The park of the medieval Palace of Woodstock, in Oxfordshire, was the site of the first recorded English royal menagerie. Henry I (reigned 1100–35), to whom this collection belonged, made Woodstock the favourite royal residence and took the wise precaution of enclosing the grounds with a stone wall 'seven miles in compass'. This wall had been built at the expense of the destruction of 'diverse villages, churches & chappels, and this was the first Parke in England'. A contemporary author, who apparently had seen the menagerie, wrote 'Wudestoc' was enclosed by Henry I 'with a wal, though not for deer, but all foreign wild beasts, such as lions, lepards, camels, linx's, which he procured abroad of other princes; amongst which more particularly, 'says William of Malmesbury, 'he kept a porcupine'. Porcupines, William claimed, were 'covered with sharp-pointed quills which they naturally shoot at the dogs which hunt them'. The veracity of this fable (first recounted by Pliny) was not put to the test, for Henry was very particular about his porcupine, a most unusual and valuable present sent to him by William of Montpellier. Henry also cherished a rare owl, another gift from the same donor. William of Malmesbury observed that Henry I was 'extremely fond of the wonders of distant countries, begging . . . from foreign Kings lions, lepards, Lynxes or camels – animals which England does not produce'.[1]

The Woodstock animals remained on the king's property for at least a century during which Henry II (1154–89) both maintained the animals there and kept a bear which he took with him wherever he travelled.[2] Foodstuffs were required in great quantity for the animals, so that when floods destroyed the usual supply from the surrounding fields of Oxfordshire in 1201, the hay 'ad nutrimentum ferarum' (for feeding the wild animals) had to be ordered and purchased from outside the county at the behest of King

Henry I owned a porcupine.
(Edward Topsell, *The historie of four-footed beasts and serpents.* 1607, tab. 456, woodcut)

John (1199–1216). In 1204 three ship-loads of animals were ordered from Normandy. It was probably at the instigation of King John that Londoners had a zoo in their midst and were given the pleasure of going to visit the King's lions and other animals in their own city. John Fitzhugh, Constable of the Tower of London in John's reign, was paid wages for the keepers of the lions in the years 1210–12. This is the first of a long list of wages for the keepers and items of expense for the animals in successive kings' accounts.[3]

The records of the payments to the lions' keepers, for their own wages and for food for the lions and other animals, recur infrequently in the records of state income and expenditure. These relate to the court, the king's palaces and estates, his armies and every other private or state transaction. Amid all the important and weighty matters detailing the running of the country, it is surprising to come across so trivial a matter as expenditure concerning the king's lions, leopards or bears and their keepers. These are to be found in the Pipe and Close Rolls (now printed and published). The Pipe Rolls were annual accounts of crown revenues sent by sheriffs to the exchequer, that were rolled round rods or pipes for storage and survive from 1130–1832. The Close Rolls were registered copies of private letters and documents that had been closed with a seal, also other copies written on sheets of parchment that were stitched together and stored rolled up.

Lion passant on 10p coin; three on a postage stamp; on the Royal Shield of England. These all show the lion *passant guardant* (in heraldic terms, a lion walking, three paws on the ground, the dexter fore-paw being elevated, looking forward and the tail displayed over the back.)

Henry III came to the throne in 1216 and reigned for 56 years. During this time he took great trouble to ensure that his collection of animals was well cared for. In 1235 he was sent a royal gift of three leopards (which later featured as part of the English King's coat of arms) by the Holy Roman Emperor Frederick II. It was an appropriate gift, but Henry did not quite know what to do with three leopards. He solved the problem by sending them to the same place to which his difficult or recalcitrant subjects were consigned; the three leopards were safely imprisoned within the Tower of London.[4]

Henry expressed great pleasure on receiving such a noble present and other princes, anxious to please or placate him, sent more animals as gifts. A camel and a lion followed the leopards. The lion occasioned a number of messages from the king to the Sheriffs of London, beginning with the command,

> 'We bid you to find necessaries for our lion and his keeper while they are in the Tower of London, and this shall be reckoned to you at the Exchequer'.[5]

This was followed by another note,

> 'We bid you to cause William, Keeper of our Lion, to have 14 shillings which he spent on buying chains and other things for the use of the same lion, and this shall be reckoned to you at the Exchequer'.

A different arrangement was made for the next arrival. A white (polar?) bear from Norway was ordered to be maintained at the expense of the Privy Purse at 4d a day (in 1251). The following year some curious additional expenses were incurred when the bear was found to need, 'one muzzle and one iron chain, to hold that bear without the water', plus, 'one long and strong cord to hold him when fishing in the River Thames'. Other accounts of the purchasing of the strong cord suggested that it was to enable the bear to wash himself in the river, rather than to catch his own meal, but whichever operation the bear performed, one wonders what exactly his keeper was doing on the bank at the other end of the strong cord.[6]

Henry III's menagerie kept growing in size until the accommodation at the Tower became cramped. The situation was further aggravated in 1255 when he had an

THE TOWER. *(From a Survey made in 1597 by W. Haiward and J. Gascoyne.)*

A Middle Tower.   B. Tower at the Gate.   C. Bell Tower.   D. Beauchamp Tower.   E. Devilin Tower.   F. Flint Tower.   G. Bowyer Tower.   H. Brick Tower.   I. Martin Tower.   K. Constable Tower.   L. Broad Arrow Tower.   M. Salt Tower.   N. Well Tower.   O. Tower leading to Iron Gate.   P. Tower above Iron Gate.   Q. Cradle Tower.   R. Lantern Tower.   S. Hall Tower.   T. Bloody Tower.   V. St. Thomas's Tower.   W. Caesar's, or White Tower.   X. Cole Harbour.   Y. Wardrobe Tower.   A B. House at Water Gate, called the Ram's Head.   A H. End of Tower Street.

elephant sent to him by King Louis IX of France. Henry had been actively engaged at the Tower, strengthening its defences and reconstructing his own palace within the walls. In February 1255 he commanded a new building to be erected, in matching brick, at the west end of the Tower,

> 'The King to the Sheriffs of London greeting. We command you, that of the Farm of our City ye cause (without delay) to be built at our Tower of London one house of forty feet long and twenty feet deep, for our Elephant'.

He added that the building should be 'made in such a fashion and of such strength as to be fit for other uses when required'. The Elephant House was partitioned into sections so that other mammals could be accommodated, including those still living at Woodstock. From now on, all of the menagerie was to be kept in London and the public allowed to visit and admire the Royal animals.[7]

The elephant caused a great stir for it is doubtful whether an elephant had been seen in this country since the time of the Romans. This specimen was brought from Wissant, a French village on the Strait of Dover near Cap Griz-Nez. It was landed at Sandwich and then taken by water up the Thames to London. Matthew Paris, the historian, said that 'the public flocked together to see this novel sight' and another author went further, stating that citizens from all over the country crowded to see it. On 11 October 1256 the King commanded the Sheriffs 'to find for the said elephant and his keeper such necessaries as should be reasonably needful'. Though the expense was to be met out of the revenues from the King's Fee Farm (an annual rent paid by Chartered Boroughs to the crown in the Middle Ages), the responsibility for feeding the elephant had fallen on the hapless Sheriffs, and they, if no-one else, must have been greatly relieved when the elephant died in 1258 and they paid the last bill for its burial in the grounds of the Tower.[7]

However, the Elephant House remained, placed between the Bulwark and the Middle Tower, that was housing other animals. It was a semi-circular Barbican almost completely surrounded by the water of the moat and, after the demise of the elephant, it became known as the Lion Tower. The keepers were also lodged there. This tower survived until the 17th century when it was pulled down.

The semi-circle of dens within the Lion Tower can be seen in the bottom left-hand corner across the moat from Thames Street. Survey of the Tower, 1597. (G. W. Thornbury and E. Walford, *Old and new London*)

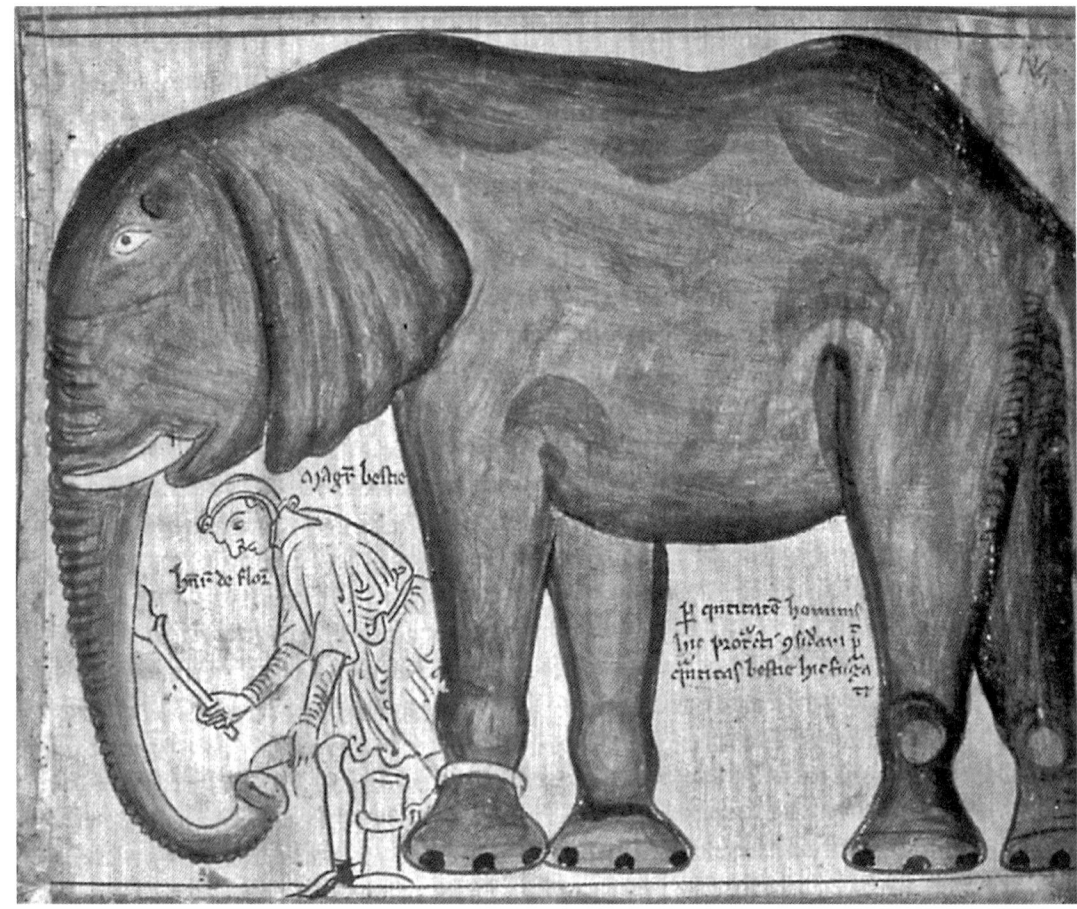

ajagr belhe

lyni: de floz

Edward I (1272–1307) succeeded Henry III and so approved of his predecessor's work at the Tower of London, that he commanded his Treasurer and Chamberlain to use certain sums of money to finish work on the ditch or moat then 'newly made about the said Bulwark, now called the Lion Tower, so called for the lions and other wild Beasts lodged therein by the king's command . . .'. Edward also built the stone causeway which crossed a small outer moat and led to the semi-circular Lion Tower. Today, this causeway is used as the modern entrance to the Tower, the present ticket office being on the site of the original Lion Tower.[8]

Edward II (1307–27) issued more orders regarding his royal beasts and their keepers. As usual, the orders went to the Sheriffs of London, while the money was taken from the

The elephant belonging to Henry III, with its keeper, drawn for Matthew Paris in 1255. The inscription between the elephant's legs states that the animal is correctly drawn in relation to the size of the man, Henricus de Flor. (Corpus Christi College, CCC MS16, folio IVa)

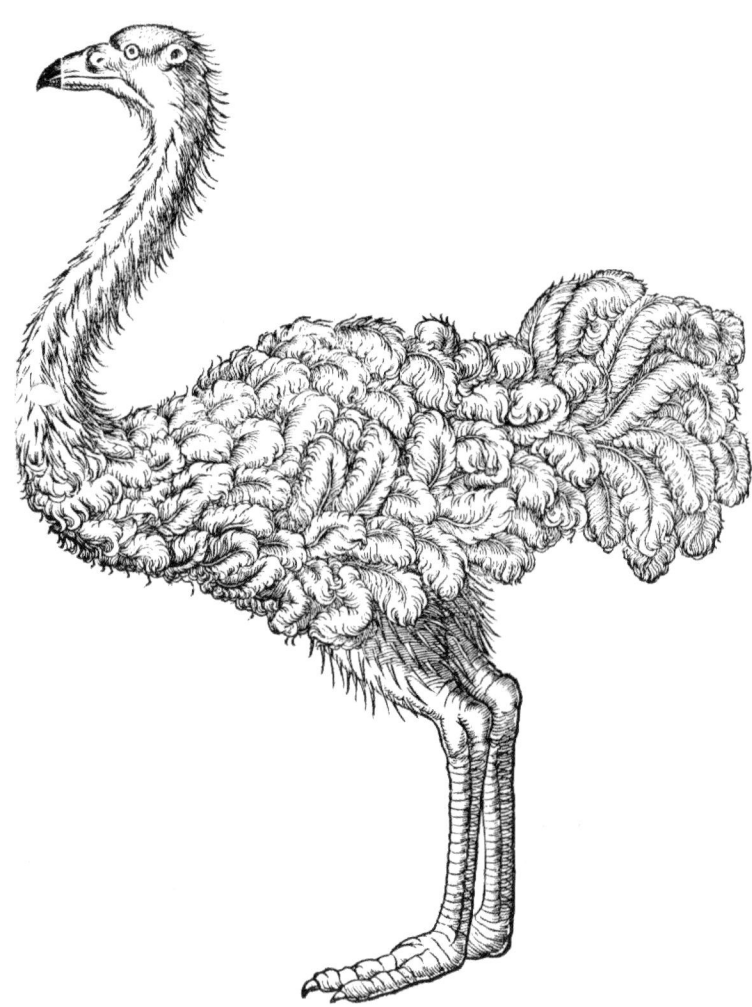

An ostrich. (C. Gesner, *Icones avium omnium*, 1560)

King's City Fee-Farm. In 1313 the lion was fed a quarter of a sheep daily and three half pence were given to his keeper Peter Fabre of Montpellier. In 1317 sixpence was allotted to the King's leopard and the keeper received the same wage as the 'lion-minder'. There were still both lions and leopards present in 1339 when 3 shillings and 1 penny was received daily for the animals, but the keeper's wages had risen to 12 pence a day. The office of Keeper of the Lions and other wild beasts in the Tower, at later periods, was granted by letters patent to some member of the nobility, but at this date the post was bestowed on a servant in the favour of the King. When these sums were carefully laid down for the animals and keepers by Edward II, the human prisoners in the Tower were allowed only one penny a day for their sustenance.[9]

There were similar references to the King's leopards, lions, bears and other mammals during the 50 years' reign of Edward III (1327–77), and another kind of animal was acquired when '2 catt lions' (or wild cats of some kind other than lions and leopards) were placed in the custody of Robert Bowre/Bowyer.[10]

Richard II (1377–99) owned two different groups of animals. He made sure the lions in the Tower were comfortable and well looked after by appointing John Evesham, one of his valets, as their keeper. Evesham took over the job from Robert Bowyer in 1382. Richard II was greatly attached to Windsor Park and delighted to visit a herd of ostriches there which, since 1380, had been cared for by a man called Jack Sparrow. Perhaps the idea of putting a sparrow in charge of ostriches appealed to the King's sense of humour. It might have been the first time a subject rejoicing in a bird-name for his surname was appointed guardian of the Royal Menagerie, but it was not to be the last.[11]

Richard I had brought a herd of black and white goats back from his crusades in the late 12th century. In the 1390s, Richard II presented his host at Blithfield Hall in Staffordshire with the royal herd of goats after a successful hunting party. His host was Sir John Bagot and the Bagot Goats, as they became known, formed part of the family crest. The goats remained semi-wild, in Bagot's Park, until the late 1970s when they were rounded up and presented to the Rare Breeds Survival Trust.

Unfortunately, during the reign of Henry IV (1399–1413), there is a gap in the history of the lions of the Tower. That Henry was interested in animals is indicated by his having brought over a leopard that he acquired in Cyprus. There is a gap in the story of the royal menageries during the reign of Henry V (1413–22). Then came a troubled period in the reign of Henry VI who alternated on the throne with Edward IV as the ebb and flow of the Wars of the Roses favoured first the Lancastrians and then the Yorkists. Surprisingly, the Tower menagerie not only survived, but flourished, during most of that time, although when Henry VI ascended the throne in 1422 he was probably not very interested in the animals. William Kent recorded that by 1436 an unprecedented absence of lions in the menagerie occurred,

BAGOT

Bagot was created a baronet 31 May 1627. His arms are 'Erm. two chevronels azure', and crest, 'Out of ducal coronet, a goat's head argent attired or', with supporters, 'Two goats argent attired or'.

'There deyde all the lyons that were in the Tour of London, the which was nought sen in no mannys tyme before out of mynde'.

A few years after this, Henry started to take an interest in animals and the French writer, Loisel, tells us the reason for this. In 1445 he married a French princess, Margaret, the daughter of René, Count of Anjou. René owned a large and famous menagerie in France. Young Margaret, who was only sixteen years old and reputedly very fond of animals, arrived at the Abbey of Tichfield, Hampshire, in preparation for her wedding on 22 May 1445. A courtier decided that no more appropriate wedding gift could be found for her than a lion. Margaret was delighted with her present and it was sent off to the Tower, where the menagerie was revitalised and reorganised. From that time onwards the post of Keeper of the Lions became one of the more important in the English court and was usually filled by someone of distinction. Henry VI gave the post to Robert Mansfield, Esquire, Marshal of his hall and subsequently to Thomas Rookes, his dapifer or steward at table. Robert Mansfield was allowed 5 pence a day, an apartment for himself and 6 pence a day for the maintenance of every lion and leopard, perhaps the only animals in residence since the time of Richard II.

During the War of the Roses between Yorkists and Lancastrians, Londoners were Yorkist and the Yorkist King, Edward IV, who ruled 1461–70 and again 1471–83, was their choice of king. He gave the office of Keeper of the Lions to Ralph Hastings, Esquire, for life. Edward prudently spent part of his reign fortifying the Tower. He built a new tower that quickly acquired the name of Lion Tower from its use when he removed the lions from their old quarters and installed them in a new home. Their dens were built in a semi-circle, with bars to each den which easily admitted the sticks and other implements used by the public to prod the animals into activity. The bars also allowed the animals' huge paws to strike back at their tormentors, as safety precautions for both humans and mammals were minimal. This new tower remained the site of the Tower menagerie until it was disbanded in 1834–35 in the reign of William IV.[12]

Richard III only reigned for two years, from 1483–45, but during this short space of time he conferred on Sir Robert

The Lion Tower in the Tower Menagerie, 1779. The semi-circle of dens round a yard was built c.1480 and remained the 'Lion Tower' until 1835. The two-storeyed cages allowed the animals to climb into an upper room.

Brackenbury, the Lieutenant of the Tower, the office of Keeper of the Lions. He also appointed a separate keeper for his bears and bulls, but these animals were for his sport rather than a part of the menagerie. The keeper of bears and bulls was frequently a different person from the keeper of the lions, since bulls, bears, and cocks, although also kept within the precincts of the Tower, were for baiting.

Another troubled period ensued, with a quick succession of monarchs who spent all their time and energies retaining the throne. The Lancastrian Henry VII at last brought peace and stability by astutely marrying Elizabeth of York in 1486, soon after his succession, so uniting the houses of Lancaster and York. This peaceful interlude lasted throughout his reign from 1485 until 1509 and immediately on succeeding to the crown he granted the office of Constable of the Tower, together with that of Keeper of the Lions, to the exalted personage of John de Vere, 13th Earl of Oxford, with a salary of 12 pence per day and sixpence for each bear. The most interesting menagerie imports to England in Henry VII's reign were exotic parrots. They were first taken to London towards the end of his reign and were exhibited as objects of great curiosity. Voyagers to Newfoundland brought back a hawk and an eagle and 'cats of the mountain' for Henry.[13]

Henry VII owned a parrot that he kept in a room of the Palace at Westminster, overlooking the Thames. The parrot learned many phrases from the boatmen and passengers on the river and frequently repeated them. One day, the parrot fell into the water and immediately called out, 'a boat, twenty pounds for a boat!' A waterman soon took it up and, restoring it to the King, demanded the reward promised by the parrot. Henry, with his usual parsimony, refused to pay that large sum. He agreed, however, that the parrot should decide between him and the boatman and asked the parrot how much the man should be paid. The parrot, in the true spirit of its master, immediately exclaimed, 'Give the knave a groat' (an English silver coin then worth four pence).[14]

Henry VII accepted some marmosets from Magdalen College, Oxford, in 1494. He presented the college with a 'she-bear' described as 'an extraordinary present' in 1504. This college has a small menagerie to this day, but houses gentler creatures.[15]

Henry VIII's activities were many and diverse, compounded of the usual royal mixture of carefully preserving some animals and enthusiastically hunting others. His menagerie was augmented by new lodgers and he also tried to establish some new species of birds in the wild state. Loisel said that he attempted to acclimatise turkey-cocks and red-legged partridges on his estates.

The most significant action taken for animals by Henry VIII, however, was to secure the site of a future wild-life reserve in central London. St James's Fields was a well-wooded, marshy area near Westminster, owned by Eton College, with a large pond called Cowfold Pool. There was also a hospice for 'fourteen poor sisters' who farmed about 160 acres of this land. Henry took great exception to their miserable dwelling house and farming activities within his view from Westminster. He got possession of this land by exchanging it for some he owned in East Anglia and then added to it another hundred acres or so from the Abbey and Convent of Westminster in 1532, thereby becoming the owner of the extensive Westminster Parklands. About 1536 the newly acquired land was surrounded by a brick wall and so became a preserve for wild animals (i.e. deer) and waterfowl. The sheet of water in the centre became known as Rosamond's Pond and the parklands were improved and made into the very pleasant royal park of St James's by Henry's descendants. Inside the park, the palace of St James's was built and is still the official headquarters of the Crown today.[16]

Henry had some natural history treasures locked away at Windsor Castle. After his death these were shown to visitors as curios. In 1599 a German tourist called Thomas Platter went to see the royal castle and wrote that,

> 'Near the Chambre de la Garde Robe in a smaller chamber we were shown a chest containing numerous very richly fashioned, worked and embroidered royal cushions, and in a lower drawer of the same chest was a longish case and in it a whole bird of paradise, which they took out for us: its back was pale yellow, and both sides were chestnut brown, all round the beak however, which was very hooked, was green. The whole bird with its tail feathers measured three of my spans in length, had very fine feathers soft as silk, & two little black thongs four spans long which it uses like claws to hook itself to trees'.

The species appears to be the red bird of paradise. The first known birds of paradise to be taken to Europe were native-dried skins, sent to the King of Spain by the ruler of Botjan (one of the Molucca Islands), on board the Portuguese navigator Magellan's *Victoria* in 1522. The Spaniards thought them to be birds from paradise rather than from New Guinea and Papuan forests and that name has been used ever since. Platter also noted,

> 'In a lower drawer of said chest lay also a natural unicorn's horn weighing twenty pounds, and one span taller than I. I could almost compass its circumference with one thumb and forefinger. In the region which seems to have been embedded two spans into the head, it was hollow and contained a nerve. They told us that Henry VIII had received the unicorn from Arabia and had valued it highly'.

In the 1532 Calendar of State Papers, among notes about the King's New Year gifts, there was 'a beast called a civet'. Later spelled sivet and zibet, these animals are a species of the mongoose family that come from tropical Africa and India. The oily musk from their perianal glands is used by the perfume industry both for its odour and ability to enhance other aromatic compounds.[17]

Henry had an entirely different kind of menagerie at Hampton Court, that was odourless, silent and static. The only maintenance required of the keeper of the king's carved wooden figures of beasts was to keep them painted and gilded. They sat on the top of posts set everywhere about the

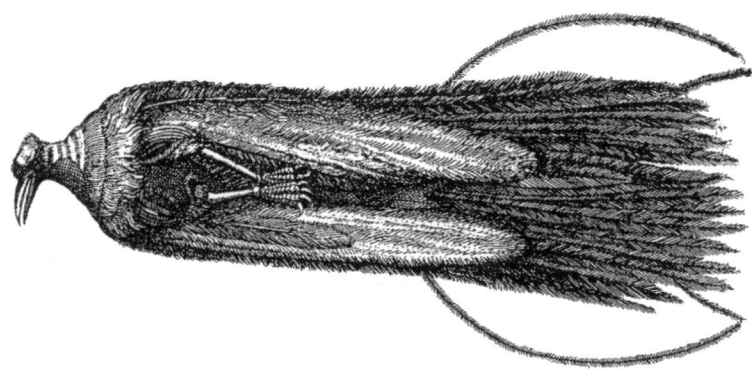

Henry VIII had a bird of paradise. Henry Vlll's bird, laid in its box, would look like the image from Ray & Willughby, *Ornithologiae libri tres*, 1676.

Henry's bird of paradise was probably the species red bird of paradise, *Paradisea rubra*. Jacques Barraband (1768–1809) painted this watercolour in 1800.

In the Calendar of State Papers, Henry VIII, 1532, vol. V: 329, among the New Year's Gifts was 'a beast called a civet.' (Thomas Bewick, *A History of quadrupeds*)

gardens. Edward More of Kingston was paid twenty shillings apiece for carving 159 of them. In one small enclosed garden alone (the 'pond garden' now the 'Privy Garden') there were '11 harts, 13 lions, 16 greyhounds, 10 hinds, 17 dragons, 9 bulls, 13 antelopes, 15 griffins, 19 leberdes, 11 yallys, 9 rams, and the lion on top of the mount'. Henry also had 'white bears, all of stone upon their curious bases'. The best his subjects could do in their own gardens, to emulate this fabulous display, was to have their trees clipped to form a menagerie of topiary birds and mammals.[18]

A plan of Westminster, drawn up in the reign of Elizabeth I by Norden and dated 1593, shows a large circular pond at the western end of the park with rivulets flowing from it. This was Rosamond's Pond. The remainder of the park was open grass with avenues and an orchard near the palace's Privy Garden. Deer were kept in the park and waterfowl collected on the pond in sufficient numbers to warrant the appointment of a 'Keeper of the Ponds in the Park of Westminster' in 1572. A German visitor, Paul Hentzner, noted that there was 'great plenty of Deer' in 1598 and Platter added that in the following year these fallow deer had 'many white ones amongst them'.[19]

Queen Elizabeth I (1558–1603) also took an interest in her Tower Menagerie and was put to some expense by its upkeep. The Gill family, Thomas and then Ralph, began their long association with the menagerie in her reign and were keepers of the lions and leopards, being allotted a small sum extra 'for burying them when they shall die', in 1586.[20] The German visitor Platter found 'all variety of creatures' in the Tower, including 3 lionesses, one lion of great age called Edward VI (from his having been born in his reign), a tyger, a lynx, a wolf excessively old', besides a porcupine and an eagle. 'All these creatures are kept in a remote place, filled up for the purpose with wooden lattices at the Queen's expence'.[21] These wooden cages do not sound very safe, either for keeping the lions enclosed, or for the public. Platter noted with alarm that 'a lion might have caught one of the party's servants, for it could get its claws through the bars of the cage in which they are fed'. When a lioness was born there during her reign, it was christened Elizabeth as custom demanded. Elizabeth the lioness died during the time of the Queen's last illness, giving rise to the legend that the lion in the Tower that bore the monarch's name, died when the monarch died.

Queen Elizabeth spent a lot on her menagerie. In one year alone the bill came to £36/14/6d for her animals, not accounting for the cost of maintaining the Indian elephant that she later received as a gift from Henry IV of France. She also employed three Keepers of the Bears to whom she paid between £12 and £15 per annum for their care. She also had some prize bulls, cocks and mastiffs, for sporting activities at the Tower. Since Elizabeth is known to have been extremely careful with money, it is clear that she was interested in maintaining a varied collection of animals, otherwise she would not have tolerated this kind of expenditure on their upkeep. However, she did not buy animals herself, preferring to graciously accept them as gifts. Jeremy Woodward complained to her Privy Council that she had refused to purchase two camels he had brought from Germany and he begged to be allowed either to sell them to someone else or to make show of them throughout the realm in order to recoup his expenses.[22] The Queen's subjects were eager to see foreign animals and they went to stare at any curiosities in taverns or gardens, or on the village green. Such early examples of animal shows usually only consisted of one very rare animal, but they aroused great curiosity and interest in the public at large.

Canaries were first seen in England in Elizabeth's reign. Louis XI of France had thought them to be wonderful little birds and filled the rooms of his castles with them and it was during his reign (1461–83) that the rapid rise of the Parisian bird markets occurred. Some Flemish owners, fleeing the Duke of Alba's tyrannical Spanish occupation, brought canaries to England in 1565. Sir Walter Raleigh introduced them to the court and the Queen about 1580. At first she was disappointed because wild canaries are streaked, dull green birds, but they sang their way into her affection. The word 'canary' entered the English language in 1576 in a poem,

'Canara byrds come in to bear the bell,
And Goldfinches do hope to get the goel'.

The Queen gave these highly vocal birds to her friends and there are still aristocratic families that keep the mummified corpses of a canary among their archives, bearing on one tiny claw a gold band with the monogram of Queen Elizabeth. We are not sure when variations in plumage were first deliberately encouraged by specific breeding, because it was not until 1709 that the first mention of variation was made. Until then, it was the vocal abilities of these songbirds that was most appreciated.

Queen Elizabeth must have acquired a taste for wooden animals from her father, for she had 34 carved heraldic beasts in her privy garden at Whitehall.

Chapter 2

'St James his Guinea Hens'
1603–1660

James VI of Scotland and I of England was a man of extremes where animals were concerned. His animal-baiting activities at the Tower of London were so extraordinary that many records of them have been preserved, but the kindlier side of his nature was equally strong as the evidence about his free-roaming pets in St James's Park repeatedly proves. James hated the Tower, with good reason since a stay within its walls had meant death to so many of his predecessors, but when he visited the Tower it was invariably to see animals put to death. The Tower drew him again and again to sample the delights of lion and bear baiting.

James moved south in 1603 on the death of Queen Elizabeth. He was already the owner of a lion sent to him by his father-in-law Charles IV of Denmark. On 3 June 1604 he took the Duke of Lennox to the Tower 'with many divers other earls and lords, and caused a lion and lioness to be put forth, and a live cock to be thrown to them; which being their natural enemy they immediately killed and sucked the blood'. A lamb was next pushed into their den, 'yet this they did not offer to hurt; but next when the King ordered a fresh lion to be baited by two mastiffs a furious battle ensued'.[1] In 1609 James took the entire court, including the Queen and her ladies, to see a fight between a bear and a lion. The bear was 'doomed to die' having killed a child which was negligently left in the 'Beare House'. 'Several lions were brought out but all, on seeing the bear, turned tail and hid in their cages. Finally, to please the King, the bear was baited to death with dogs'.[2]

The King had appointed Edward Alleyn (1566–1626) to be Master of the Bear Garden in 1604. He organised the bull-baiting exhibitions for the king, also bear-baiting and the King's favourite sport where three mastiffs fought two lions. The baiting was done in the semi-circular enclosure built round the Lion Tower. Alleyn had as unpleasant a reputation as his master after he had acquired an interest in the baiting house at Paris Gardens in Southwark in 1594. Four years later, when the post of Master of the Royal Game of Bears, Bulls & Mastiff Dogs fell vacant, he had attempted to secure it in partnership with Henstone, a groom of the Chamber to Queen Elizabeth. They failed then, but succeeded in purchasing the post from the holder in 1604, after which Alleyn held it until his death in 1626. Alleyn, it should be noted, was also a famous actor and one of the founders of the Dulwich College, so he too had his better side.[3]

James's and Alleyn's attempts to provoke animosity between animals were not always successful and it is pleasing to note that a spaniel placed in the lion's cage got on so well with the lions that it took up residence with them permanently and lived amicably with them for many years, adding yet another curious spectacle for the public to gaze at when visiting the Tower Menagerie.[4]

In May 1604 the room where the lions were kept in the tower was enlarged and a lioness had whelped. There was further breeding success in 1605 when both young lions and leopards whelped. The young rarely reached maturity, probably because of faulty feeding.[5]

The King revived the menagerie in 1604, adding many other non-combatant animals to its number. There were more animals there than in the time of Elizabeth, including at least 6 lions. James granted letters patent in 1613 to his keeper of the lions, Robert Gill, 'that thenceforth no person should at any time carry any lions or leopards into any part of England to shew them for gain upon such forfeiture as by any laws may be inflicted on them'. This was to be invoked ten years later when Thomas Warde was warned and prohibited by the Vice-Chancellors of Oxford and Cambridge, but still had 'gone about the country with a lion which he showed in Oxford and at Stourbridge Fair in Cambridge and other places, charging admission. He then parted with it to Martin Brocas and John Watson, who in like manner carry the same about now, notwithstanding he has grown so fierce that he almost killed a child, and bit his keeper so that he lay eight weeks of the sore'.[6] This attempt to prevent anyone other than royal servants from showing animals was doomed to failure.

Some of James's animals may be seen in Wenceslaus Hollar's engravings, but the animals depicted there and the detailed references to others, (frequently gifts from foreign monarchs) which are found in the contemporary accounts of visitors who went to see his menageries, are more often descriptive of the free-roaming pets lodged in St James's Park.[7]

James kept the ground uncultivated in St James's Park and in this wild area he established a new kind of menagerie. During his reign the area was extended by the addition of Spring Gardens between the park and Charing Cross, with butts, bathing ponds, pheasant yard and a bowling green as entertainments.[8] The Spring Gardens, attached to the King's Palace at Whitehall, were so called from a jet of water that sprung up with the pressure of the foot and dowsed who-ever unwittingly trod on it, another 'entertainment' for by-standers. William Walker was granted the office of keeping the houses and yards for pheasants in 1608. The pheasant yard was a breeding-place and in July 1614 a charge was made 'For two clucking hens to sett upon the pheasant eggs iiijs' (i.e. four shillings).[9] Many waterfowl were lured into captivity by decoys installed by the King and he also received presents of ducks from abroad. They were housed on separate ponds near the Vine Garden attached to the Palace, one pond being reserved for two cormorants which were trained to catch fish for their owner. Some old receipts are still extant for payments made in 1614 'for cleansing and scouring the pond' (by casting up the mud onto the banks) and a man was engaged for nine days mowing and clearing the nettles about the pond-head and the duck-ponds.

James had some unusual birds in the park. A visitor, Monsieur Monconys, remarked on seeing a 'quessa-ouarra' or cassowary there and in a book of *Crudities* by Thomas Coryat published in 1611 there is a list of London's remark-able sights, compiled by Henry Peacham, which included,

> 'St James his Guinea hens, the Casowary, moreover, The Beaver in the Park (strange beast as ever any man saw, Down-shearing willows, with teeth as sharp as a handsaw)'.

A curious footnote regarding the cassowary explained that it was 'an East India bird at St James's in the keeping of Mr Walker, that will carry no coales, but eat them as whot [=hot] as you will'. Feeding hot coal to a bird was not done, but the Tower animals were kept warm by open coal fires

The Guineahen was described in 1655 by Moufet and Bennet, in *Health's improvement*, 'There are some which lately brought hither certain chequer'd Hens & Cocks out of New Guinea, spotted white and black like a Barber's apron whose flesh is like to the flesh of Turkies'. (C. Gesner, *Icones avium omnium*, 1560).

and the bird may have helped itself to one or two pieces. The Dutch spice traders had brought the first live cassowary to Europe in 1597 from the Moluccas. Coryat was the first to record its presence in England in 1611.[10]

The beaver is not mentioned elsewhere, but the fact that a few years later the park was largely made up of grass plots and avenues and there were few trees left would be adequately explained by its activities 'down-shearing' the willows and other species.

Apart from the birds, James had a remarkable assemblage of mammals roaming in the Park, not to mention two crocodiles that had a separate pond near the Vine Garden. His delight in wild animals was soon known in foreign courts and presents began to arrive. In July 1613 an Ambassador from Savoy presented him with a tiger and a lioness, and a lynx that unfortunately died in transit. The King of Savoy also shipped over a tame 'ounce-leopard' which, on the very day it arrived, had the temerity to attack a pet fawn nursed by a woman employed specifically to rear it. Four years later, in November 1617, a Russian envoy brought white hawks and some live sables among other gifts from Czar Boris of Muscovy. Sir Thomas Roe returned home from his embassy to the Great Mogul at Delhi in 1619 bringing with him 'two antelopes, and a straunge and beautifull kind of red deare'.[11]

The East India Company ship which transported these deer was only one of many which coped with the problems of keeping mammals and birds in sufficiently good health

John Evelyn wrote in his diary on 22 October 1684 about a 'living crocodile brought from some of the West Indian Ilands in every respect resembling the Egyptian crocodile'. (Edward Topsell, woodcut in *History of four-footed beasts and serpents*, 1658).

The axis or Ganges deer brought to England in the East India Company's ships for the royal menagerie. (Thomas Bewick, *History of quadrupeds*).

during the long sea voyage to England, in order to present them alive to the King. The Company had been incorporated by Queen Elizabeth on the last day of December 1600 and carried many 'curiosities' home from the east over the following two centuries.

James I enjoyed fishing with cormorants. His Master of the Cormorants, John Wood, was paid £30 in April 1611, 'For his trouble in bringing up and training of certain fowls called Cormorants, and making of them fit for the use of

James I enjoyed fishing with cormorants. Joseph Wolf drew this scene 'Cormorant fishing' when the sport had been revived in the 19th century, G. E. Freeman & F. H. Salvin, *Falconry*, 1859.

fishing'. In 1618 James had a house and ponds made at Westminster and stocked the ponds with one hundred each of carp, tench, barbel, roach and dace for the purpose of cormorant fishing. He also fished with cormorants at Theobalds, his country house in Hertfordshire.[12]

The King of Denmark, Holstein and Norway (King James I's father-in-law) sent mammals and birds. Some black, or very dark brown, deer which came from the north, were released by James in a Scottish forest and a forest in the vicinity of London. Captain Newport brought a wild boar from Hispaniola, and the Virginia Company handed over some flying squirrels as a gift. But, once again, it was an elephant that aroused the greatest interest and comment.

There is nothing quite so lovable as an elephant, so daunting and powerful when seen from the front and so ridiculous from the rear. Apparently the exact date of this particular elephant's arrival was not known sufficiently accurately because the King was at Theobalds in Hertfordshire when it arrived in London, accompanied by five camels. James had been warned by the Duke of Buckingham, in a letter, of their dispatch, but the animals arrived before full preparations had been made for their reception. The King of Spain sent them for him and in July 1623 James had to issue a set of emergency orders stating that the animals were to be well fed and housed in the King's Mews (now the site of the National Gallery, London) and that nobody was to be allowed to inspect the elephant, but the camels should be taken daily to St James's Park to graze. They were later sent to Theobalds where special quarters were prepared for them.

The elephant, as that belonging to Henry III, proved to be a very expensive animal for which to cater. It was allowed four keepers, two English and two Spanish. The Spaniards, who had come over with it, insisted that from September to April it must be given a gallon of wine each day. It is to be hoped that it also had unlimited access to water, for an elephant needs to consume fifty gallons of water daily to maintain its weight. The cost of its maintenance was estimated at £275/12/- per annum (not to mention the present of £150 to the Spanish official who delivered it in London) and Richard Weston was moved to exclaim that the Lord Treasurer would be little pleased with any further presents which 'cost the King as much to maintain as a whole garrison of men'. This elephant did not conveniently die after a short while, but lived on to be mentioned in a play of 1639 (*The City Match*, IX: 137), when it was still one of the sights of London along with 'camels, dromedaries, etc'.[13]

Apart from these regal gifts, Englishmen sent abroad on various missions brought home suitable presents in order to obtain the favour of the King. James's favourite, the Duke of Buckingham, was sent on the 'Jean de Paris expedition' to Spain, with the young Prince of Wales, to court the Infanta. They went in disguise, but made themselves so conspicuous in every way that no-one was deceived by the Prince's false name, Jean de Paris, and they only contrived to make themselves and their mission look ridiculous. The young Prince Charles, the future Charles I and the 'babie' of the letter below, was twenty-three years old at the time, and very much in the hands of the all-powerful Duke who was to conduct the negotiations and report to the King.

Besides finding a suitable bride for the prince, Buckingham was also set the task of procuring some animals for the King's collection and in particular he hoped to bring James a lion from Madrid, where Bristow was the English ambassador. Bristow was acutely embarrassed by the escapades of the two young men and despaired of persuading the Spanish king to allow the Infanta to marry the Prince of Wales. The other part of the enterprise was more successful, however, as Buckingham told the King in what must be one of the most remarkable letters ever written to an English sovereign by a subject,

> 'Sir, Four asses you I have sent. Tow hees and tow shees. Five camels, tow shees with a young one; and one ellefant which is worth your seeing. These I have impudently begged for you. There is a Barbarie here come with them, I think for Wat. Ashton. My Lord Bristow sayeth he will send you more camells. When we come ourselves we will bring you horses and asses anoufe. If I know whether you desire mules or not I will bring you them, or deere of this countrie eyther. And I will lay waite for all the rare coler burds that can be hard of. But if you do not send your babie jewels enough, I'le stop all other presents. Therefore louke to it'.[14]

The elephant proved to be a costly success, and the camels enjoyed their freedom at Theobalds. In addition, the twenty-three year old 'babie' got his jewels and there were enough for Buckingham to have a share too. As for the asses and the reason they should be so desirable, Thomas Pennant explained when he wrote in 1766, 'This animal, tho' common in all parts of these islands (now), was entirely lost among us during the reign of Elizabeth, Hollingshed informing us (p.109) that in his time "our lande did yeilde no asses"'.[15] Another author, George Edwards, added that the ass was familiar before the time of Elizabeth as far back as Ethelred (brother of Alfred the Great, ruled 866–871) when a mule or young ass was worth twelve shillings. How we came to lose this species from our fauna was not explained.

Two years after this importation of asses and camels, elephant, horses and birds, the 'babie', still a bachelor, succeeded to the throne.

Charles I (reigned 1625–49) was a man of very different character from his father. For one thing, his tastes were much more refined. His main interest lay in works of art, while in natural history he favoured plants rather than animals.

He did not indulge in acts of violence against animals. Nevertheless, having inherited the unusual menagerie from his father, Charles was obliged to make provision for the imprisoned animals. All began well, for a lioness whelped in the Tower in June 1625, 'which some take as a presage that all things are like to succeed as in the former time'.

In the second year of his reign he issued an order, dated 31 January 1627, for £75/5/10d a year to be paid for life to Philip, Earl of Montgomery, 'for keeping the Spring Gardens and the beasts and fowls there'. The cormorants were still thriving under Mr Wood 'the Master of the Corvorants' and they were said by Ray and Willughby, in their *Ornithology,* to have been kept hooded like hawks until they were taken to the river to fish. A leather thong round the lower part of their necks prevented them from swallowing any fish which they caught. When five or six had been captured and stored in their gullets, they were called to hand by the keeper and sat on the fist, while they regurgitated the fish 'a little bruised with the nip the bills had given them'.[16] When they had finished fishing, the cormorants were allowed to eat part of the catch. Since this account was written in 1676, it is probable that the cormorants had bred and increased in number, or been replaced with new stock over the intervening years. They were a feature of the collection of birds in St James's Park for much of the 17th century, even surviving the Commonwealth period.

The East India Company still obliged the King by bringing exotic creatures home in their ships. In 1631 Captain Weddell brought back a leopard for Charles I and a cage of birds for the Queen. The factor at Patna was trading mynah birds as early as 1620 and the cage of birds might well have contained one or more of this talkative species.[17]

Charles I seems to have taken little interest in the Tower animals and very few records have been handed down to us concerning the history of St James's Park during his reign. The one significant reference comes from the account of Monsieur de la Serre, a Frenchman attached to the court of Queen Henrietta, who commented in 1638 that 'This Park is full of wild animals but as it is the place where the ladies of the court usually take their walk, their kindness has made the animals so tame, that they all submit to the power of their charms, rather than to the pursuit of dogs'.[18]

Queen Henrietta Maria had pet monkeys, in which she took special pleasure, but their antics were only just tolerated by the rest of the court, like those of her dwarf Jeffrey Hudson who was only 3'9" high. A delightful portrait of the Queen, painted by Van Dyck, included her dwarf holding onto one of her monkeys.

If Charles I had found little time to attend to the animals in the Park and Tower during the last few troubled years of his reign, Cromwell might have been expected to have even less time for such frivolities. So few animals seem to have survived the period of fighting that one suspects that many had gone to provide a meat dish for Roundhead and Cavalier soldiers alike. The deer had certainly disappeared from St James's and Cromwell, rather surprisingly, took the trouble to re-stock the Park from the deer in Bushey Park and Hampton Court at the cost of £300 in 1652.[19]

The remains of some of the former inhabitants found a scientific use when John Tradescant gathered together the first natural history museum in England. He proudly proclaimed in a catalogue of the contents of his Lambeth Museum, under 'CLAWES' of birds, that he owned, 'A legge and claw of the cassowary or Emeu that dyed at St James's Westminster' some time prior to 1656. One doubts that the remainder of this particularly tough bird had been eaten, rather that the claw and leg were the only parts that had survived because of the lack of knowledge of how to preserve specimens at that date.

The Tower Menagerie, according to Howell in 1657, was still in existence under the care of Mr Robert Gill who 'hath the place (i.e. post of Keeper of the Lions) now and hath had it many years', but nothing further is known of the fate of its occupants during the Commonwealth period. This lull in the fortunes of foreign mammals in Britain was to last many more years, because Charles II, though a great naturalist, was above all else a lover of fine birds, of all species and varieties.[20]

An innocent delight in birds was shared by everyone, even Cromwell, and though the royal collection of animals may have suffered, people made up for this by having all kinds of birds in their houses. The importation of live birds increased greatly and many new aquatic species began to grace lakes and ponds all over the country. The seed-eating species, such as parrots and canaries, being more easily fed, both in transit and in this country, were the ones that were kept in the home. These were greatly sought after and prized. The canary was known as the sugar bird because it fed happily on sugar cane and was brought from the Canary Islands initially. The Spaniards had a monopoly on the trade with canaries, but at some time during the 1650s a Spanish ship loaded with canaries and bound for Leghorn was ship-wrecked off the Italian coast and the birds escaped and flew off to Elba, where they found the weather and climate to their liking, settled down and bred and multiplied. From this source, many of them were shipped to the European mainland and subsequently transported to England.

People in the Commonwealth period made up for the lack of curiosities at the Tower by flocking to see any strange animal advertised as being on view at an inn or shop in town. Evelyn went to Greenwich specially to view the lemur exhibited there in June 1657 and wrote in his diary,

'I saw at Greenwich a sort of Catt brought from the East Indies, shaped & snouted much like the Egyptian Ratoone, in the body like a Monkey, & so footed: the eares & Tail like a Catt, onely the taile much longer, & the Skin curiously ringed, with black and white: With this taile, it

A ring-tailed lemur *Lemur catta* originally brought home on an East Indies ship but which was picked up in Madagascar or Comoro. George Edwards called it a Maucauco and said it had been brought home 'from Madagascar by Captain Isaac Worth Anno 1748. I kept it alive in my House for some time'. (Wood engraving from Thomas Bewick, *History of quadrupeds*).

wound up its body like a Serpent, & so got up into trees, & with it would also wrap its whole body round; It was of a wolly haire as a lamb, exceedingly nimble, and yet gentle, & purr'd as dos the Cat'.

With such rare treats Englishmen had to be content until the time of the Restoration.

Chapter 3

'His Majestie desires no more Cassawarrens' 1660–1685

Charles II arrived back in England from exile in May 1660 and took up residence in Whitehall, along with a large number of King Charles spaniels that over-ran the apartments. Evelyn said that the King 'tooke delight to have a number of little spaniels follow him, & lie in his bed-Chamber, where often times he suffered bitches to puppy & give suck, which rendred it very offensive, & indeede made the whole Court nasty & stinking'.[1]

The King soon discovered St James's Park with its clear fresh air so conveniently near to his palace apartments and within a year he had grown so fond of the place and enjoyed walking in the park so much that he had plans drawn up to make it into a really beautiful area, as much as possible like the elegant gardens he had known at Versailles. He had the swamps and ponds channelled into a long strip of water which became known as the Canal and planted trees thickly round the largest and deepest pool, called Rosamond's Pond. The native birds must have found this greatly to their liking for it gave them additional security and nesting places in the centre of London.

Charles established a colony of ducks and foreign waterfowl on the Canal. He also had made a pheasant walk (on the site now occupied by Marlborough House) where his peacocks, partridges, guinea-hens, pheasants and other birds were kept. By the side of the south-east end of the Canal there was a small island, with a number of channels and rivulets. The islets these formed were covered with reeds and shrubs to provide safe places for nesting waterfowl.

The largest of the islands was called Duck Island which came under the supervision of a pond-keeper who had a salary of £30 a year. West of Storey's Gate on the south side of the park ran Bird Cage Walk, the origin of whose name has puzzled many historians. It is known that Charles had

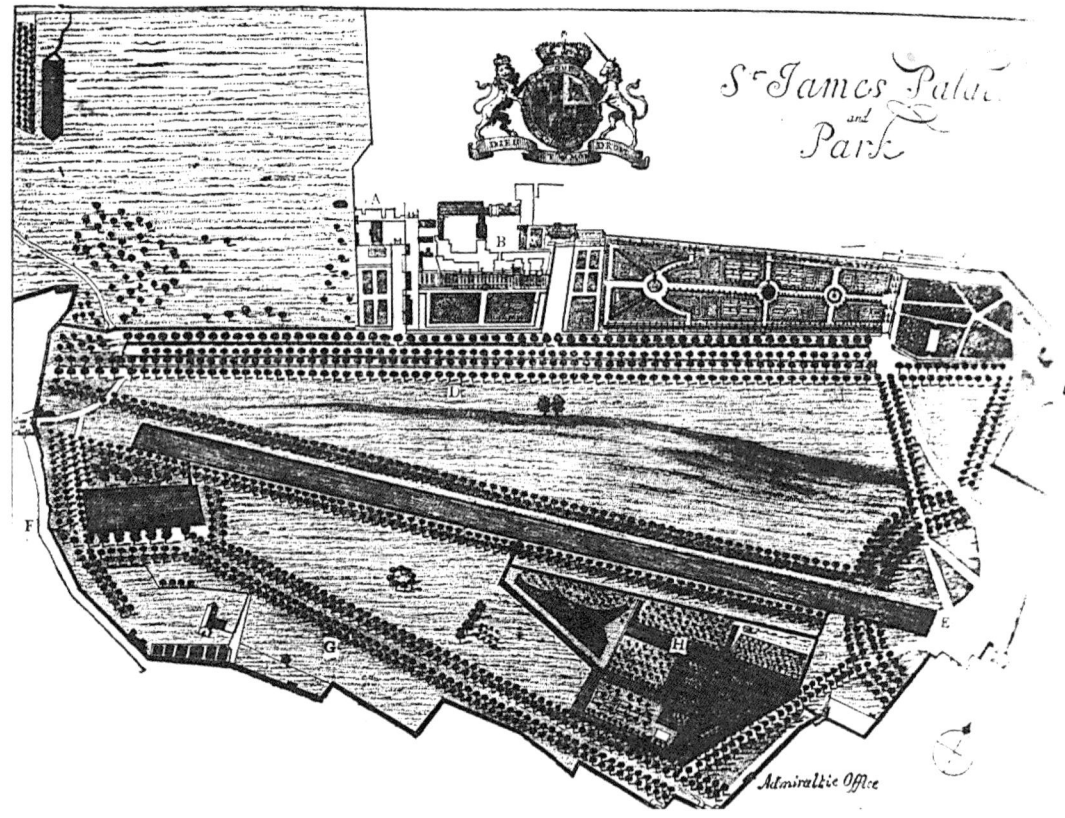

many bird cages situated in and around the park, from references to them in journals and poems of the time, but no picture of them has been traced 'suspended from the trees' in Bird Cage Walk as some writers described them. The name originated before Charles' time, for Wheatley stated it was, 'Given to the south side of the park between Buckingham Gate and Storey's Gate from the aviary established there in the reign of James I'.[2]

By the end of 1661 Charles had made noticeable progress with his improvements and Pepys commented with some surprise in his diary for 18 August, 'Lord's Day . . . and then to walk in St James parks and saw great variety of fowle which I never saw before'. By this time there were parrots and cassowaries and an aviary of some description had been erected, according to Letters Patent dated 1661, which referred to 'an house and yards in our parke at St James's, built for keeping of pheasants, gunny hens, partridges, and other foule within our said park'.

The straight canal through St James's Park, c.1665. The canal was altered c.1770 by Capability Brown, and then re-formed nearly to its present shape with islands and willow trees in 1826. A Cleveland House. B St James's Palace. C The Spring Garden. D The Mall. E The Canal. F Rosamond's Pond. G Birdcage Walk. H Duck island and the Decoy. (G. W. Thornbury and E. Walford, *Old and new London* vol. IV: 54).

The keeper of the volary or aviary was Edward Storey, 'from whom or his house is named Storey's Gate', but this evidence is as suspect as the statements about Birdcage Walk and, unfortunately, the truth as to the origin of both names may never be known.

Edmund Waller senior, a poet who visited the park about the same time as Pepys, voiced his approbation of the alterations made by the King in a poem with the title 'On St James's Park as lately improved by His Majesty', of which a part said,

'For future Shade young trees upon the banks
Of the new stream appear in even ranks'.

and Waller looked forward to the day on which they would have grown sufficiently so that,

'Free from impediment of Light & Noise
Man thus retired his nobler thoughts employs'.

On Monday 3 January 1663 Charles gave audience to two imposing visitors from Russia. The event was reported in two newspapers, *Mercurius Publicus* and *King's Intelligencer*. At the end of their audience the two ambassadors offered presents from the Tsar Alexis that,

'were as followeth: From the Great Lord Emperor and great Duke Alexee Michalivich Six Goshawks One persian horse, skins of sables, ermin garments etc. One tassel of goshawk, Two faulcons, one living martin, one Gire falcon One grey stone-horse, One Pelican: from Duke Feodor Alexee-vich one tassel of Goshawk, Two faulcons, one living Martin, one Pelican, one Crane'.

The gyrfalcons and tassel (i.e. male) goshawks would be housed in the King's mews in the care of the Master Falconer, Sir Allen Apsley. At this time Charles had 34 falconers, but when some economies had to be made in the King's household in August 1667 this department was cut back, though Sir Allen retained his job. The pelicans were such a success and delighted both the King and the public so much, that to this day pelicans are kept in St James's Park, as a memorial to Charles who first established them there over three hundred years ago. They are replaced if they die without having produced any young to keep a presence on the lake.

Pelicans have lived in
St James's Park from the time
of Charles II.
Melchior de Hondecoeter
(1636–95).

Sir Thomas Browne's son, Edward, lived in London and, like so many other residents in the capital, he found a walk in St James's Park much more interesting after the Restoration because of the number of birds there. Charles insisted on sharing this pleasure with his subjects, against the advice and wishes of his counsellors, who were afraid of plots to assassinate him, and they worried incessantly when they saw him strolling unconcernedly in the park among strangers and foreign visitors. Edward Browne wrote in his journal on 25 February 1664, 'This night I walk'd into St James his Parke, where I saw many strange creatures, as divers sorts of outlandish deer, Guiny sheep, a white raven, a great parrot, a storke . . .' According to Monconys there were two white ravens there in 1663, apparently free to come and go as they pleased. Peter Munday made a long list of the species that he saw during the time he resided on Tower Hill, from 1657 to 1663, and besides the species mentioned by Browne, he found,

> 'shovelars (i.e. Spoonbills) . . . outlandish geese, ducks etts., of severall shapes, collurs and sizes. Among the rest claegeese, lesser than our ordinary sort, being blacke with some white about the breast (probably claik-geese, our barnacles), etts.

Canada goose and spur-winged goose. (Thomas Bewick, *History of British birds*).

A great number of our ducks and mallard, widgeon and teal, pewetts (i.e. black-headed gulls), etts. which swimme and fly to and fro, frequenting the severall ponds. They have little hutts or cabbins or boards fitted for them to breed'.[3]

Ray and Willughby, the two 17th century scientists who wrote the first illustrated English systematic textbook on ornithology (*Ornithologia libri tres,* 1676), described Canada, brent, barnacle and spur-winged gambo geese from 'examples among the King's water-fowl in St James's Park'. They were exceptional in that they had no difficulty in recognising the various species, while most of the authors writing about the birds and mammals in the royal collections were not scientists and so frequently merely gave generic names such as ducks and geese and then resorted to '&c' or, rather more quaintly, 'etts'.

Peter Mundy made a better attempt to itemise the animals, as,

'Elke, of whose skinne buffe (i.e. leather) is made, fallow deers, allso Indiann antelope, a kind of deere, allsoe another sort which I have seene in India of a yellowish collour with many white spots in ranckes (a cheetul?); a small kind of goates from Guinnea etts'.

Evelyn confirmed that all these were present and added 'Robucks and Arabian sheepe'.[4]

In Charles II's reign the first list of all the known mammals and birds, in alphabetical order with English, Latin and Greek names, was published in 1668. Its author, Walter Charleton, had seen several species of royal birds in St James's Park, including a 'white parrot with a tuft of red feathers on his head for a crest', and in the 'Zootrophia Regis' he had seen 'Emeu the Cassoware', and a pelican 'Regis nostri Vivario' from the Muscovite emperor along with 'Anser Chilensis'.[5]

The East India Company (founded in 1600) presented Charles with many deer and antelopes, but they found it more difficult than they had expected to get the sexes of the deer in balance for breeding purposes and instructions had to be given to the servants of the Company 'for the spotted deere, that they be most females of which send some by every shipping'. This was in March 1676, to which came the reply two months later, 'Wee . . . now send you by these

shipps some deere, male and female; the latter whereof are hard to be procured'. Their efforts having met with some success, a consignment of 8 deer, 2 antelopes and one elk was shipped home the same month (January 1677).[6]

Charles was very fond of the gentle members of the deer family and much preferred them to the ferocious animals favoured by his forbears. He did, however, own one of the most ferocious of all bird species, a cassowary. Judging by his description, Mundy had taken a long hard look at one of these vicious birds,

> 'At a place near St Jameses house I saw a cassawarws, a strange fowle somewhat lesser than an estridge, the body about four foote high, very big in the head and like a turkey, black shining feathers or spriggs, narrow and long, which uppon him appear like soe many long haires, sleeke and smooth. It hath two feathers and one quill, of which I have some to shew. It hath some appearance of wings or pinions, but of no use, as the dodo etts'.[7]

Francis Barlow (1626-1704) painted cassowaries several times; here (in his *Birds and fowls*, 1665) one is shown with an ostrich, peacocks, pheasants and a monkey. The Dutch spice traders brought the first live cassowary to Europe in 1597 from the Moluccas.

One can have too much of a good thing, however, and in 1676 Charles rebelled at the number of cassowaries which were being sent to him. Writing to his colleagues in Surat, the East India Company scribe warned, 'His Majestie desires no more Cassawarrens'.[8]

Mundy saw another bird in the aviaries which he thought to be like 'a shee bustard of a fine grey collur, as big as a turkey hen, I thinck they are of those wee calle at Dantzigk Awerhaens, the cocke black, the hen gray, as the hethcock and hen'. This rather mixed-up account suggests a female capercaillie. Evelyn gave a clearer description of the birds that he saw in an amusing entry in his diary for 9 February 1665,

'I went to St James' . . . where I saw various animals, and examined the throat of the Onocrotylus, or pelican, a fowl between a stork and a swan, a melancholy water-fowl, brought from Astracan by the Russian Ambassador. it was diverting to see how he would toss up and turn a flat fish, plaice or flounder to get it right into his gullet at its lower beak, which, being filmy stretches to a prodigious wideness when it devours a great fish. Here also was a small waterfowl, not bigger than a moorhen, that went almost quite erect, like the penguin of America; it would eat as much fish as its whole body weighed; I never saw so unsatiable a devourer, yet the body did not appear to swell the bigger. The Solan Geese here are also great devourers, and are said to exhaust all the fish in the pond. Here was a curious sort of poultry, not much exceeding the size of a tame pigeon, with legs So short as their crops seemed to touch the earth; a milk-white raven; a stork, which was a rarity at the season, seeing he was loose, and to fly loftily; two Balearian cranes, one of which have had one of his legs broken and cut off above the knee, had a wooden or box leg and thigh, with a joint so accurately made that the creature could walk and use it as well as if it had been natural; it was made by a soldier. The Park was at this time stored with numerous flocks of severall sorts of ordinary and extraordinary wild fowl, breeding about the decoy, which for being near so great a city, and among such a concourse of soldiers and people, is a singular and diverting thing . . . There were withy-pots or nests, for the wild fowl to lay their eggs in, a little above the surface of the water'.[9]

Solan Goose is a name long used for the gannet. Evelyn's note of the presence of Canada geese in England, at St James's Park 9 February 1665, is the first for this species.

Quite a number of the birds had been brought from the East Indies at Charles' special request. Within a year of his Restoration, messages had gone out to Surat and Madras asking the personnel of the East India Company in the trading settlements there to collect rare birds and mammals to present to His Majesty. The first consignment arrived from Madras in November 1661 from whence 'two greate and one small antelops, two pellicans, and two noorees or Macasser parrots' were despatched. Over the following months and years, many spotted deer were sent and occasionally a specific request was received from the Court, like that of 1669, for 'any small parretts, about the bignes of sparrows, which are called noories, or any other of the like nature which are rarities and pleasant to the eye or eare'. The Company forwarded a searching enquiry to Surat in 1671, which included a message from Charles which read,

> 'Wee have received an intimation from his Majestie to procure for him such sortes of fowles as are exprest in the words following: The severall sorts of water fowles of broad bill kind and larger sorts, such as may be kept with English bread or corne or such feed as is in England: That it bee carefully enquired into to know their naturall feed: That they may bee or such sorts, large and the most beautifull and as are not in these parts, and such as used to the land waters and not alwaies upon the see'.

This letter says much for Charles' genuine concern for his birds in that he took so much trouble to investigate their feeding habits in order to keep them in a healthy condition. He was also shrewd enough to realise that fresh-water birds would be easier to keep in the conditions he had available in the park, whereas sea-birds would not flourish. His concern over the welfare of his birds appears again in another letter, written in March 1676. This letter went to Surat and informed them there that,

> 'He also desires the large bird with a crown upon its head, comonly called the crowne bird or East India peacock; a bird like a crane, but different in couller: a bird less then a goose, being finer featherd, comonly called an East India

goose; any sort of wild fowles as duck, mallard, teale, widgeons, etc. soe that they are different in couller from ours and will feed upon any sorts of grayne which we have in England. What you can procure of any of theis sorts, or any fine wild fowle, sent by the first ships, being very acceptable to His Majestie'.[10]

On receiving this letter, the 'several factors' around Surat, decided to give a few facts on migration and the habits of the 'copple-crowned' or crested bird of which the King was so fond, by way of explaining their difficulties in procuring them,

'As to water foule with broad bils, and those Indian geese with copple crowns, they do not breed in these parts, but come only at certaine seasons: soe that, though they are often shott by fowlers, yett never taken young, soe as to send home or breed up. Last yeare wee sent you two large birds caled sarusses, and now alsoe sent you two more by these shipps. They are much esteemed by these great men, and kept in the kings court; their nature being to keep strict watch, standing on one leg all night, and, if any noise or accident hap-ens, they take the alarum. Wee hope they will please you'.[11]

The sarus cranes were the species *Grus antigone* and on arrival in London they would have been accommodated in the poultry-house along with other exotics in the park.

When Charles wished to relax, he took a stroll in the park and fed the ducks. Colly Cibber, the poet, wrote of Charles, 'Even his indolent amusement of playing with his dogs and feeding his ducks in St James's Park (which I have seen him do) made the common people adore him'.[12] His subjects shared his love of animals and also admired his bravery in walking among them in the park, despite rumours and counter-rumours of plots to assassinate him. The fear of a 'popish plot' to kill Charles was ever present and very real in their minds. The general alarm is evident in the story concerning one of Charles's subjects who shared his monarch's love of birds. 'There were lately several bullets, to the number of 40 shot into the King's gallery and garden; the Politicks judged there was treason intended . . . but at last it is found to be an ordinary fellow that keeps tame pigeons, which it seems his neighbour's cats are very lickorish of; he, to be revenged, watches to kill all cats with his stone-bag, and some of his shots have reached into Whitehall'. (Letter vignette written in 1670).

All the birds and mammals cost a lot in upkeep and the bills for the making of the decoy in the park, providing willow baskets for nesting purposes and grain to feed the ducks, are extant,

'Charles R – The Workes and Services comprised in this Account, were done by our direction, May 30, 1671.

To Edward Maybank and Tho. Greene for digging the Decoy, and carrying out the earth and levelling the ground about the said Decoy   128.2.11½d

To Edward Storey, for wyer and other things used about the Decoy, and for 100 Baskets for the Ducks   8.9.0

To Oliver Honey for paving the feeding place for the Ducks and breaking ground   1.10.0

To Sr George Waterman for several Netts for the Decoy   15.3.0

To James Rimes for plants, sets, and 400 Bolts of Reeds for the use of the Decoy   15.11.0

To Edward Storey for money paid to sundry workmen for settling the Reeds and Polles round the Decoy and wyering it   9.10.0

To Sydrach Hilcus for ye contriving of the Decoy in St James' Parke   30.0.0

For oatmeal, Tares, Hempseed, and other corn for the Birds and Fowles from September 1660 to June 24, 1670   246.18.0

To William Thawsell for fish for the Cormorant, the 12th of March 1661   1.13.0'[13]

In addition, the pond-keeper or Governor was paid £30 a year. Duck Island, within the channel of the Decoy, had a succession of Governors, starting with the appointment of the appropriately named Sir John Flock, who had been with Charles in exile and remained a faithful follower throughout that difficult time. After his death, the post remained vacant for a while and then a new governor was granted the post by a rather ingenious, but not very honest ruse. The Chevalier de St Evremond,

'Having solicited various ministers and lords for some royal post with a salary attached, and no offer being forthcoming, he met the king one day in the Park and threw himself on his knees to thank the King for his kindness in his new appointment. The King could not remember having granted him a post, so Evremond assisted his memory by saying, "Your Majesty is all the more great in not remembering the instances of your benevolence; but his Grace of --- and my Lord ---, who both are present, assured me they had solicited Your Majesty for me: I know your royal kindness of heart, and cannot doubt they have succeeded."

"You shall succeed yourself," replied Charles, "if you will tell me what you desire, that is now in my power to grant". "I love to feed the ducks here in your Majesty's Park; make me Governor of Duck Island, and I shall be the happiest man in the three kingdoms"'.

Contrary to his custom, Charles for once used his royal prerogative and St Evremond was appointed on the spot.[14]

This story conflicts with another account of the same episode, written by Uffenbach in 1710, and after considering the authenticity of both in view of the character of St Evremond, as outlined by Uffenbach, the reader may decide for himself which seems the more likely story. Uffenbach dined out on the 29 June while staying in London, and wrote,

'On this day at dinner there were various strangers at table, who related the following particulars of Her. S. Evremont; that, although he was indeed a philosopher without religion, all loved him for his 'genie et honetete': that he was not only kindly to human beings but also to dumb creatures, keeping several birds and even more dogs; he even used to feed the dogs that ran past his window, so that even after his death hordes of them would look expectantly up at it. Therefore the King, who liked him greatly, made him keeper of the small cage-birds and birds (because he would accept no other office) and gave him a pension of two hundred pounds a year'.[15]

Uffenbach also noted that he visited St Peter's or Westminster Church four days later and found the tomb of Mr S. Evremont and quoted the Latin inscription 'made tolerably well of white and black marble' which hung from a pillar.[16]

The post was bestowed on other servants in succeeding reigns and besides this tradition, others begun by Charles were also continued. Duck Island is still a bird reserve today, where the keeper of the birds in St James's Park has a small hut and rears orphaned ducklings and tends sick birds taken to him by Londoners who find birds in need of help and attention. The pelicans are replaced when necessary, often by gifts as of old, for example, an eastern white pelican was sent by the Amir of Bahawalpur and an American white pelican by the Governor of Louisiana, after World War II. Pepys's opinion of the Park is still true today, for if there is one place in London where you can guarantee to find people smiling happily, it is the area near the bridge over the lake in the middle of St James's Park, where the ducks and gulls, sparrows and pigeons gather and are hand-fed by passers-by. 'Creed and I walked round the Park', Pepys said on 26 April 1666, 'a pleasant walk, observing the birds, which is very pleasant'. This is still true, thanks to Charles II.

Charles also cared about wildlife outside the safety of the Park and, when he could ensure freedom from disturbance by issuing an order to that effect, he would do so. For example, he ordered the preservation of 'the game of heron and wild fowl on the Thames from Windsor to London'. He attempted to establish red-legged partridges in the park at Windsor by sending 'Mr de Mouchant, Gamekeeper to the King of England' to France in October 1673 to collect them, but they all soon died. It was not until two introductions were made in the 1770s, using imported eggs to be hatched under domestic fowls here, that red-legged partridges bred and became feral. They were introduced on the estates of the Marquess of Hertford at Sudbourne near Orford, Suffolk, and nearby on Lord Rendlesham's estate.

The Tower Menagerie was of little interest in comparison with the activities in St James's Park, consequently the references to the menagerie in the literature of the period are few in number. Mundy wrote that in September 1660 'a lyonesse whelped three young ones in the Tower: not one in thirty years before, but they all died within a fortnight'.[18] Since lions and lionesses born at the Tower usually took the name of the reigning sovereigns, it is likely that no further cubs arrived on the scene because two imported animals, brought from 'Tunis in Barbary' as late in the reign as 1682,

Red-legged partridge. (Thomas Bewick, *History of British birds*).

were christened Charles and Catherine. (Barbary lions became extinct in 1922).

The lions were a constant attraction, however few in number. On 3 May 1663 Pepys went,

> 'To dinner to my Lady Sandwich; and Sir Tho. Crewes children coming hither, I took them and all my Lady's to the Tower and showed them the lions and all that was to be shown, and so took them to my house and there made much of them; and so saw them back to my Lady's – Sr Tho. Crewes Children being as pretty and the best behaved that ever I saw of their age'.

Pepys enjoyed taking people to see the lions, or indeed, anything and everything in any part of London which might give rise to some interest or excitement. He was completely amazed, therefore, when a man up from the country, called Will Stankes, was obstinately disinterested and Pepys exclaimed in despair,

> 'but Lord, what a stir Stankes made with his being crowded in streets and wearied in walking in London, and would not be wood [i.e. wooed] by my wife and Ashwell [his wife's companion] to go to a play nor to White-hall or to see the lyons, though he was carried in a coach. I never could have thought there had been upon earth a man so little curious in the world as he is'.[19]

A cockatoo strikes Mr Povey. Samuel Pepys showing some children the Tower lions. (*Everybody's Pepys*, G. Bell, 1926).

In 1681 the lions had a very poor year. Narcissus Luttrell recorded in his diary for 21 February, 'Three of the four lyons in the Tower are lately dead, and this news gave a rhymster the excuse to publish "The Lyons Elegy, or verses on the death of the 3 Lions in the Tower"'. The situation was remedied eleven months later. At the end of November 1681 a caravan headed by the Moorish Ambassador, 'Alcaïd Mohammed Ohadu (or Ahmed Hadu) approached the British fort at Tangier across the sandhills ... escorted by Ali Benabdula and two hundred horsemen, and followed by his retinue bringing presents for the King of England, including two lions and twenty ostriches'. On 9 December the Moorish Embassy set sail for England and arrived at Deal twenty days later. On reaching London, the Moroccan Ambassador was received by the King and Queen in the Banqueting-house where,

> 'he came up to the Throne without making any sort of Reverence, bowing so much as his head or body: he spake by a Renegado English man, for whose safe returne there was a promise; They were all clad in the Moorish habite Cassocks of Colourd Cloth or silk with buttons & loopes, over this an Alhaga or white wollan mantle, so large as to wrap both head & body, a shash or small Turban, naked leg'd & arm'd, but with lether socks like the Turks, rich Symeters, large Calico sleev'd shirts &c: The Ambassador had a string of Pearls odly woven in his Turbant; . . . Their Presents were Lions & estridges &c; Their Errant, about a Peace at Tangire &c'.

The King received the deputation and the presents with decorum, though he afterwards laughed at the ostriches. He soon found, however, that twenty of those mirth-provoking birds were too many to keep in confinement peacably and, 'gave them away to any of his courtiers who would accept them', saying 'he knows nothing more proper to send by way of return than a flock of geese'.[20]

The Merry Monarch was in tune with the humour and affections of his subjects in so many ways, his love of birds, but one example.

Chapter 4

'The two-legged cat is dead'
1685–1714

The Merry Monarch died in 1685 and was succeeded by his dour, dull brother James II. Narcissus Luttrell's diary recorded an unfortunate incident during the short reign of this unhappy monarch. In February 1686, 'a woman that lookt after the lions at the Tower putting her hand to(o) near the old one he caught hold of it and grip'd it so hard that it was forc'd to be cut off to prevent a gangrene, but she died of it in a little time'. Looking after lions seems a strange job for a woman in the 1680s.[1]

James made himself unpopular when he ordered all the animals, other than deer and cows, to be removed from St James's Park and transferred to the Tower Menagerie in 1687.

During the earlier and happier days of James's life, when his children were young, there were many pets in his household. Peter Lely, when painting a portrait of James's three to four year old daughter Anne, depicted her wearing a feathered cap and holding a piece of string to which a flying great tit was attached. James II's other daughter, Mary, was also painted by Lely, but as the goddess Diana drawing her bow and followed by her greyhound. This is a complete reversal of their interests and characters as adults, for it was Mary (who became the wife of William III) who was very fond of birds, while Anne followed the hunt with great enthusiasm.

After James fled the country in 1688, Mary and William reigned jointly in Britain, while William was also monarch in Holland. In the grounds of their Dutch palace, Honselaersdyck, William established a small menagerie in succession to another collection of mammals and birds which Charles II's favourite sister, Mary, the mother of William III, had formed. The animals included a spotted Indian cat, an elk, and 'several fowles most of them brought from England'. Charles II sent presents to his sister and exchanged other birds and mammals with some from the

Dutch royal menagerie. The list of species at Honselaersdyck reads much like the categories mentioned by visitors to the English royal collections – ostriches, gazelles, etc. Were the ostriches in Holland some of those surplus to requirements which the Moorish Embassy had brought for Charles? In Holland William had a chameleon, a species unknown in Britain, which had been presented to him by his favourite minister, William Bentinck, afterwards created Earl of Portland when he went to live in England. In 1674 the Dutch menagerie had been augmented by Charles's gift to his niece and nephew of a lion and a tiger. The intermediary in the exchanges was the British Ambassador George Clifford who would find this part of his duties perfectly congenial for he was every bit as enthusiastic about animals as his royal master. He had several species 'decorating his lawn' just as many other of Charles's subjects had built their own volaries, or walk-in aviaries. When Dutch William and his wife were called to England in 1689, this was another characteristic they had in common with their Protestant subjects.

The Dutch couple's other residence, Het Loo, had a remarkable aviary full of exotic and unusual species and Mary was greatly distressed at having to leave them and the gardens. The Het Loo aviary was used by the outstanding Dutch painter Melchior d'Hondecoeter as the basis for some of his splendid canvases accurately portraying dozens of non-European as well as more common species. Bentinck brought six of these large paintings to England where they were installed at his country seat, Welbeck Abbey. They illustrate peacocks, swans, a blue pigeon, a cassowary and waterfowl. (More of these lively birds may be seen in canvases in the Mauritshuis at The Hague and Rijksmuseum in Amsterdam.) Some of d'Hondecoeter's paintings include exotic mammals taken to Holland in the late 17th century, including deer, an elephant, sheep and goats. Among other animals, many of them brought by Dutch spice traders in the East Indies and Moluccas, was the first live chimpanzee to reach Europe. This was called 'Enjocko' and placed in the Het Loo menagerie in 1641. Another anthropoid, the orang-utan, was first delivered alive to the same collection, belonging to the then Prince of Orange. It had been collected by his scientific adviser who doubled as museum director at The Hague and head of the Het Loo menagerie, Aernout Vosmaer. The female orang-utan only lived a short while

A Virginian nightingale, or red cardinal, from Eleazar Albin's small picture book, *A Natural history of English song-birds*, 1737: 84. It was an imported North American bird.

and then caught pneumonia in the damp, cold climate of Holland. This was the fate of a number of the animals in the Prince's menagerie where the death rate was high.

Queen Mary had many other pet cage birds indoors, among them a cockatoo, a Virginian nightingale (red cardinal) and two little green birds with red heads.

It was a wrench leaving their pleasant kingdom of Holland where both were loved and respected and having to move to London. They took with them some of their pets which softened the blow and Mary introduced the English to the idea of keeping 'Dutch Mastiffs or Dutch Pugs' and also goldfish. On one occasion Mary offered one of her favourite, beautifully plumaged birds to the ailing Duke of Gloucester (her sister Anne's son and the heir to the throne) in order to cheer him up. He, however, politely refused to accept the bird, not wishing to deprive his aunt, knowing how fond she was of her pets.

Once they had settled in England, William took just as great an interest in the welfare of the ducks in St James's Park as Charles II had done. He may not actually have fed them himself, but he had a small house built on Duck Island to act as a hide and retired there to drink tea and to observe the activities of the numerous species on the ponds. The Park then supported 'curious birds, deer and some fine cows' and one of the white ravens still frequented the park and could usually be found at the end of the canal towards Westminster, at least up to 1695. William also followed Charles's example in forbidding the killing of birds by issuing a special command, 'that none presume to keep a fowling piece, gun, setting dog, net, trammel, or other unlawful engine, wherewith to destroy or kill, or in any way disturb the game' within the vicinity of the park.[2]

Of the Tower Menagerie in this reign we have but few glimpses, but an English lady traveller and diarist, Celia Fiennes, visited the Tower and said, 'in another part is kept severall lyons which are named by the names of the kings, and it has been observ'd that when a king has dyed the lion of the name has also dyed; there are other strange creatures kept there, leopards, sables, etc which have been brought from foreign parts'. The idea that a lion died in the same year in which the king after whom it was named also died, was often repeated by the lions' keepers to visitors to the menagerie, but is not borne out by the facts. It may have happened once, at the end of the reign of Queen Elizabeth I, so giving rise to the legend, but we know that other lions lingered on well past the demise of their royal namesakes.[3]

William III escaped out of London to Hampton Court whenever possible. He had an aviary there, by the banqueting house, variously named in documents as a menagerie,

Goldfish were first introduced into England about 1691. Charles Lennox (1701–50) Duke of Richmond, sent one jar to China to collect goldfish for his ponds at Goodwood House. By the 1750s they were so common as to be kept at Vauxhall in the 'purling basons'.

a pheasant yard, or, more mundanely, a henhouse. Exotic birds were kept in cages arranged in a semicircle for which a piped water supply was laid to some newly built cages in 1701.

Goldfish were first introduced into England about 1691, the Portuguese having had them many years before this and British ships collected them from Lisbon in large earthenware jars.

After Mary died in 1694, William reigned alone until 1702. He was asthmatic and did not care for the mists and smog in London any more than the cold damp climate of his native land. His animals shared his dislike of the conditions in which they were held captive. Their numbers were on the decline and, under his successor, the St James's Park animals declined further.

Queen Anne was a less amiable person than her sister Mary and was the last of the unhappy Stuarts to reign in England. She was concerned with her immediate family, her bossy friend Sarah, the Duchess of Marlborough and her duties as Queen, but little else besides. Her duties always seemed beyond her capacity to deal with adequately and tactfully. One of her first actions was to restrict the use of St James's Park as a public recreation ground, incurring great displeasure. The Park was only open at certain times and the common people not encouraged to enter it. The aristocratic Zacharias Conrad von Uffenbach, a bibliophile, connoisseur and traveller from Frankfurt, wrote notes on his travels in England in 1710. On 8 June he wrote,

> 'the first day of the Whitsun holiday, we walked in the afternoon in St James Park. This extremely pleasant walk, famed wellnigh throughout the world . . . Since not only some of the finest English cows but also a considerable number of red deer graze there, it is called a park, although there is no real woodland but merely avenues. There are no birds to be seen, such as were to be found here formerly'.

The last statement is rather sweeping, the truth being that the great variety of exotic species was no longer there, although our native ducks were still present.[4]

Anne appointed the landscape gardener Henry Wise as Deputy Ranger of the Park. He widened the canal in 1703 by some twelve feet at a cost of approximately £1,800, but the birds, after this disturbance, were neglected and left to their own devices. Dean Jonathan Swift took his constitutional walk there every day and frequently referred to the Park in his letters, but not to the animal inhabitants, and so it would seem that it had become a place of recreation for humans, rather than a pleasant oasis in the city for other fauna.

Anne's interest in the deer in St James's Park turned out to be purely political. In January or February 1711 she decided to make a present of spotted deer to the Emperor of Morocco and ordered Wise to immediately ship ten brace from the royal parks to this potentate. Wise demurred, mainly because at that time of the year several of the does were pregnant and they might travel badly or die in the heat. He was over-ruled and, as he had predicted, several of the does died on the voyage. The Moroccan Ambassador in London, on hearing of their fate, was at first upset and then became angry and finally abusive and threatening towards the Queen. There would be reprisals, he reported, against captured Britons if his master did not receive instant replacements. Wise packed off more of his charges to the 'Descendant of the Family of Ottoman whose Reign May God Perpetuate to the Day of Judgement'. This regal person then let it be known that if sixty-nine British prisoners were to be released (on the basis of one Christian in exchange for two Moors) then he must have the replacement deer 'with the utmost expedition'.

The Queen had no alternative but to agree to this demand, but she did manage to get some change out of the deal beside the release of the prisoners. The emperor condescended to send her a phoenix (?) which died, with an eagle, which died, two lions, one of which died and a tiger. The mythical phoenix is said to rise from the ashes a new creature, but on this occasion the unfortunate bird was doused by water on board during the long and windy sea voyage.[5]

The Tower Menagerie was faring a little better. Stow wrote that in June 1704 the animals exhibited there were 6 lions, 2 leopards or tigers, 2 cats of the mountains, 3 eagles, 2 Swedish owls presented to Charles II and a jackal. By 1708 the same figures are given for all these species with the exception of the lions, now increased to eleven. This is accounted for by an entry in Luttrell's diary for 6 July 1708 which reads, 'An ambassador from the emperor of Morocco is arrived here and has brought with him 5 lyons as a present to the queen'. Later another lion was presented, this time by the Consul of Algiers.[6]

Uffenbach drove to the Tower on Tuesday morning, 17 June 1710 and said,

> 'We were then taken into the old house where foreign wild beasts are to be seen. We found, however, only the following: four lions, in whose cage there was a dog; they are so used to him that they do him no harm, and he lies beside them quite calmly, which is amazing; but I think that if the lions had been given nothing to eat for a long time, the dog would have to suffer for it. The lions were only of medium size. There was further a tiger here and two wolves, which, as is known, are a rarity in England, as so much indeed as the lions. Also two Indian cats, which were extraordinarily large and savage, but in other respects not unlike our own. The two-legged cat is dead. There are two eagles, of which one, as the keeper of these animals assured us, was forty years old'.[7]

No further explanation as to why the cat had only two legs was given. Oddities and malformations occur naturally, although they were sometimes contrived for exhibition purposes. That was probably not the case with a Tower Menagerie specimen.

After the Queen's only son died in 1698, there would be little pleasure for her in going either to the Tower Menagerie or the Park. During her reign there occurred two other deaths, in quick succession, which may have caused little stir at the time, but the memory of them has been preserved through history to modern times. Charles II's former mistress, Louise de Kerouailles, died in 1702 and her devoted African grey parrot did not long survive her. The beautiful Louise, Duchess of Richmond, was modelled in wax and her effigy placed alongside those of Queen Mary, Queen Elizabeth and Lord Chatham, at Westminster Abbey. The Duchess had left instructions for her grey parrot's care and its future preservation, so that when it died it was preserved and reunited with its mistress, now in effigy. Sophie la Roche, visiting Westminster Abbey in 1786, found them together and explained,

> 'The custom of exhibiting wax figures of important personages, clad in the costumes of their day, struck me as

The African grey parrot was the companion of La Belle Stuart, Louise Kerouaille, Duchess of Richmond and Lennox, for forty years. They died within a few days of one another in 1702. (George Dawson Rowley, *Ornithological miscellany*, 1876–78).

extremely queer. A beautiful Duchess of Richmond seems to come towards one, when the doors of her cupboard have been opened, fan in hand, in her court dress of green velvet embroidered in gold, as seen a hundred years ago; her stuffed dog and parrot are by her side'.[8]

This group, including the stuffed parrot, is still in existence in the Abbey precincts today and may be seen in the Norman Undercroft Museum. The parrot is believed to be the oldest extant preserved bird specimen in the world.

Chapter 5

'Reign in my Duck Island'
1714–1760

George I was far more interested in Hanover than in his new kingdom of Britain. Nor did he care for his royal parks or his collection of animals in the Tower of London, but we have some amusing accounts of the activities of the animals held there during his reign.

A Frenchman called César de Saussure visited England early in the eighteenth century and found much to interest him in London and to write about in his letters to his family living in exile at Lausanne. He returned to Switzerland in 1729 and found that his accounts of life in the English capital had been read not only by his family, but also their friends. He added further notes on subsequent visits to England. The full text was published first in English in 1902 and his descriptions of life in London at the time he was writing make the city sound most attractive.

First he visited St James's Park and wrote a lively account of how it appeared to a stroller in September 1725,

'St James's Park contains several avenues of elm and lime trees, two large ponds, and a pretty little island; in a word this is an enchanting spot in summer time. Society comes to walk here on fine warm days, from 7 to 10 in the evening, and in winter from one to 3 o'clock. English men and women are fond of walking, and the park is so crowded at times that you cannot help touching your neighbour. Some people come to see, some to be seen, and others to seek their fortunes; for many priestesses of Venus are abroad, some of them magnificently attired, and all on the look-out for adventures, and many young men are not long in repenting that they have become acquainted with such beautiful and amiable nymphs. The ponds are covered with wild ducks and geese, deer and roe-deer are so tame that they eat out of your hand, and there is little danger of being attacked in the park or in the neighbourhood of the Palace, for should the offender be taken up in any of these privileged parts, the laws would condemn him to lose his hand'.[1]

The following June, Saussure enlarged this picture and reminds us how rural in aspect London was in the first years of the 18th century,

> 'Nothing is more beautiful than the road from London to Kensington, crossing Hyde Park. It is perfectly straight and so wide that three or four coaches can drive abreast . . . When you look from one end of the road to the other the effect is charming. In this (Hyde) Park and in St James's there are numbers of buck and roe-deer. These parks being separated by Piccadilly only, the animals can wander from one to the other'.[2]

Saussure also visited the Tower, though with less enthusiasm because of the manner in which it was kept. In December 1725 he described how, after entering,

> 'In the first inclosure you must see the King's menagerie, this being a small and rather dirty place containing ten lions, a panther, two tigers, and four leopards, each in his own den or cage. Last time I went we also saw a quantity of curious birds, but what amused us most was the sight of four young lions a few months old, born in the Tower, and as they were too young to be ferocious, they allowed us to fondle and caress them as if they had been little dogs. I also saw what I considered to be a very curious and extraordinary animal, which the keeper called a "Tiger-man". It was a very big monkey, its face, hands, and feet resembling those of a man more than those of any monkey I have ever seen, and it had a small white beard, giving it quite the appearance of an old man. Its hide was striped like that of a tiger, especially on the back, with handsome, well-defined, white, red, and black stripes. We were told that this animal was very intelligent, and I will give you a proof of this. One day, the poor beast being ill, a little wine was given it, which seemed to do it good. The rogue found it excellent, and having remarked that no wine was given him unless he was ill, he feigned sickness two or three times in order to receive the coveted remedy: this little scheme answered at first, but one day his keeper, seeing him leap about with mischievous

Three tame lion cubs, born in the Tower of London, illustrated in *Curiosities in the Tower of London*, published by Thomas Boreman in 1741. Boreman said he had held them on his lap and they were not restrained in any way while they warmed themselves by the open fire.

joy after drinking the wine, discovered the trick and beat him soundly. We were told that the captain of a ship belonging to the East India Company had brought this 'tiger-man' some months before from the island of Sumatra'.[3]

This monkey, apparently a mandrill, found the Tower far too cold, and died about six weeks after Saussure had seen it.

George I died in 1727 and was succeeded by George II and his consort, Queen Caroline. They had rather more to do with their animal dependants and brought two other parks into use as habitats for their unusual, imported species. The new parks were at Windsor and Richmond.

Edward Jesse was Deputy Surveyor of Richmond Park and lived at the Farm House. He was the author of *Gleanings in Natural History* (published in 1832) in which he tells the story, often repeated to him by his father, who had also been a keeper in the park, that in the reign of George II there was a large flock of wild turkeys kept there. In this flock there were no fewer than 2,000 birds which,

'fed on acorns, of which they must have had an abundant supply, since the park was then almost entirely wooded with oak, with a thick cover of furze . . . Stacks of barley were also put up in different places in the park for their support; and some of the old turkey cocks are said to have weighed from 25 to 30 pounds. They were hunted with dogs, and made to take refuge in a tree, where they were frequently shot by George II. I have not been able to learn how long they had been preserved in the park before his reign but they were totally destroyed towards the latter end of it in consequence of the dangers to which the keepers were exposed in protecting them from poachers, with whom they had many a bloody fight, being frequently overpowered by them'.[4]

Cape geese were kept on the large ponds in Richmond Park and had their nests on the island in one of the ponds. Rats were a nuisance however and kept stealing their eggs, so the geese took to building their nest in some oak pollards near the water and, Jesse reported, 'they conveyed their young to safety from these elevated nesting-sites'. The ponds were known as Pen Ponds. There was to be an even

Four Tower of London menagerie animals, in *Curiosities in the Tower of London*, published by Thomas Boreman in 1741.

more remarkable acclimatization experiment in this park, but that story must wait until the next reign.

At Windsor in the Great Park, both peafowl and guinea fowl were released and 'perfectly succeeded, the fowls requiring no more care or feeding than the pheasant'. George II's third son, William Augustus, the Duke of Cumberland, was appointed ranger of Windsor Forest and Great Park. His main hobby was the breeding of race horses, many of which were painted by the two artists Paul Sandby and Sawrey Gilpin. The Duke's other hobby was collecting wild animals which he kept in a semi-free condition in Windsor Park. His father gave him an elephant and a zebra that were allowed to roam in large enclosures within the park. He also had some lions and tigers, and Horace Walpole after inspecting them thought them to be 'so delicious!' He would not have written that, had he waited a little while to hear of the adventures of one of the tigers. Mrs Delany told her sister about it in a letter dated 9 June 1757,

> 'We went directly to the Duke's Lodge . . . The menagerie is not stored with great variety, but great quantities of Indian pheasants, the gold kind, blue and white, and the common sort. The wild & foreign beasts are all sent to the Tower. A terrible accident happened not very long ago – the tiger got out of his den and tore a boy of 8 or 9 years of age to pieces; the mother was by and ran upon the beast, and thrust her hands and arms into its very jaws to save her child; the keeper got her away, safely, but the poor child was destroyed; upon which accident the Duke sent them to the Tower as the only fit place for such fell beasts. There is a dromedary – an ugly creature, it is kept in a yard by itself; it made a hideous noise and frightened the horses. I forgot to name among the birds two eagles, a young eagle of the sun (not come to its beauty) and a horned owl that looked as wise as a judge in his robes'.[5]

During George II's reign, the two artist brothers, Thomas (who was acting as deputy ranger and lived at the Lower Lodge) and Paul Sandby, created the lake, Virginia Water. They also supervised the planting, road-laying and lawn-making which so greatly added to the beauty of this large open space. The planting had matured by the time George II's great grandson (George IV) came to the throne and this part of the country then became the site of an even larger menagerie than that owned by the Duke of Cumberland.

Queen Caroline read a great many books on a wide range of subjects. She had a cave or grotto in Richmond Park called Merlin's cave, where she could retire to the small library kept there in order to read in peace. This gothic thatched building had a custodian called Stephen Duck. What more appropriate person could the Queen have found to become the new Governor of Duck Island in St James's Park?[6] There had already been the royal appointments of Sir John Flock, Mr Webb, Jack Sparrow and Mr Martin as custodians of royal mammals and birds, but surely Stephen Duck for the Decoy

Portrait of Stephen Duck, the poet. (Frontispiece of the 1753 edition of Stephen Duck's *Poems*).

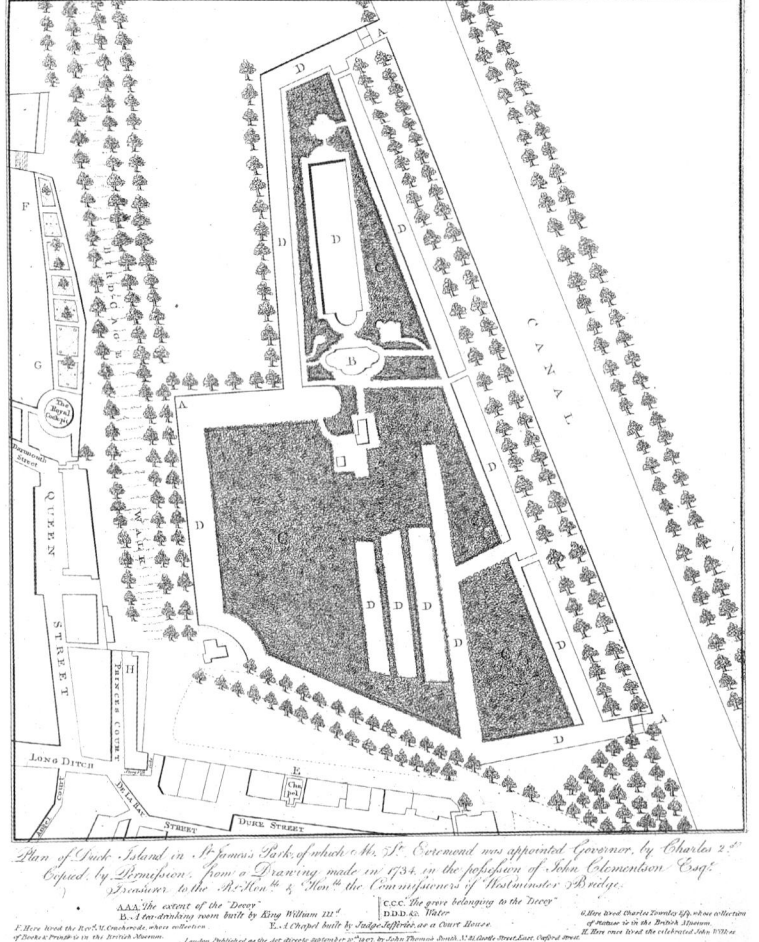

Plan of Duck Island in St James's Park of which Mr St Evremond was appointed Governor, by Charles 2d. Copied by Permission, from a Drawing made in 1734, in the possession of John Clementson Esqr. Treasurer to the Rt Honble & Honble the Commissioners of Westminster Bridge.

A.A.A. the extent of the 'Decoy'.
B. A tea-drinking room built by King William IIId.
C.C.C. the grove belonging to the 'Decoy'
D.D.D. &c. Water
F. Here lived the Revd S.W. Crackenrods, whose collection of Books & Prints is in the British Museum.
E. A Chapel built by Judge Jeffries, as a Court House.
G. Here lived Charles Townley Esq, whose collection of Statues is in the British Museum.
H. Here once lived the celebrated John Wilkes.

London, Published as the Act directs September 30th 1807, by John Thomas Smith, N. 31 Castle Street East, Oxford Street.

Duck Island, a drawing made in 1734, published in 1807 in John Thomas Smith, *Antiquities of Westminster*, captioned 'Plan of Duck Island in St James's Park of which Mr St Evremond was appointed Governor by Charles 2d'.

and Duck Island was the best choice of all. He had a varied career and was nicknamed the Thresher Poet, became a Yeoman of the Guard in 1733, was admitted to Holy Orders and preferred to the living of Byfleet in Surrey and finally ended his own life by drowning in the river Thames near Reading in 1756. This odd person commenced life as a farm labourer, hence the 'Thresher' and wrote doggerel verse which attracted the attention of the Queen, who probably read his poetry in Merlin's Cave while it was in the custody of the poet himself. Stephen Duck is remembered to this day. Each year on 1 June, the annual Duck Feast at Charlton, just south of Salisbury, attended by twelve 'Duck Men' is presided over by the 'Chief Duck' wearing a tall hat decorated with the figure of a thresher and his flail and trimmed

St James's Park 1753. The long straight canal made c.1662, where the wildfowl were to be seen, with Buckingham House at the far end. Baron Bielfeld referred to the Canal and Duck Island, when he saw them in 1741, 'On one side I beheld a spacious basin, covered with clamorous ducks and every other aquatic fowl. In the midst of this basin rises an island that is ornamented with an elegant building'. This view was painted by Stevens after Canaletto. The duck decoy, known as Duck Island, lies behind the fence on the left.

with duck feathers. Since 1734, when Lord Palmerston gave a piece of land whose rent paid for the feast, the combined toast has been to 'the health of the Rev. Stephen Duck and Lord Palmerston'.

St James's Park was visited in 1741 by Baron von Bieldfeld and regularly toured each morning by him to marvel at 'le spectacle de la campagne, de la guerre, de la ville, et de la cour' and also to see the ducks and other waterfowl. He crossed to Duck Island in the decoy, picked flowers there and admired the building which had been associated with St Evremond and his successors.

The ducks living on Rosamond's Pond in the Park, saw some strange sights during this reign and frequently had their own domain rudely invaded. Larwood tells how,

'Rosamond's Pond was railed in and prevented a number of accidents of the sort that occurred on 6 Jan. 1730. In a great fog a couple of chair-men lost their way while crossing the park and the first man fell into the Pond dragging the chair and its occupant in after him. It was only with the greatest difficult that the lady was rescued'.

At a later date, the ducks lost their pond completely, for this same land was emptied and cleaned 'by an engine raised upon piles in the pond,' invented by Hugh Roberts of Flintshire. It was said to discharge 30 tons of water in a minute and cost about £400. The following notice was fixed to one of the trees to warn those attempting suicide,

Rosamond's Pond, before fencing and after
(a) An unfenced Rosamond's Pond (to the left of the canal), the straight canal after being altered by Capability Brown c.1770 and Buckingham House centre right.
(b) Rosamond's Pond c.1745, now fenced, looking eastwards toward Westminster. Part of Birdcage Walk now runs over the site of the pond.

'This is to give notice to all broken hearts, such as are unable to survive the loss of their loves, and are come to a resolution to die, that an engineer from Flintshire having cruelly undertaken to disturb the water of Rosamond's Pond in the Park, gentlemen and ladies cannot be accommodated as formerly'.[7]

The writer of this warning then made an alternative suggestion to the would-be suicides, directing them instead to the basin in the Upper Green Park which was 'of depth sufficient to answer the ends of all sizes and conditions'.[8]

Queen Caroline apparently suffered from depression too. She put saffron in her tea to ward off the miserable symptoms and drank dandelion tea and other infusions. Her idea that saffron might be a cure for depression may have come from her visits to the pet shops in St Martin's Lane. The bird dealers gave saffron to canaries when moulting, either to perk them up, or in the belief that the new feathers would become more glowingly yellow and thus render the birds more expensive for prospective buyers.

In 1739 General Churchill was made Deputy Ranger of St James's Park and this appointment provoked Sir Hanbury Williams to write an 'Address to Venus' on the General's behalf, imploring the goddess to,

> 'Quit Paphos and the Cyprian Isle
> And reign in my Duck Island'.[9]

Churchill was succeeded in 1751 by Lord Pomfret and Horace Walpole similarly could not resist sniping at him in a letter he wrote informing his friend and correspondent Sir Horace Mann, 'My Lord Pomfret is made Ranger of the Parks, and by consequence my Lady is Queen of Duck Island'.

Early in George II's reign a guide to the Tower was published for the benefit of visitors. The booklet was issued in 1730 and described the scene on entering the Tower when the visitor would immediately 'see on the right the figure of a lion painted over the door' and for 3d he could go in and see the lions, panthers, eagles, vultures and other caged exhibits.[10] In August the following year a litter of young lions was whelped from a lioness and a lion who had himself been born at the Tower six years previously. Another lioness, who died 4 September 1733, had annually produced a litter of young ones in the Tower for several years and was very elderly.[11] The Keeper of the Lion Office in the Tower was a Mr Martin who was related to Sir Joseph Martin the wealthy, eminent Turkey merchant. The relationship bore fruit for the menagerie when '2 Apes from Turkey' were brought in some time during this reign. George II did not appoint Mr Martin's successor himself, but left it to his minister, Sir Robert Walpole. Walpole's choice fell on John Ellis, a 'face-painter' or portraitist who had materially aided him in the formation of the magnificent Houghton art collection. Houghton Hall in Norfolk was the home of the Walpoles, later created the Earls of Orford.[12]

In 1739 a costly new addition to the menagerie, an animal of voracious appetite, was put on show. It was a Bengal rhinoceros, which cost nearly £1,000 initially to purchase and ship to England. It ate great quantities of hay and grass and also received a daily ration of seven pounds of rice and three pounds of sugar, the whole lot being divided into three meals a day.

Dr Samuel Johnson was almost as eager for visitors to London to go and see the lions in the Tower as Pepys had been a century earlier and he always asked them if they had been. By 1754 it was certainly worth a visit, for there was so much more to see. Visitors even had a choice in the manner of paying for their entry. Members of the public were either admitted after paying 3d, or upon providing a cat or dog 'to serve as nourishment for the lions'. Maitland gave a long account of the exhibits at this time, March 25 1754, but some of them are difficult to recognise under their contemporary names and description, e.g. 'Two Egyptian Nightwalkers'. Other dubious species were 'Man-Tygers' of which there were two, one 'neither so large nor so dexterous' as the other, which was just as well because the larger animal was very bad-tempered and obstreperous. He had acquired,

> 'an admirable art of throwing Stones and will throw any Lead or Iron that happens to be within his reach with such force as to split stools, bowls or any such wooden utensils, in an hundred pieces. When he came over, he killed a poor boy on board the ship that brought him by throwing a canon shot of nine pounds weight at him, upon some disgust'.

Despite this waywardness he was 'fed in the nicest manner, with as good bread as the Keeper eats at his Table . . . He has a stool to sit upon, is as big as a boy of 10 or 11 years old, and has many actions nearly approaching to those of the human species'. Besides these two mandrills, there were the '2 Apes from Turkey, three beautiful tigers, and a fine leopard'.[13]

Among the birds were several eagles brought from different parts of the world and a golden eagle 'which has been kept here upwards of ninety years'. Maitland enthused over 'A horned owl' (eagle owl?) whose 'head seems full as big as that of a cat, its eyes large, having circles round them, of

The quagga is now extinct, the last one, a female in the Zoological Society Gardens, purchased from Carl Jamrach on 5 March 1831, died in 1872 and no more were known after 1883. It was first described by Tachard in 1685 as a wild ass. In 1827 Sheriff Parkins owned a pair of quaggas which had been taught to pull a carriage that he drove in Hyde Park and other fashionable places. (Jacques-Laurent Agasse, *A Male Quagga from Africa*. Royal College of Surgeons).

a bright shining gold colour'. He then gave details of the owl's beautiful feathers. An ostrich had been presented to George II by the Dey of Tunis. The remaining animals were two bears, the lion Pompey and his seven-year old lioness Helen, a tyger cat ('this last a beautiful creature, larger than the largest Boar Cat, delightfully coloured and fierce beyond description', identifed in other sources as a 'Shargoss' or caracal and a margay and a ratel!), a jackal and a 'Guiny Rangoon much more beautifull than those from America'. Thomas Bewick named an animal from the Tower as a sand bear, but John Hunter identified this as a raccoon. The raccoon was fond of oysters and was kept in good fettle on them.

Having given visitors an anticipatory thrill and fright with these tales of ferocity, Maitland spoiled the effect by admitting,

'All these creatures are regularly fed with food proper for them, and as carefully tended, as if they were indeed a royal Dignity. This takes off much of their savage nature and makes them tame and submissive; and perhaps, contributed not a little to disappoint the expectations of King James I when he made trial of the fierce nature of the Lion'.[14]

The year in which George II died, aged seventy-seven, the elderly lion Pompey also died and was erroneously reported as being over seventy years old, far too long a life-span for a lion.

Prince George, who succeeded his grandfather as George III in 1760, had owned a female quagga which lived several years in a house at Kew. George Edwards in his *Gleanings of Natural history*, published in 1758, wrote about,

> 'this curious animal which was brought alive, together with the male from the Cape of Good Hope; the male dying before they arrived at London. The noise it made was much different from that of an ass, resembling more the confused barking of a mastiff-dog. It seemd to be of a savage and fierce nature; no one would venture to approach it, but a gardener in the Prince's service, who was used to feed it and could mount on its back'.[15]

The future King was thus already used to owning exotic animals before he took over the responsibility for the royal menageries.

Chapter 6

'The hillifents and the pye bald ass'
1760–1820

George III was the first of the Hanoverian Kings to show any real interest in his animal subjects and Queen Charlotte shared his enthusiasm for them. 'Farmer George', as he was often called, was a countryman at heart and liked nothing better than to escape to the informality of his farms and estates where his mammals and birds were kept in relative comfort. During his very long reign, 1760–1820, the study of natural history received a tremendous boost from increased trade and the discovery of Australia. Many species new to science were introduced and many more living specimens shipped home from all parts of the world. Following the precedent set during the famous circumnavigation of the world by Captain James Cook in 1768–71, when Joseph Banks was on board as the expedition's naturalist, other ships' complements frequently included botanists and zoologists who brought home new and interesting species, some of them alive.

Captain Cook attempted to maintain the health of his crew and prevent scurvy by taking greenstuffs on board and he also took his own goat. Sophie La Roche was disappointed when,

> 'The rain deprived me of a visit to Greenwich Park and Captain Cook's goat, which, after accompanying him on his voyage round the world and supplying him with fresh milk, had also earned the recognition of the marines and permission to spend the remainder of her days amongst the tars, where she may eat her fill without disturbance'.[1]

This idea was put to good use by other captains when conveying young mammals home from foreign countries. It was easier to capture and transport cubs who were more tameable than their wild parents, but cubs needed milk while they were being weaned.

George Stubbs painted a kangaroo from a skin in 1771 or 1772 for Sir Joseph Banks, which was engraved for this first published picture of the species. (Hawkesworth, *Voyages for making discoveries in the Southern hemisphere*, vol. 3, plate 20, 1773). Thomas Pennant wrote of the first live specimen in his book, *History of quadrupeds*, 1793, 'In the spring of the present year, I had opportunity of observing the manners of one brought into the capital alive'.

In the wake of Captain Cook's voyages, a most remarkable and successful experiment took place. When Arthur Phillip (1738–1814) took the first fleet to Australia in 1789, comprising a ship-load of convicts to settle the colony, plus supply ships with food and ammunition, he was appointed Governor of the new country. On reaching land, Phillip set about organising the new Australians and their guards so that the colony could become self-sufficient. He sent out parties to discover what the countryside near Botany Bay had to offer by way of native plants and animals for food. He was brought some kangaroos and in 1792 sent the first live kangaroo to England, to be presented to George III as a present 'from the Governor'. William Bullock described what happened next. The kangaroo, he said,

> 'May be considered in some degree as naturalised in England, several having been kept for many years in the Royal domains at Richmond which have, during their residence there, produced young, and promise to render this most elegant animal a permanent acquisition to the country'.[2]

The first kangaroo to be born here was the subject of a letter to Banks, from David Dundas, who wrote on 30 December 1793 from Richmond, describing the young kangaroo born in the gardens there, and the behaviour of its mother.[3]

The royal family would have been delighted with the antics of their kangaroos and when the princes and princesses were given their regular lessons in natural history, what pleasanter way could there be to learn than from the real, living animals? The lessons must have been lively affairs when they visited the Tower, St James's Park and Richmond Park. They also had access for their indoor studies to specimens which the Queen asked Dr S. C. T. Demainbray to collect and prepare for their instruction. In reality, Dr John Hunter prepared many of their specimens and a cabinet of natural history objects gradually accumulated and grew to some proportion at Kew Palace. It was transferred many years after the King's death to King's College Museum in 1843 and preserved there under the name 'George III's Museum'.

The King's farming interests were extensive and he greatly encouraged the new scientific methods of breeding to improve farm animals for wool or meat. He reclaimed land in Windsor Great Park and created the Norfolk and Flemish Farms, then made them examples of the most approved systems of agriculture of that age. He employed the services of Sir Joseph Banks to import merino sheep from Spain for his farms. Sir Joseph's first two, a ewe and a ram with iron collars bearing his address stamped on them, arrived in 1785. Two years later George III asked Banks to obtain merinos from Spain for him, not only to improve his flocks in Richmond Gardens, but to improve the country's

Merino sheep, (David Low, *The Breeds of the domestic animals of the British Isles*, 2 vols 1842, plate X11). The most successful breeders in 1842 were Lord Western and Mr Bennett MP for Wiltshire.

wool, which he regarded as 'A most national object'. Since wool accounted at that date for almost one quarter of the nation's exports, this was no exaggeration. British manufacturers had for generations been importing the close-set, silky merino wool from Spain to mix with English wool to make a very fine cloth.

It took many years to obtain more merino sheep and build up flocks on private estates, but finally, in 1804, there were sufficient to hold a public sale. At this sale, John Macarthur purchased eleven sheep for his flock in New South Wales. Whereas the merino experiment had no lasting effect in England, despite all the King's and Banks's efforts, the merino was the breed on which the extraordinarily successful Australian wool industry was built. Of all the acclimatisation and improvement schemes with animals in the late 18th and 19th centuries, this was one of the most successful, but not in England.

By the early 1800s, the King's and Queen's scattered menagerie was quite large and if we add to this the animals in the care of their grown-up children, it was even more extensive. They had, of course, inherited quite a large collection of animals at the Tower and during the sixty-year reign many more specimens arrived as presents for the King and his family. One of the first gifts was brought by Captain Booke Samson of the *Hardwicke*, an East Indiaman. This was an elephant from Bengal, which was presented in the name of the East India Company in September 1763 and received by the King 'with great regard'. The elephant was pampered. It had two attendants who had come from the East Indies, one called Senetal who was resplendent in a rose-coloured lustrine Turkish robe and cap, and his servant Newran who wore a chintz cotton mantle. The elephant was wrapped in a blue fringed cloth which had a lining of red baize to keep it warm and a headpiece with a crown embroidered on either side. The stables for the elephant and a zebra stood outside the garden wall on the south, beside the road we know as Buckingham Palace Road, but when the weather was fine they were put to graze in St James's Park where the public was allowed to visit the 'Queen's animals'.[4]

In 1767 Lady Mary Coke 'went to visit the Queen's Elephants. The Men that have the care of them told us the three Dukes had been with them in the morning. 'Tis

A female zebra caused great excitement when it arrived in London from the Cape of Good Hope, a gift to Queen Charlotte in 1762. It was housed in a paddock at Buckingham Gate, where the public was allowed to view it. An account of this first zebra in Britain was published in *London Magazine* XXX1, July 1762, with an engraving. George Stubbs's oil painting (now in the Paul Mellon Collection, Yale Center for British Art) was exhibited in 1763.

wonderful what exceedingly intelligent Animals they are; they were perfectly obedient to every order that was given them'. Among other visitors were some less kindly authors, who used the animals as the pretext for scurrilous lampoons and artists who adopted them as characters in order to produce caricatures of notorious public servants. The zebra was one of these subjects. It had been presented to the Queen and at first was exhibited in The Mews, but later it usually could be seen grazing in the paddock near Buckingham House, where it was the object of much curiosity. Too much, for 'owing to the rudeness of the populace, the zebra and an elephant which had been exhibited at the same place, were removed to the menagerie in the Tower'.

In 1763 George Stubbs painted this male mountain zebra (*Equus zebra*) from the Cape of Good Hope, the first to be seen in England. Stubbs painted it, as he did the famous racehorses of the day, side-ways on, which was the perfect position to show the pattern of the stripes.

Smollet's novel *Humphrey Clinker*, published in 1771, includes a comment by the Welsh waiting woman, who described her visit to London and St James's. She said she had, 'seen the Park, and the paleass of Saint Gimses . . . and the sweet young princes, and the hillifents and pye bald ass, and all the rest of the royal family'. The family was fond of walking in the park, like Charles II, and enjoyed visiting their animals.

Foreign animals were now to be found in travelling menageries and, when they died, they were preserved and took on a second career earning gate money for their owners in museums. The Queen's irritable female zebra was such a nuisance that she was sold to one of the menageries in 1773, but soon died and ended up preserved and mounted in Sir Ashton Lever's museum in Leicester Fields. This museum also obtained '3 specimens of young lions, bred in the Tower of London' which were bought for £1 and 2 shillings when the museum was sold in 1806.

The Tower Menagerie had become so popular that several new guides and accounts of the inhabitants were published and ran into a number of editions. One of them gave a clear description of what the menagerie looked like at this time,

> 'On entering the Tower, the King's Menagerie first presents itself; for when you have entered the outer gate, and passed what is called the Spur-guard, you see the keeper's house just before you, and over the door where you enter, is the figure of a lion; there you ring, and for 1 shilling each person, you will be admitted to see the Wild Beasts'.[5]

It required another shilling to view the Regalia and a further two shillings to see the Spanish armour, quite an expensive outing in 1806. Having paid,

> 'At your entrance you come to a range of dens in the form of a half moon. These dens are rooms about 12 or 13 feet high, divided into three apartments, a large one above, and two below. In the upper apartments the beasts generally live in the day, and at night retire to the lower to rest. You view them through large iron grates, like those before the windows of a prison; so that you may see them with utmost safety, be they ever so ferocious'.

Nearly all the animals had names, so visitors were introduced to Princess Didon who was a 'perfect beauty' of a lioness aged six and in the prime of life. Jenny, at fourteen, was the 'greatest age attained by any of the lions kept at the Tower over the last 500 years'. (Alas, poor Pompey, already forgotten). She was the mother of nine lion cubs, offspring of a lion named Marco who had died. Most of the cubs died at the teething stage when they were subject to 'convulsions'. It was very rare for young lions to be reared in captivity at this period, owing, no doubt, to insufficient privacy for the nursing female and lack of vitamins in their diet. They were kept in a warm room for the first year and the keepers found them adorable and tame, but as their strength increased, so did their unpredictability. Two of Jenny and Marco's cubs were called Nero and Nancy. Apart from a lioness Helen, who was seven years old in 1761, there was a 'virgin but has a lover', coyly unnamed.

Other lions in this reign were one from Senegal in 1775, reported in the *Gentleman's Magazine*, 2 Asiatic lions, another so tame 'that the keeper kisses him and goes into his den' which had been sent by the Emperor of Morocco, Miss Fanny, a lioness bred in the Tower and Miss Fanny Howe, who was whelped on the glorious 1st of June 1794 and named after the gallant admiral, Richard Howe, who

Tower Menagerie 1820 The arrangement of the dens in a semi-circle around a yard at the Tower of London. The walkway over the upper storey gave spectators a view down into the yard when the animals were let out for exercise. (G. W. Thornbury and E. Walford, *Old and new London*, vol. 11: 85)

Thomas Rowlandson's cartoon published December 1799 and called 'The Monkey Room in the Tower'. The descriptive booklet of 1794 *The Tower Menagerie* referred to a 'school of monkeys'. The larger monkey is probably Jumbo, a baboon. Strype spoke of a 'school of apes' in 1754, when there were 'two Egyptian night-walkers' among them, and 'two apes from Turkey'. The keeper and his wife are on the left of the picture, the caricatured visitors to the Tower are on the right.

gained a great victory over the French on that day with the Channel fleet off Ushant.[6] A Barbary panther had been named Traveller and Henry was a 'Royal Tiger' brought over in the *Pitt* East Indiaman, presented to Her Majesty by Secretary Nepean and, 'had a little dog constantly with him'. No-one had thought of a name for a, 'Ring-tail'd Tyger from Bengal brought by Admiral Reynier for Her Majesty', but the leopards had all been christened. They were very variable in the markings on their coats, so that the young Duchess from the Malabar Coast was dull compared with Miss Nancy, 'a bright spotted leopardess sent from Anjango, by Governor Hutchinson'. The Prince of Wales owned two leopards and a leopardess called Miss Maria and Masters Bobby and George. But the beautiful black panther was the lady who caught everyone's eye, including that of the naturalist and author Thomas Pennant, who, after seeing her in 1787, wrote that this specimen which came from Bengal was 'wholly black with round clusters of small spots of a glossy and most intense black on the body and the tail hung several inches beyond the length of the legs, and was very full of hairs'.[7]

The large cats were always the favourites, many accounts listing them in detail and then tailing off with such phrases as, '. . .and other animals etc'. We are more fortunate with the 1806 account, *An Historical Description of the Tower of London and its curiosities*, which elaborates on the other inhabitants, for example, a young wolf from Mexico 'sent in a flag of truce from Adml Masserano in Spain', a hyena from the Cape of Good Hope and a very large African deer from the same area, 'brought home by Genl. Dundas and only ever one brought to England'. Sophie La Roche saw the hyena and said that its movements 'were the most impassioned and persevering – it is indeed an ugly, fearful and revolting animal'.[8]

The raccoons and jackals had bred successfully in the Tower and a white fox had come all the way from 'Owhyhee' (but how it had got to Hawaii was not explained), while an 'Eagle of the Sun' occasioned an apologetic note at the bottom of the page about some 'kids – food of eagles'. The lambs, hares, fawn and pheasants might well also have served as meals for other carnivorous inhabitants. Sophie said that the eagles 'were perched sorrowfully beneath the trees, fastened to thongs, looking to the sun and airy regions above'. She was not too sure whether she was enjoying her visit to the menagerie, for she seems to have let her imagination run out of control and she became sorry for the animals,

> 'The all-black tiger, which Mr Hastings brought with him from the East Indies, is most handsome, but his tigery glance all the more horrible. Monkeys I always loathed when I saw them even though I realise, that like hyenas, they belong to creation'.

Sophie visited the menagerie in 1786. The monkeys were no longer present two decades later.[9]

One wonders if this 1806 list is complete, for other writers remember having seen bears there, including 'a large bear from the north', confirmed elsewhere in the phrase 'bears black and white'. The 1792 edition of a *Guide to the Tower* included some monkeys and two black bears from North America and says that Sophie's much disliked hyena had come from the East Indies – a vague term used in a blanket way for anything arriving on an East Indiaman whatever its place of origin, either Far, Middle or Near east or picked up at an African port on the way home. The same guide remarked on an ostrich which had died recently and a post mortem had revealed '80 nails in its stomach'.

In the last year of George III's reign, 1820, another booklet was published called *A Visit to the Tower being an Account of several Birds and Beasts*. The odd mixture of animals in this is unlikely to form a comprehensive record of the state of the menagerie at that date, but the animals named are different from those in the usual accounts. It is quite short, 'The Lion,

Elephant, Horse, Owl (barn, with quotation from Grey's *Elegy*), Bull, Sheep, Robin Redbreast, Sow, Whale, Dog, Cat, Squirrel, Rat'.

On 9 March 1768 Lady Mary Coke visited the Tower and found one lion which,

> 'was packed up in a large wooden box to be sent on board a ship that waited for it, as a present to the Nabob that made the King a present of diamonds & pearls to the value of eighteen thousand pounds; it seems to me a very inconsiderable return for so magnificent a present on the part of the Nabob'.[10]

While the Tower Menagerie had been attracting so much attention, the royal park at St James's had received a face-lift. An alteration in the landscape had been effected which deprived the birds of some living space. They had never had as much peace on Rosamond's Pond as elsewhere in the park and in May 1770, after a great storm the previous year with much flooding from both the pond and the canal, as well as most of the stagnant water round the duck pond, work was commenced on filling in Rosamond's Pond. Larwood said that,

> 'The house on Duck Island was spared for a time for the King having heard that Mr Drury who was keeper of the island, was sadly distressed at losing his house, kindly gave instructions that it should remain standing as long as Mr Drury lived'.

This was the little house which William III had built as an observatory and had been lived in, prior to Drury's occupancy, by a flat-footed keeper called Webb and so had acquired the name of Webb's House.[11] The wood growing on the island and on the undulating ground around Rosamond's Pond was to be felled and cleared away before Michaelmas 1772. The park at this time still had a countrified air and milk-women grazed their cows there at 2 shillings and 6 pence a week in the 1770s, and 3 shillings later.

A famous London character, Jack the mute swan, lived in and around the Duck Decoy. He was thoroughly spoilt by Queen Charlotte, who fed him with warm white bread and he was fussed over by other Londoners. Though sensible enough not to bite the hand that fed him, Jack could be vicious on occasion and had killed several dogs and once

The milch cows and milkmaids in St James's Park by the park rails. Mr Grossly, a French visitor, in 1765 commented on the park where 'The cows are driven about noon and the evening to the gate which leads from the Park to the quarter of Whitehall. Tied in a file to the posts at the extremity of the grass plot, they swill passengers with their milk, which being drawn from their udders on the spot, is served, with all the cleanliness peculiar to the English, in little mugs, at the rate of a penny a mug'. (G. W. Thornbury and E. Walford, *Old and new London*, vol. IV: 84).

nearly killed a boy who baited him beyond endurance. This rogue lived through four reigns.[12]

Queen Charlotte's feeding of the swan at St James's is reminiscent of Charles II's habit of publicly feeding the ducks. The Queen also had a number of birds in her private apartments. The portraits of the Queen and six of her children, painted by John Zoffany in 1770, show William, Duke of Gloucester on the left, holding a sulphur-crested cockatoo. The Queen also owned a weaver-bird and would willingly have given it to replace a weaver-bird belonging to the cultured, elderly Mrs Delany in order to spare her grief over the death of her bird, had the two been of the same species. They were so different that the exchange could not be made.

King George and Queen Charlotte were fond of their small house at Kew. Princess Caroline of Ansbach had been given the southern part of Kew Gardens by her husband, George II and in 1761 George III similarly presented the estate to his new queen, Charlotte of Mecklenburg-Strelitz. They used it as a summer retreat and employed Capability Brown to re-design the surrounding landscape. About 1770 Queen Charlotte's new cottage was built at the centre of a menagerie with pens for exotic mammals and birds. In 1801 this was described as having 'a Kangaroo, a native of New Holland; the males of these are chiefly kept in pens, which form a square inclosure, in which the females with their young are permitted to range'. There were also buffaloes, a duck pond and pens for golden pheasants. This menagerie had been built in 1760 by Sir William Chambers for Princess Caroline.[13]

Their small house at Kew, which was run on simple lines, had few staff to intrude on their privacy. In 1806 the menagerie housed their children's pets. Besides kangaroos there was a fine blue nylghau from India, Algiers cows, a 'hog like a porcupine in skin', jerboas and a crown bird in the aviary.

Horace Walpole was curious about Chambers's buildings at Kew and apart from the numerous temples 'all of wood and very small', he particularly noted the 'Aviary, & a Chinese building in the Menagerie'. The Chinese style portion formed the centrepiece of the Menagerie and housed exotic birds and waterfowl. Pheasants from China and Tartary, many small foreign birds and gold fish lived there at various times.[14]

The hardier birds, perhaps British species and pheasants, which lived outside in the aviary have not been recorded in detail, but John Smith in his history of the Royal Garden at Kew said, 'Queen Charlotte, shortly before her death, gave orders for the aviary which she had to be left open, and the birds to be dispersed through the neighbourhood'. The site of the menagerie was flooded over when a lake was made in the 19th century.

The King and Queen taught their children to love animals and when they grew up, three of the princes took an especial interest in them and formed collections of their own. The Prince of Wales developed the greatest interest and we shall note the fortunes of two royal menageries under his reign as George IV. The other two sons with menageries were Ernest Augustus, Duke of Cumberland, and Frederick, the Duke of York. The Duke of Cumberland was an unpleasant man and an appalling martinet, but if his relationships with

(a) The old menagerie and its Chinese style pavilion built at Kew by Sir William Chambers 1760 to house the Kew Palace kangaroos, 'Pheasants de Chine, Pheasants de Tartary'; many small exotic birds and goldfish, at the end of the 18th century. (G. E. Papendick, *Kew Gardens, a series of 24 drawings on stone*, c.1820. Picture of Kew Aviary).

(b) The elaborate aviary at Kew, built by Sir William Chambers in 1763. (*Plans, elevations, sections and perspective views of the garden and buildings at Kew in Surrey, the seat of H. R. H. the Princess Dowager of Wales*, 1763. The aviary, E. Rooker, sculp).

people left much to be desired he had a soft spot for birds and made a collection of exotic species in the 1820s.[15]

George III's second son was Frederick (1763–1827), the Duke of York. In 1790 he bought a house at Oatlands Park near the site of the ancient royal palace of that name, some three miles from Weybridge in Surrey. He paid £45,000 for it and shortly after he took possession of the house it was burnt down. The Duke had it rebuilt in a sham Gothic style. Oatlands had been the country palace where Anne of Denmark, Queen of James I, had died. James I used it as a hunting lodge and Queen Anne visited it frequently and lived there for a while. She was very fond of dogs, particularly small Italian greyhounds which can be seen in Van Somer's portrait of her. Now history was repeated,

(a) Nero, a lion from Senegal exhibited in September 1814, drawn by Edwin Landseer, etched by his brother Thomas for *Twenty engravings of lions, panthers and leopards.* In 1820 Edwin dissected a lion from Exeter 'Change and produced several large paintings of lions. In 1859 Landseer was given a government commission to sculpt four lions for Trafalgar Square. While doing them, he haunted Regent's Park Zoo lion enclosure, sketching and then modelling them in miniature.

(b) John Ballantyne painted Landseer (his dog beside him) while sculpting the stone lions for Trafalgar Square, an eight year task. (National Portrait Gallery, London).

for the Duke of York married a Prussian princess in 1791 and Frederica Charlotte Ulrich Catherine (the eldest daughter of Frederick William II) went to Oatlands and there installed scores of dogs. It is said that she had a hundred at one time, but usually their number was around the forty mark. Despite this eccentricity, men of wit and learning, as well as the leading politicians of the day, willingly accepted her invitations to Oatlands, for she was a most attractive woman of decided personality, great charm and with much better manners than the rest of the royal family. Everyone loved her, for she was extraordinarily kind to the children, tenants and pensioners on the York estates. In her case, the love of animals was an extension of her genuine love and concern for people. The guests at Oatlands found her husband's penchant for playing whist almost non-stop a sore trial, but when they could escape from the card table they enjoyed the novelty of playing with the monkeys which lived in small houses on the tops of poles in the duchess's menagerie. Other creatures were kangaroos, ostriches and parrots. The ostriches were 'painted from nature' by Henry Bernard Chalon (1770–1849) 'Animal Painter to the Duchess of York', and exhibited at the Royal Academy in 1816.

The Natural History Museum in London, owned by William Bullock, exhibited a number of specimens from her collection after their much lamented demise, for example, 'The Royal Cuckoo C. regius', and one of the diminutive and delicate monkeys, the striated or sanglin Monkey (common

The menagerie of Frederica, Duchess of York at Oatlands, with wallabies, zebu, goats, peacock, black swan. (Edwardian copy of early 19th century print).

marmoset) which the duchess succeeded in breeding about 1815 or 16. Her kindness to birds was sensed by the wild birds at Oatlands and they joined her captive birds to share in the liberal fare provided for them. Even the rooks, when driven from the surrounding fields by the attacks of kites and fowlers, sought sanctuary under her protection at Oatlands, where they estabished an extensive colony. Lord Erskine, who frequently visited the Duchess, wrote,

> 'At Oatlands, where the buoyant air
> Vast crowds of rooks can scarcely bear
> What verdure paints returning Spring!
> What crops surrounding harvest bring
> Yet swarms on every tree are found,
> Nor hear the fowler's dreaded sound.
> And when the kite's resistless blow
> Dashes their scatter'd nest below,
> Alarm'd they quit the distant field,
> To seek the park's indulgent shield;
> Where, close in the o'ershading wood,
> They build new cradles for their brood,
> Secure – their fair protectress nigh,
> Whose bosom swells with sympathy'.[16]

However, dogs were always her favourite animals. Having so many always around her was distressing for others because of their dirty habits and for her on account of the frequency of their deaths. Her special dog-cemetery is now in the grounds of Oatlands Park Hotel. Peter Eduard Stroehling's portrait of the Duchess of York included four dog portraits, a greyhound, St Bernard and poodle and one of indeterminate breed. Farington, in his diary 8 June 1794, wrote, 'A Fire happened at Oatlands yesterday which damaged some of the art buildings. The King had been there, & brought back a little dog belonging to the Duchess of York, who seemed more anxious abt. her animals than abt. the House. She has 18 dogs. The King observed that affection must rest on something. When there were no children animals were the objects of it'.[17]

When she died in 1820 she was genuinely mourned and missed by all her friends, tenants and, one suspects, her numerous pets.

Chapter 7

'The very pink of politeness'
1820–1901

George IV eventually owned one of the finest collections of mammals and birds ever found in the care and keeping of a British monarch. He not only revived the fortunes of the Tower Menagerie and made improvements in St James's Park, but also constructed a private menagerie for his own pleasure at Windsor.

St James's Park took on a new lease of life, largely owing to the employment of the King's architect John Nash to remodel the canal. In January 1827 he converted the straight canal into a lake, with irregular margins and an island at each end. The old decoy and its Duck Island were destroyed and so the new island at the eastern end of the lake was promptly adopted and named 'Duck Island' by Londoners. Jack the Swan had been transferred from the Canal when his old haunts around Duck Island had been destroyed and this redoubtable old bird was further upset when the Ornithological Society of London introduced all kinds of new and foreign species to invade his territory. Jack gave them a hard time and life became hectic for the ageing swan, but Jack still invariably came off best in his many fierce and furious encounters with the newcomers. He survived to see another two monarchs come to the throne.

The Tower Menagerie had been greatly neglected during the last ten years of George III's reign, because of his illness, so that by 1822 nothing more than one grizzly bear called Old Martin, one elephant and a few birds remained. Alfred Cops was appointed Keeper in that year and with great enthusiasm and expenditure (for the first time animals were bought for the Tower) he set about filling the empty dens, constructing new ones and making improvements in the layout of the accommodation. He joined the two courts or yards, where the animals were kept, into one very large room 70' long. He was quickly rewarded by the public who went there in droves to see the fine spectacle of over 600

Old Martin, the Tower of London's grizzly bear. (Wood engraving from E. T. Bennett, *The Tower Menagerie*, 1829.

89

mammals and birds, which were present by 1829. He was an excellent keeper in all respects and only one accident occurred while he was in charge. The secretary bird pushed its head and long neck through the bars of the hyena's cage and was promptly deprived of both in one bite.

The full extent of the menagerie was recorded in a book published in 1829 (*The Tower Menageries*, by Edward T. Bennett), which had some excellent illustrations of the animals drawn by William Harvey (a former pupil of Thomas Bewick) and engraved on wood by Branston and Wright. The book was dedicated to George IV. Naturally, some new lions were given top priority and Cops would have been thrilled to have two cubs, a male and a female from Bengal, so that he could boast of having both African and Asiatic species at the Tower. The cubs had been reared on goat's milk on the long voyage to England. The Tower also had an Asiatic elephant, of which Cops was very proud and the differences between this and the African species were carefully pointed out. These differences had only just been discovered by the eminent French professor of comparative anatomy, Baron de Cuvier.

The Emperor of Morocco (a more amiable character than the ruler in Queen Anne's time) obliged by sending presents of lions and the East India Company ships still faithfully ploughed the seas with dangerous and awkward animal cargoes packed alongside their legitimate trade in the holds and on deck. The Company ships were still not allowed to transport animals for private or commercial sale, except for the King.

Similarly, some contributions came home aboard ships from America trading for the Hudson's Bay Company including a 'clouded black wolf'. Many of the animals that were shipped from foreign countries were caught young, then spoilt and petted by the sailors while roaming free on deck and subsequently took great exception to being cooped up in cages in the gloomy atmosphere of the Tower. The author of the book, Edward T. Bennet, said that a tigress and a caracal snarled and spat and turned 'sulky' when confined after their sea voyage to England. Such animals also acquired odd habits and food preferences, for example, a tiger liked to have soup served before his meat course and a Burchell's zebra, which was frequently allowed to run loose through the Tower, would race away from its keeper and

Thomas Bewick's wood engraving of a caracal, an African lynx (*History of quadrupeds*). This animal was in the Tower of London menagerie in 1829.

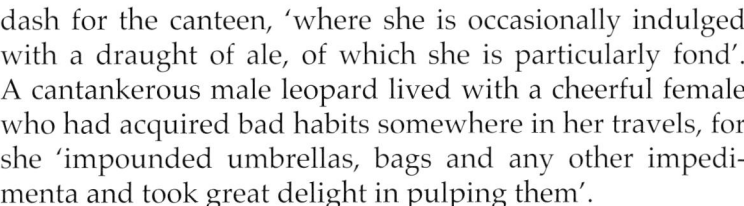

The llamas in the Tower of London. (Wood engraving from E. T. Bennett's, *The Tower Menagerie*).

dash for the canteen, 'where she is occasionally indulged with a draught of ale, of which she is particularly fond'. A cantankerous male leopard lived with a cheerful female who had acquired bad habits somewhere in her travels, for she 'impounded umbrellas, bags and any other impedimenta and took great delight in pulping them'.

Working with Mr Cops must have had some hilarious moments, particularly when dealing with the llamas from Peru,

> 'Those in the Tower Menagerie have a particular fondness for carrots; and if one of these is abstracted from them while they are eating, their anger is immediately aroused, and they spit, as it is termed, with the greatest vehemence, covering with their saliva a surface of three or four yards in extent. One of the animals in the cut is represented in the act'.[1] (see figure)

Some different members of the cat family were now on show and the public could see jaguars, puma, ocelot, and cheetahs. The pair of cheetahs had been bought by Mr Cops from a ship's crew returning from Senegal. The smaller cats were watched very carefully by the keeper, for a good reason as Bennet reported that, while a male 'Civet or Musk Cat' which had been born in the Tower over 12 months before had still not 'deposited any of its perfume', two female Javanese civets had been guilty of depositing 'large quantities of civet'. 'Perfume' is a misnomer, for the civet's deposit is a foul-smelling substance used only in tiny quantities as a fixative for aromatic oils to create perfume.

Mr Cops had some snakes and to both the India boa and anaconda listed in the book, the same scientific name, *Python tigris*, was attached. The anaconda was fed with a fowl or rabbit once every five or six weeks. The number of rattlesnakes present sounds distinctly alarming, over one hundred 'varying in length from 4 to 6 feet and differing very considerably from each other both in colour and markings'.

The variety of birds is much greater than formerly with two different species of macaw, a sulphur-crested cockatoo, and a Virginian horned owl, besides the foolish secretary bird which took too close a look at the hyena. Of some significance was the short note about the hen pelican

John Evelyn (*Diary* 19 September 1657) wrote 'I saw at Dr Joyliffe's 2 Virginian rattlesnakes alive'. These were some of the earliest seen in England. They were named *Crotalus horridus* by Linnaeus, indicative of the dislike humans have for this snake. (Wood engraving from E. T. Bennett, *The Tower Menagerie*).

who sat tightly on three eggs while her mate fed her. This is an early breeding record for a member of this species held in captivity.

There were many other interesting animals too numerous to itemise here. Among the notes that Bennett compiled for each species, are references to where the animals had been collected and who had donated them. In addition, there was some traffic between the Tower Menagerie and George IV's own private menagerie, which is reminiscent of the bad old days when difficult subjects were put out of harm's way in the Tower of London. A Malayan rusa deer (*Cervus equinus*, Cuvier) had been presented to the King and kept, along with another of the same species, in an enclosure at Windsor. As both, however, happened to be males, they disagreed violently, so,

Malaysian rusa deer fighting one another. George IV had two which fought so furiously that one was 'dismissed royal service, and condemned to the captivity of the Tower'. When alone, it became extremely tame. (Wood engraving from E. T. Bennett's *The Tower Menagerie*).

> 'it was found absolutely necessary to separate them; and our animal, as the most outrageous of the two was dismissed royal service, and condemned to captivity in the Tower'.

Emus and kangaroos became far too numerous on the royal estates, because they were so well acclimatized that they bred freely, and so those that were quarrelsome were sent off to the Tower to relieve the crowding at Windsor.

No King had owned such a magnificent collection of mammals, reptiles and birds in the Tower Menagerie before George IV, so it was ironical that he, of all our kings, should have chosen to have his own private menagerie. This was situated near Sandpit Gate, Virginia Water, in Windsor Great Park. However, George IV had for many years been lampooned, ridiculed, libelled and maligned by cartoonists and pamphleteers. In addition, when he finally became King, after waiting in the wings for so long as Regent, he, who had once earned the reputation for being the most elegant, well-dressed man in Europe, was now obese and ungainly and in his hour of triumph, King at last, all he wanted to do was to hide away at Windsor and not show himself to his highly critical, rude subjects. For his own amusement, he collected a menagerie in a corner of the park where his great-uncle the Duke of Cumberland had once formerly had his menagerie and he drove from the Castle in his phaeton to visit them. He objected to being stared at while indulging in this simple pastime and so he had several new roads

George IV in his phaeton
(Engraving by Melville,
published by J. Dickenson in
1830).

cut, for his own special use, through the beautiful park
to Sandpit Gate. Any visitor who wished to see the royal
menagerie was wise to restrict his visiting to the two open
days, Monday and Saturday, when he could see the animals
free of charge. Any wrong planning and an arrival on any
other day when the King might drive into view resulted in
visitors being peremptorily turned away.

One such visitor, Prince Pückler-Muskau, drove through
Windsor Great Park on 20 August 1827 to the royal stables
to see the first living Nubian giraffe which had arrived in
England nine days before. This 'Cameleopard', as it was
then called, had been sent to George IV by Mohammet Ali,
Viceroy of Egypt, and lived for a few months at Windsor
before it died. Its limbs were deformed by the treatment
it had received at the hands of the Arabs on the overland
journey from Sennar in Sudan to Cairo. It had been carried
on the back of a camel huddled into a more compact shape
by having its legs tied up with cords. This appears to have
been the normal mode of transport adopted by the Arabs at
this time, because another specimen which arrived for the
Surrey Gardens (at a later date) appears to have suffered
the same kind of damage. The merchant vessel conveying
the giraffe had cows on board to supply milk for it and
the whole lot were disembarked at the wharf by Waterloo
Bridge on Saturday 11 August 1827 and kept in a warehouse

The entrance to George IV's menagerie at Sandpit Gate, near Windsor. (Charles Knight, *Menageries*, vol.1. 1829).

until the following Monday when Mr Cross took them, with their two Arab attendants, to Windsor in a caravan. The giraffe was given a spacious paddock, this being one of the best elements of the king's menagerie, the intelligent manner in which his animals were housed. They had large, open sheds in spacious paddocks, which had plenty of trees to provide shade and fresh browsing.

Prince Pückler-Muskau managed to secure,

'a sight of the giraffe, which was led out before us by two Moors who had accompanied her from Africa . . . she used her bright-blue tongue like a trunk, in which way she took from me my umbrella . . .'[2]

But if the Prince had timed his visit to see the giraffe with great care in order to avoid the displeasure of the King there was one little girl who had no need to fear meeting him, for she was his heir. Seven-year old Princess Victoria was in the park, with her mother, on 1 August 1826, when they met the King in his phaeton and she was lifted into it and taken by her 'Uncle King', as she called him, to see his menagerie. She wrote down an impression of him, 'large and gouty but with a wonderful charm of manner'[3], although she made no reference to the many kinds of deer, wapitis, zebras, kangaroos, birds of prey, members of the parrot family, emus, peafowl of all varieties, cranes and ibises, which she must have seen. Perhaps she was also introduced to the King's

Known as early as 1398 as a Camelopard because it 'hathe the head of a camell . . . and speckes of the Perde' or leopard. Drawn from nature and on stone by A. B. van Worrell, this lithograph was published by Hullmandel in 1827 and dedicated to the king. The giraffe was 2 years old and 10'8" high when painted with its keeper at Cumberland Lodge by Meadow Pond.

Sandpit Gate menagerie in 1825. The elderly man is thought to be John Clark, keeper of the menagerie, who died on 8 October 1827, aged 65, and was buried at Old Windsor. He is surrounded by the mammals and birds at Sandpit Gate: a gazelle, small deer, wallaby, pony, zebu, peacocks, an emu, macaw and cockatoo. An engraving after the painting by John Frederick Lewis (1805–76) who had practised drawing animals in the menagerie at Exeter 'Change.

favourite cockatoo, described by the author W. J. Broderip as a bird who 'was the very pink of politeness' (in his *Zoological recreations*, 1847).

One purpose of the establishment of the menagerie at Sandpit Gate was to form a fine collection of quadrupeds and birds suitable for domestication. Included in their number were llamas, which were introduced frequently after 1810 in an attempt to breed them, but with little success, chamois deer, another failure, other deer and antelopes which proved hardier, kangaroos which bred in great numbers, ostriches and emus which reared young, and quaggas and zebras which were great favourites with the public.

Emus seem to have caused many problems and the way in which they were given away and passed from one owner to another reminds us of Charles II's similar experience when he tried to give away his excess ostriches to any of his

courtiers who would have them. George IV sent some emus to the Tower, some to the Zoological Gardens in Regent's Park, where they had an enclosure near the entrance in 1829 and then presented his physician Sir Henry Halford with two fine specimens. When Sir Henry got them home to his estate at Wistow in Leicestershire they proved every bit as mischievous and destructive as their previous owner had discovered them to be, but Sir Henry put up with them 'in consideration of their royal donor'. He also showed a nice sense of humour by choosing 'Two emeus proper each gorged with a coronet composed of crosses pattée and fleur-de-lis or' as supporters for his coat of arms when this privilege was granted him by the King.[4]

We know that George IV himself had decided he had too many emus from an exchange of letters between him and the author Sir Walter Scott. In 1827 a couple of emus had been sent to Sir Walter by an Australian who admired the novelist's books. On their arrival Sir Walter went out to look at them and was quite taken aback to discover that they were six feet tall.[5] His efforts to get rid of them by

A view of the Zoological Society of London Gardens in Regent's Park, taken from the emu enclosure in 1831, lithographed by James Hakewill. Under the Royal Charter, 1829, the new society's purpose was stated to be to advance the study of zoology and animal physiology and to introduce new and curious subjects of the animal kingdom.

transferring them to the Royal Menagerie were abortive. As Charles II might have replied to such a suggestion, 'His Majestie desires no more Emus'.

George IV had several wild cats at Windsor. Two artists painted portraits of them, John Frederick Lewis (1805–76), whom the King employed to paint sporting subjects, and J. L. Agasse, a Swiss artist who worked in London. Lewis painted and then made seven etchings of lions and a tigress (published by W. B. Cooke in 1824–25). In 1825, Agasse made a beautiful study of two clouded leopards (*Neofelis nebulosa*), whose greyish fur had brown and black lines, streaks and blotches.

Owing to an event of great significance which occurred in 1826, future monarchs and other private individuals had no need to satisfy their wish to become acquainted with different members of the animal kingdom by keeping them on their own estates at their own expense. The idea of a Zoological Society was circulated among scientists in a prospectus of 1825 proposing that,

> 'a collection of living animals, belonging to the Society will be established in the vicinity of the metropolis; to which the Members of the Society will have access as a matter of right, and the public on such conditions as may be hereafter arranged'.

In 1826 the society was formed, with premises at 33 Bruton Street, London, and the officers appointed. When the officers moved into their new quarters some animals moved in with them, among them a 'wanderoo' monkey who occasioned a pained note in a report made by the clerk,

> 'that a book of vouchers has been partially destroyed by one of the monkeys kept in the office, which had occasioned a deficiency of 78 vouchers for annual contributions'.[6]

It must have been a great relief all round when the cages and houses in the Regent's Park were ready to receive the animals in 1827. The Zoological Society steadily acquired a much bigger, better menagerie than any private individual had previously maintained. The Zoological Gardens were opened to the public on 27 April 1828. George IV retained his own menageries at Sandpit Gate and the Tower of London until his death two years later and so it fell to his successor and brother, King William IV, to decide what to do about them. William wisely adjusted to the new situation and agreed to become Patron of the Zoological Society. He also made arrangements to present his collection of 63 mammals, 88 birds and several reptiles, including a boa constrictor which had nearly killed its keeper, to the new zoo. They were removed in 1830, the mammals comprising 14 wapitis, 3 axis and 2 sambur deer, 11 American roe deer, 3 gnus, 2 nylghaus, 2 llamas, 4 cashmere and 3 Barbary goats, 1 Cape ram, 7 zebus, 2 mountain and 2 Burchell's zebras, 1 wild boar, 1 peccary, 2 hybrids between both species of zebra and the common ass, 13 kangaroos. The birds comprised 1 king vulture, 2 sea eagles, 1 peregrine, 4 macaws, 2 great-eared owls, 2 cockatoos, 1 scarlet lory, 2 golden parakeets, 1 rosebill parakeet, 5 widow birds, 11 emus, 1 curassow, 42 peafowl of different varieties, 4 crowned crane, 1 scarlet ibis and 7 cereopsis geese. Queen Adelaide added 3 alpacas to this gift, but it is not clear where these animals had been kept, or how she had acquired them. The high number of deer and animals bearing fine wool coats is evidence of the interest in acclimatising animals for economic reasons as food and clothing.[7]

In 1831 William IV decided to present the Royal Collection in the Tower to the Zoological Society. This must have been a harder decision to make, because he was breaking a six centuries' old tradition. The disposal of this collection was also more difficult to effect, for not only was it larger than it had ever been in its history, but the Zoological Society was

Early in the reign of William IV an unscheduled and fatal combat took place in the Tower of London when a battle royal broke out between a lion, a tiger and a tigress. The lion was killed. (Coloured engraving by S. Maunder, 3 December 1830).

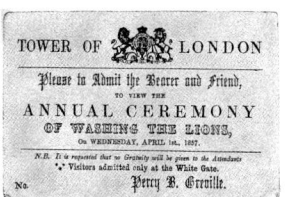

Ticket giving admittance for viewing the annual washing of the lions in the Tower of London menagerie, dated 1 April 1856. Some members of the gullible public fell for this practical joke each year. This ticket is for 1856 when the menagerie had been dispersed and closed for twenty-one years.

not ready to absorb another large collection so soon after receiving the first from the King. Consequently, the Tower Menagerie was not fully dispersed until 1835. The Lion Tower was then removed and all traces of the menagerie, first established in the Tower of London in the early 1200s, disappeared with it.

Not all the animals in the Tower were transferred to the London Zoological Gardens. Some duplicates were taken to Dublin for the new Zoological Society gardens at Phoenix Park and others were offered to Edward Cross, the commercial menagerie owner, who accepted a few of them. The Cape lion, cheetahs, Tibetan bear and a deep-blue macaw were sold to private individuals.

By the time Queen Victoria ascended the throne in 1837 there were no animals in the Tower and an empty menagerie at Sandpit Gate. Henceforth, when the Queen and later monarchs were presented with wild animals by fellow monarchs, they transferred them to the Zoological Gardens for safe keeping.[8]

At first, the Queen only had household pets at Buckingham Palace, which the Zoological Society Superintendent Abraham D. Bartlett took care of in her absence and tended when they fell sick. Among these was a favourite parrot. When the young composer Mendelssohn visited the Palace on 9 July 1842, to give the Queen a music lesson, he was ushered into the room where this parrot was kept in its cage. Before the Queen sang one of his songs to his accompaniment she told him, 'But first we must get rid of the parrot as he will scream louder than I can sing'.[9]

In 1839 Sir Edwin Landseer painted a picture of the Queen's Skye terrier with a macaw and lovebirds and it would appear that a succession of members of the parrot family were kept by the royal couple and their children throughout Queen Victoria's reign. Landseer painted a picture of a lory given to Princess Victoria in 1836. The pet birds were quite safe from cats; the Queen loathed them and banned them from all royal residences. Dogs were favoured and the Queen usually had half a dozen at a time which went from one residence to another. These included collies, Skye terriers, Spitzes and a fox terrier, while the Prince Consort had a favourite greyhound called Eos. These frequently appear when painted in the royal portraits.

Gradually, in the 1840s, as the number of young princes and princesses grew, the pets also increased. More exotic species were added to the royal possessions until the Queen had aviaries at Buckingham Palace and Frogmore and paddocks for mammals at Windsor and Shaw Farm, while some animals, for example, nylghaus, roe deer and angora goats, roamed free in Windsor Great Park. The number of species is wide and the rarity of some remarkable. She was sent gifts by the Earl of Derby from his menagerie at Knowsley, near Liverpool, and by Lord Hardinge from his at South Park, Tunbridge Wells, in Kent, and exchanged animals with them to form pairs for breeding purposes. The Queen also requested from the Earl of Derby a piece of alpaca wool, of 12 yards, from the 3 specimens he had sent. Lord Hardinge donated tragopans to Prince Albert and, when visiting Buckingham Palace Gardens in 1848, saw a young monal pheasant recently hatched there.

The Queen believed that possession of an animal rendered the owner responsible for its well-being so that kennels and stables were clean and hygienically maintained. The Windsor farms, the Home, Flemish and Shaw Farms, all near Windsor, housed fat stock and produced prize stock of cattle. A buffalo lived at Shaw Farm for some years, sent to the Queen as a calf. A pretty albino pony was purchased by the Queen from Hengler's Circus to please the Princes of Battenberg.

We know of several species from paintings commissioned from artists. Thomas Landseer executed an engraving of the Queen's Brazilian marmosets c. 1842. Charles Burton Barber painted a watercolour of wild boars at Shaw Farm with their cross-bred striped piglets, also her Spanish cattle at Osborne (which the Queen had purchased in 1881). The wild boars lived in Windsor Forest in an enclosure alongside some curious long-haired white Canadian pigs. The boars were killed and dressed by the royal chefs for the Queen to send to members of the Royal family as Christmas presents.

In the gardens at Buckingham Palace some exotic pheasants were kept and some bred, including monal, golden, and tragopans. Rare birds such as black-necked swans from Valparaiso, Chile, graced the irregularly shaped, three acre lake created in 1825 when William Townsend Aiton, superintendent of Kew Gardens, re-designed the gardens for George IV.

Animals for domestication were greatly valued, the Queen being particularly interested in llamas, alpacas and white goats from the Outer Hebrides from whose wool a dress, soft and warm, was made for her. Lord Hardinge gave Prince Albert two pairs of goats from Tibet. They were brought from Tibet on the Kashmir frontier, sent by Gulab Singh (whose Jammu dynasty was established in 1846 by British influence) as the tribute goats which he was bound to supply on demand, and had a long journey first to Simla, then Calcutta, Egypt and so to London. Some goats were sent to Windsor in 1848. Cashmere shawls became very fashionable in Victoria's reign.

When the male nylghau died, 'his widow' was reported as going, 'loose about the Great Park and is very tame and harmless', along with roe-deer also in the plantations. Prince Albert later accepted a pair of nylghaus to run loose in Windsor Park with Angora goats. In 1842 some Canadian wapiti were obtained from 'the Upper regions near the Great Lakes among the Chippeway Indian (Wa-pi-ti being in fact nothing more or less than a Chippeway word for Elk)'. They were put into the custody of Mr Lewis, the Queen's animal keeper. The stag died two months later 'much to the Queen's annoyance' and she did not 'seem much encouraged to be extravagant in purchases for her Menagerie'. Like Queen Elizabeth I, she liked to be presented with animals for her collection, rather than buy them.[10]

The following year, Queen Victoria received a small genet brought back from the Niger expedition, believed to be the only specimen then in England.

Some different white goats were sent by the Shah of Persia, but the Queen was not sure what to do with these and finally put them on the Great Orme, Carnarvon, North Wales where they became feral.

Close to Frogmore House, in the Little Park, Windsor, the Prince Consort had an aviary built facing a sunny slope and surrounded by shrubs. The group of buildings included a Keeper's House which had a small apartment where the Queen and her children used to go to drink tea. They could look out onto a large basin of water where the ducks bathed and a fountain splashed and view a cluster of eighteen pens of fancy poultry. These were not only kept for ornamental purposes, but the white dorkings provided all

the eggs served at the Queen's breakfast table. A penful of gold-spangled Hamburghs belonged particularly to Prince Alexander of Battenberg (a German aristocrat and relation of the Queen, uncle to Earl Louis Mountbatten of Burma) who was very proud of the handsome birds. From the birds raised in the aviary every year, about one hundred were kept for stocking the pens, the remainder being fattened for the Castle. Fancy birds included some seventy pigeons, principally Jacobins, and some owls and pure white doves belonging to Princess Beatrice. Cinnamon turkeys and golden pheasants bred successfully. Princess Beatrice also took cages of birds from residence to residence, hers were canaries, while the Queen had linnets in cages at the castle and eagles lived in a large aviary at the Head Keeper's Lodge.

C. R. Stanley designed the extensive range of aviary and poultry farm buildings built in 1845 at Frogmore, Windsor, under the direction of Prince Albert. Behind the fountain a milkmaid is surrounded by small birds, with pheasants, cranes and ducks on the terrace and lawn.

Fellow aviculturists, interested in the different breeds, were permitted to visit the collections, for example the Reverend Edmund Samuel Dixon of Cringleford acquired an admission ticket in 1850 to the poultry collection at Windsor. He discovered a dark, almost black, guinea fowl whose 'speckles on most of the feathers are obliterated and

The Cottage on Duck Island, built for the Ornithological Society of London. (Lithograph by I. B. Watson, the architect, 1841) The bird-keeper's lodge is a cottage orné reminiscent of the previous century's rural ornamental cottages.

the birds look much as if they had been dipped in an ink bath'.[11]

Prince Albert had contacts with the naturalists of the day and took a keen interest in all the new imports and experiments in domestication. After his death in 1861, there were fewer animals in the collections. When the Queen died forty years later, Edward VII sent the Windsor Menagerie animals to the Zoological Society gardens. The gift comprised: 2 Spanish cattle, 1 Grévy zebra, 3 Nubian goats, 1 black-faced kangaroo, 1 yellow-footed kangaroo, 3 zebus and 3 St Kilda sheep. An American bison fell down dead during the operation of boxing it for transit. The only birds transferred to the Zoo were 2 Somali ostriches.[12]

From now on, presents of lions and tigers from foreign princes were not so welcome and they were passed on to the Zoological Society of London. Victoria's eldest son, Edward Prince of Wales, contributed presents to the zoo following his overseas tours. When he received a gift of five lions and two zebras from Emperor Menelik of Abyssinia, on the occasion of his coronation as Edward VII in 1901, he presented them to the zoo.

Here the story of the royal menageries in England ends, but there is a swan song. Jack the Swan was still reigning supreme in St James's Park in 1839 when he was reputedly almost seventy years old. One day a gaggle of geese arrived and were immediately in conflict with old Jack. This time, there were too many attackers for him to deal with and he

Thomas Bewick's magnificent wood engraving of a mute swan.

DEATH OF A CELEBRATED CHARACTER.—(From a Correspondent.)—At the beginning of last week departed this life "Old Jack," the gigantic and venerable swan with whom the public have been so long acquainted on the canal in the enclosure of St. James's-park, at the advanced age of nearly 70 years. Old Jack was hatched some time about the year 1770, on the piece of water attached to Old Buckingham-house, and for many years basked in the sunshine of Royal favour, Queen Charlotte being extremely partial to him, and frequently condescending to feed him herself. When the pleasure gardens in St. James's-park were laid out, Jack was removed there, and his immense size, sociable disposition, and undaunted courage, have often excited the admiration of the Public. Jack's strength and courage were indeed astonishing; frequently has he seized an unlucky dog who chanced to approach to the edge of his watery domain by the neck and drowned him, and on one occasion he seized a boy of about 12 years of age, who had been teasing him, by the leg of his trousers and dragged him into the water up to his knees. Jack, however, never acted on the offensive, but always on the defensive, and if not annoyed was exceedingly tractable. But the march of modern improvement affected poor Jack as much as it had done thousands of more pretending bipeds. The Ornithological Society was formed, and a host of feathered foreigners found their way on to the canal, with whom Jack had many fierce and furious encounters, and invariably came off successful. But a legion of Solan geese at length arrived, who commenced hostilities with Jack immediately. Despising every thing like even warfare they attacked him in a body and pecked him so severely that he drooped for a few days and then died. The body of poor old Jack is to be stuffed for one of the scientific museums.

The obituary for the Mute Swan, Old Jack, from *The Times*, 9 July 1839.

was severely pecked. He drooped for a few days before he finally died. Jack's obituary appeared in *The Times* on 9 July 1839, and an obituary for his life-long mate Jenny, a mere sexagenarian, appeared eleven days later.[13]

TRAVELLING AND COMMERCIAL MENAGERIES

Chapter 8

'The Keeper called it a Dodo'

From very early times, foreign animals and curiosities were exhibited in Britain for the entertainment of the public. A small sum was charged by the owner of the animal for the privilege of viewing each exhibit. In addition, the animals were trained to perform tricks, monkeys being the perfect subjects for this kind of treatment. A picture of a tumbling ape, drawn in the 14th century, is in a manuscript in the Bodleian Library. A monkey was exhibited in 1572 riding on the back of a horse. This animal caused Thomas Cartwright, a Puritan (1535–1603), some anxiety because he complained to Parliament about the Vicars who 'If there be a bear or bull to be baited in the afternoon, or a jackanapes to ride on horseback, the minister hurries the service over in a shameful manner, in order to be present at the show'. However, in 1699 Members of Parliament proved themselves to be equal sinners with the clergy in this respect. During a debate in Parliament the old East India Company lost its business against the New Company by ten votes as so many of its supporters were, 'absent by going to see a Tyger baited with dogs'.[1]

Some of the earliest exhibitions of animals took place in inn yards. The inn was a focal point in the community and the natural place to take a leisurely view of the animal, and discuss it with one's neighbours. Apart from the fairly regular appearances of bears and monkeys, there were occasional exhibits of very rare and unusual species, either shown by an itinerant owner, or purchased by the inn-keeper himself as an added attraction to his tavern. In the ports such rarities were of more frequent occurrence, since the sailors bringing mammals, birds and snakes from foreign countries which they had visited wanted to get rid of them quickly on landing, or else show them for profit. Company ship owners, like those of the Hudson's Bay, East India and African Companies, were very strict about cargoes and only permitted gifts for the monarch (officially) to be transported in their vessels, but other ships were free to bring whatever they could find and sell their curiosities on arrival home.

One of the most remarkable and rarest of these curiosities was the now legendary bird the dodo. This bird was once alive and well, and in London too!

Sir Haman Lestrange saw it and wrote,

> 'About 1638 as I walked in London street, I saw the picture of a strange fowle hong out upon a cloth, and myselfe with one or two more then in company went in to see it. It was kept in a chamber, and was a great fowle somewhat bigger than the largest Turkey Cock . . . The keeper called it a Dodo'.

Lestrange watched the bird swallowing pebbles as big as nutmegs and described it as being 'coloured on the underside like a young pheasant and darker on the back'. This bird might well have been the one bought after its death by John Tradescant, who had it stuffed and put among the specimens of unusual creatures in his museum at Lambeth. Tradescant's catalogue of his possessions in 1656 listed, 'A Dodar from the island of Mauritius . . . It is not able to flie being so big'. The dodo became extinct before the end of the 17th century. The Englishman Benjamin Harry, first mate on the *Berkley Castle,* is believed to have been the last person to see a live dodo in Mauritius in the year 1681.[2]

Most of these early exhibits were of single specimens, mainly because living birds, mammals or reptiles were difficult to transport on long sea voyages under sail and few arrived in a healthy state. Not sufficient was known about the feeding requirements of animals for fodder of the correct kind to be put on board for them. Putting them in cages below deck meant a lack of fresh air and also exercise. On deck they were subject to wind, rain and cold. Ships' captains were not always cooperative in accepting responsibility for such difficult cargoes. Just occasionally there was a spectacular success, such as Lord Berkeley's elephant, sent from the East Indies and landed at Whiteford 3 August 1675. George, Lord Berkeley, was a director of the East India Company, hence this exception to the rule banning loading ships with strange and noisome cargoes. He found the animal a great charge to his purse and proposed selling the elephant by 'the candle at the East India House, sett up at £1000 and to advance £20 every bidding'. According

The Dutch landed in Mauritius in 1598, and imported some dodos to Europe. The Portuguese name 'Dodo' came to us from a letter written to Sir Edward Altham 18 June 1628, 'A strange fowle, which I had at the Iland Mauritius, called by ye portinalls Do Do'. George Edwards painted it, (*Gleaning of natural history,* 1757, vol. VI, plate 294) with a guinea pig and said of the small mammal, 'they are bred tame about London and feed like Rabbets'.

to a trade advertisement in the *City Mercury* 2 November 1675, the elephant was 'now to be seen at the White Horse Inn over against Salisbury Court in Fleet street'. This was probably the same animal that the coin dealer Thoresby and his friend Elkana Boyse went to see two years later at Southwark.[3]

We do not know for how much the elephant was sold, but the tale of a rhinoceros and its sale in 1684 has survived. Evelyn wrote a very lengthy and detailed account of this first rhinoceros brought to England, after he saw it on 22 October 1684, and later when the animal was auctioned. He thought it looked like 'a greate coach overthrowne', which was an apt description since coach bodies were then made of thick leather. At the auction it was knocked down to an over-enthusiastic bidder for the enormous price of £2,320.[4] The bidder then got cold feet and refused to pay up, and no one would bid at a second auction, so the rhinoceros was placed at the Bell Savage Inn on Ludgate Hill for viewing 'at twelve pence apiece, and two shillings those that ride him'. It was reported that the takings amounted to fifteen pounds a day, but by 1686 the charge to see the rhino had dropped to two pence. Evelyn proceeded from the rhinoceros to view 'a living Crocodile brought from some of the W: Indian Ilands . . .' and thought it was then 'not yet 2 yards from head to tail', but envisaged that 'If he grow, it will be a dangerous Creature'. Evelyn was getting bored with seeing camels in 1661 for he wrote in his diary, 'There was a Camel shewn in our Towne, newly brought from the Levant, which I saw, as I had done others'.[5]

The next rhinoceros to be shown in England was described in the *Daily Advertiser* on Saturday 5 December 1741. 'To be seen at the Unicorn in Oxford-road opposite Argylle St. A large Rhinoceros. 6 years old 5′ high, 12′ round the body. 12′2″ from nose to rump. She travelled a thousand leagues from the Great Mogul's Dominions to Bengal, from whence she was brought here on board the *Shaftesbury*'. This mammal had a 'large horn on her nose' and was proudly reported as being 'the only complete Animal of the kind that has been seen in England these 85 years, according to the best information that has been received'.

During the reign of Queen Anne, a huge Lincolnshire ox, 19 hands high, was on view at the White Horse Inn 'Where the great white elephant was seen'. About the same period,

A rhinoceros was first seen in London in 1684, another in 1741, noted in *Daily Advertiser* Saturday 5 December, 'To be seen at the Unicorn in Oxford-road opposite Argyll-street. A Large Rhinoceros'. (Wood engraving by Thomas Bewick, *History of quadrupeds*).

the Adam and Eve tavern (a notoriously rowdy place situated where the Euston Road was crossed by the junction of the Hampstead and Tottenham Court Road) owned a long room with an organ, tea gardens, grounds for skittles and Dutch-pins and a miniature menagerie in which a monkey, a heron, some wildfowl and parrots lived.[6] There was also a small pond for goldfish, which had been introduced as pets by Queen Mary when she came over from Holland a few years before. The Adam and Eve was famous for this menagerie, plus its cream teas and gardens. It was a pleasant walk out from the city and the resort of pleasure-seekers until the end of the 18th century when 'the character of the visitors deteriorated' according to Wheatley.

The New Wells, near the London Spa, had a small zoological garden in 1739. Visitors could see a fine collection of large rattlesnakes, one of them 'having 19 rattles and seven young ones'. A young crocodile was there, having been imported from Georgia and American darting and flying squirrels 'which may be handled as any of our own', and a cat 'between a tiger and the leopard, perfectly tame, and one of the most beautiful creatures that ever was in England'. The admission charge to this show was one shilling.[7]

The prices of admittance were quite high, but had the advantage of keeping the 'common sort of people' away. The kind of visitors preferred is evident from an advertisement in a newspaper of 19 August 1807,

'The Proprietor of the two wonderful Siboya Serpents, now exhibiting at the large rooms No. 22 Piccadilly, begs leave to inform the Nobility & Gentry, and others, that from the numerous applications he has received of Noblemen & gentlemen to see those extraordinary Reptiles devour their Prey, they will have a public dinner on live Rabbits this day, at 3 oClock, which is expected to be attended with a numerous assemblage of Ladies and Gentlemen. Admittance each person 2 shillings'.

Inn-keepers could never be quite so particular about their clientele, but they tried to set the tone of their inn by having side-shows and if these had a vaguely educational flavour, so much the better, although the chance to earn extra income was the over-riding consideration. By the mid 18th century a single animal was no longer sufficient to draw the crowds and the Rose and Crown near the gates of the Spring Gardens, Greenwich, owned a small menagerie and went to the lengths of issuing a catalogue of the exhibits. The catalogue included 'a large and beautiful camel which has come from Grand Cairo, Egypt' which was nearly 8' tall and nearly 2 years old and which only drank some water once in sixteen days; a 'surprising hyaena, from the Coast of Guinea; a male panther from Buenos Ayres; & a young riobiscay from Russia'. The catalogue quaintly concludes, '& several other creatures too tedious to mention'.

Extravagant claims were used to entice the public and enhance the status of the animal being exhibited. A Peruvian llama exhibited in the Haymarket in London was claimed to be 'the first that has ever been offered to the inspection of a British Public' in 1805 and Thomas Shore went so far as to offer a reward of £500 to 'any Person who ever saw in any other Travelling Menagery a Black Tyger. His being the ONLY ONE in Europe'. Thomas Pennant took a more dispassionate and scientific view of a fierce and ill-natured lion-tailed baboon (*Simia veter*) exhibited in London, noting that its tail was the exact length of its back and its beard reached entirely up the cheeks as far as the eyes.[8]

Other town-dwellers had rare opportunities to see wild animals. In 1783 an inn-yard in Norwich gave temporary shelter to a lion, a hunting tiger, a porcupine, a wolf, wanderoo (macaque) and female satyr, or Aethiopian savage (orang-utan).

Thomas Platter, an Elizabethan doctor of medicine, in his *Travels*, 1599, said, 'In one house on the Thames bridge I also beheld a large live camel'.
(Edward Topsell's camel, tab. 73 *Historie of four-footed beastes*, was a two-humped bactrian, but he said he knew of 'divers kind according to the country where they breed, India, Arabia, and Bactria' i.e. in Central Asia).

Exciting as these sights of rare animals might have been for those who could get to the inns and showrooms and afford the entrance fee, it was the travelling menageries that aroused the greatest interest and attracted the crowds. The coming to town of a travelling menagerie was advertised in the local newspapers, or with posters on hoardings for several days in advance. The event was looked forward to with eager anticipation in the surrounding villages and countryside. The time of their arrival often coincided with the fairs held in market towns. The cages were mounted on wheels and pulled by teams of horses from one end of the country to the other. Occasionally, they also crossed to Ireland. From small beginnings these menageries grew in size until they were regular features in the 19th century. Even when they ceased touring and were succeeded by circuses, the circus proprietors found they earned additional income by putting their performing animals on show between performances, so great was the appetite of the public for displays of wild animals.

The story of the travelling menageries is closely linked with the history of the fairs held in London and provincial towns from Medieval days to the end of the 19th century. They formed an integral part of the noisy scene where trade and barter were combined with eating and drinking, entertainment, sports and contests of various kinds.

Bartholomew Fair in Smithfield was the oldest, longest-lived (c.1123–1855) and most famous fair, as well as being most often mentioned in connection with the exhibition of wild animals. A booth or stall holder enjoyed not only great prestige, but earned a good return in terms of hard cash. The fair was held over three days in early September. Some wandering Indians made snakes manoeuvre up silk ropes to the sound of music in 1778. Alongside, there were pelicans from Egypt, a panther from Turkey, a noble vulture cock 'having the finest tallons of any bird that seeks his prey', a beautiful large Bengal tiger and the 'right man tyger brought from Angola by Captain Dalbiac in the Portfield East Indiaman'.[9]

As the 18th century drew to a close the sights had become more daring and spectacular. The spectacle of 'the keeper's head in the lion's mouth' began to thrill audiences and at that time arose the story of the keeper asking, 'Does he whisk his tail?' to which his understudy outside the cage replied, 'He does, mate'. 'Then I am a dead man', came the muffled reply.

By the 19th century, Bartholomew Fair was large enough to accommodate two, even three menageries, each of them showing a good profit at the end of the three days. The menageries attending in 1828 were Wombwell's which headed the list with takings of £1,700, Atkin's with £1000 (each of them charging 6d admission) and Morgan's which earned £150 by charging 3 pence admission. This indicated the popularity of the wild beast shows in a London fair at a time when Londoners also had the Tower Menagerie, the Zoological Society's newly formed collection and the Exeter 'Change's wild animals to visit within the boundaries of the capital.[10]

On each occasion, when we meet up with menageries at the fairs, both ludicrous and perfectly normal exhibits are to be found in close proximity, with no hint that the owners or sight-seers found this at all strange. Time and again, deformities are billed as equal attractions with magnificent specimens of rare animals. The camel exhibited in 1650 appeared no less strange to its viewers than 'the child born back to back with a live bear'. In 1788 a foreigner exhibited some snakes at Bartholomew Fair, but these would have caused no more stir than a two-headed ox or three-legged sheep, or a four-legged goose. Some abnormalities were genuine, some faked. Ben Jonson gives a very detailed picture of Bartholomew Fair in his comedy (1614) of that name. Among the sights was a black eagle, a black wolf, a huge hog, a bull with 5 legs, a musical hare that played the tabor and dogs that danced the morris. An ape had been trained by a juggler to walk over a chain for the King of England and go back for the Prince of Wales, but refused to move for either the Pope or the King of Spain.

These mixed elements made the fairs very popular with courtiers and slum-dwellers alike. Pepys was just one sight-seer who could not resist going to the fair, though he found the humans attending just as curious as the animals exhibited, and twice in his diaries expressed mixed feelings about his presence there,

> 'To Bartholomew Fair . . . at seeing the monkeys dance, which was much to see, when they could be brought to do, but it troubled me to sit among such nasty company'

and again, on 4 September 1663,

> 'And at home made my wife get herself presently ready, and so carried her by coach to the fair and showed her the Munkys dancing on the ropes; which was strange, but such dirty sport that I was not pleased with it. There was also a horse with hoofes like Rams hornes – a goose with four feet – and a cock with three'.[11]

The ancient sport of baiting animals still persisted in 1701 where it took a curious form at Bartholomew Fair. *The Postman* for Tuesday September 9 announced, 'The Tiger in Bartholomew Fair, that yesterday gave such satisfaction to persons of all Qualities by pulling the feathers so nicely from live fowls, will at the request of several persons, do the same this day: price 6d each'.

St James's Fair, held in May in Brook Field, quickly acquired the name of May Fair. It was situated in the district between Park Lane and Berkeley Square, by grant of James II, to commence on May 1st and continue for fifteen days. An attempt to suppress it in 1709 did not entirely succeed, for it revived and the wild beast shows, jugglers, stage-players and side-shows crept back and were tolerated by the first three Georges until about 1770. The temporary lull in Queen Anne's reign, however, proved a set-back for the actor-manager William Pinkethman, who had got hold of a large elephant in order to sit in state on its back to advertise his performances. *The Tatler* (no.20) of Will's Coffee-House 25 May 1709) announced,

> 'May Fair . . . that Fair is now broke, as well as the Theatre (Royal) is breaking. But it's allow'd still to sell Animals

Miles Menagerie at Bartholomew Fair in the late 18th century. Stephen Polito took Miles as his partner in 1798, and they exhibited at fairs together from 1799. (A Rowlandson print, engraved by Dalziel Brothers).

there. Therefore, if any Lady or Gentleman have occasion for a Tame Elephant, let them enquire of Mr Pinkethman, who has one to dispose of at a reasonable rate. The downfall of May-Fair has quite sunk the price of this noble animal, as well as of many other Curiosities of Nature. A Tyger will sell almost as cheap as an Ox; and I am credibly informed, a man may purchase a cat with three legs for very near the value of one with four'.

Pinkethman's strollers were popular actors at Bartholomew and Greenwich Fairs and at Drury Lane, where he was greeted familiarly as Pinkey, so he did not lose too much by Queen Anne's suppression of the rowdy merry-making at May Fair.

Greenwich Fair (held 12–14 May and also 11–13 October from the mid 18th century up to 1856), though originally a cattle fair, soon developed into the usual conglomeration of stalls for general sales, entertainments, eatables, wax-works, theatricals etc which was typical of the country and London fair and, of course, the menagerie wagons rolled up to claim their pitch. John Evelyn (on 18 June 1657) saw,

> 'a sort of Catt brought from the East Indies, shaped & Snouted much like the Egyptian Ratoone, in the body like a Monkey, & so footed: the eares & taile like a Catt, onely the taile much longer, & the Skin curiously ringed, with black and white: With this taile, it wound up its body like a serpent, & so got up into trees, & with it, would also wrap its whole body round: It was of a wolly haire as a lamb, exceedingly nimble, & yet gentle & purr'd as dos the Cat' (A ring-tailed lemur).

When the Thames froze over, there was no better way of celebrating the event than to hold an impromptu frost-fair on the ice. The Thames froze sufficiently hard for such fairs to be held in 1608, 1683–84, 1688–89, 1709, 1715, 1739–40, 1768 and 1789. Evelyn was a visitor to the 1683–84 frost fair and Charles II and his court also went to share in some of the fun. The first member of the famous Chipperfield circus family began with a performing bear on the frozen Thames in 1683. The frivolity quickly came to an end when a thaw set in and everyone scrambled to get off the fast-disappearing ice. If this occurred in the night, the booths

Bewick knew the black-tailed or common marmoset, *Hapale jacchus*, as the 'Mico, or fair monkey'. The fairground showman's monkey was usually either a green monkey or this marmoset from South America. The scientific name adjective *jacchus* gave rise to the nickname of Jacko and Jackanapes for monkeys from their first earliest importation in the late 15th century to Spain and Portugal.

and stalls floated off down river before their owners could rescue them. Although wild beast shows were held during the frost-fair, there is no record of a menagerie afloat, so it is likely that the animals, being too dangerous to risk under such conditions, were taken off each night.

Pepys also visited Stourbridge Fair, the largest of the English fairs, held in September for two weeks, near Cambridge. It was the Vanity Fair of John Bunyan's *Pilgrim's Progress*. Lady Spencer shared some of Bunyan's feelings about fairs and gives a lively account of a fair she encountered at Portsmouth 25 July 1809,

> 'The street was one continued rattle and gingle, produced by bells ringing, organs grinding, wild beasts roaring, and all the variety of noises attending booths, crockery shops, giant, dwarfs, monkeys, women without leggs, girls with pink eyes, fat children, and two-headed cows, which, besides puppet shows and dancing dogs, were drawn up in battle array, to be looked at by the shoals of drunken people of every sex and age, who were reeling and bellowing about from one sight to another'.

Lady Sarah Spencer apparently lost some sleep over this fair.[12]

Anyone wanting to see some foreign animals, for whatever purpose, had little choice other than to push his way into the caravans housing the menageries in the fair grounds, after paying his shilling. In the last years of the 17th and in the early 18th centuries, the reward for such an effort would be the sight of a tiger or lion, perhaps an ostrich or cassowary, a leopard from Lebanon, an eagle from Russia, an opossum from Hispaniola, or who knows what else? The unpredictability added to the pleasure of the visit and serious naturalists such as Sir Hans Sloane, as well as artists, did not let such rare opportunities slip them by. They not only went to see the animals, but took steps to make drawings of them and included them in records of specimens known to science in their day.

George Edwards, who worked for Sir Hans Sloane, making drawings of rare mammals and birds for him, visited fairs for this purpose. He was searching for imported natural history rarities and was rewarded in 1752 by the sight of a crowned eagle. 'Its keeper told me it was brought from the coast of Guiney in Africa'. About the same time, two other specimens of the magnificent crowned eagle (*Stephanoaetus ornatus*), in a private house on Garlick-hill were seen by Edwards, perhaps from the same shipment.[13]

Most of these very small groups of animals were toured for short periods by proprietors whose names we do not know. We catch glimpses of them on the road only when an accident occurs, or a diarist has seen them. Evidence of one early travelling collection in Malmesbury, Wiltshire, occurs in a gravestone inscription. Hannah Twynnoy died 23 October 1703 after being attacked by an animal that escaped from a travelling menagerie. The inscription reads,

> 'In bloom of life
> She's snatched from here
> She had not room
> To make defence
> For Tyger fierce
> Took life away
> And here she lies
> In a bed of clay
> Until the Resurrection Day'.

In the middle of the 18th century there were no fewer than three travelling menageries visiting fairs in the summer. During the rest of the year the showmen showed their animals in inn yards. London newspaper advertisements for 1748 itemise the animals on show in these menageries, which were still on a small scale. The largest was Perry's, showing at the White Horse Inn, Fleet Street, 'a large he-lion, a he-tiger, a leopard, a panther, two hyenas, a civet cat, a jackall or lion's provider, and several other rarities too tedious to mention. To be seen at any time of the day, without any loss of time'. The second was to be viewed at 'the Flying Horse, near the London workhouse, Bishopsgate Street, from eight in the morning till nine at night', and this also had a 'he-tiger' with a young leopard, a civet cat, hyena, and a 'man-tiger' (mandrill) from Angola. The third collection was at the White Swan, Holborn, advertised as 'a collection of the most curious living wild creatures just arrived from different parts of the world'. These were a young camel from Egypt, hyaena, 'he-panther from Buenos Ayres' (i.e. a jaguar) and a young riobiscay from Russia, which species, several times advertised by menagerists both in this and the next century, still defies identification.

It was not until the last half of the 18th century that a travelling menagerie of any size, owned by Pidcock, took to the roads of Great Britain and Ireland. John Pidcock was first on the road, then succeeded by his son Gilbert. This collection was small when it was first assembled in the 1770s, but grew in size. As early as 1769 the wild beast show of Bartholomew's Fair was that of Pidcock who took the animals out of his collection at Exeter 'Change for the days of the fair. Gilbert Pidcock and his wife Sarah lived in the parish of St Leonard, Shoreditch, in the 1790s, where their children were baptised. At that time he housed a menagerie at Exeter 'Change, a building in the Strand, during the winter and took it, or part of it, touring in the summer months. The Exeter 'Change menagerie charge was high, 2 shillings and 6 pence for admission, but the contents rivalled the collection in the Tower in the number of species exhibited.

Thomas Bewick awaited Pidcock's appearance in Newcastle-on-Tyne with impatience because he required mammals to draw and engrave on wood for his book *A General history of quadrupeds*. This was published in 1790 and he had gathered illustrations of foreign animals when Pidcock took his collection north in 1787, when he made a magnificent drawing of a tiger 'allowed to be one of the finest creatures of its kind ever seen in England'. The following year Pidcock's lion was drawn and in 1789 Bewick wrote to his brother of the animals visiting Newcastle that year, that they consisted,

> 'of various kinds of the Ape tribe, Porcupine, Tiger Cat and Tiger, Greenland Bear, and one of the finest Lions

Dancing bear with monkey on its back being led between towns to perform. (Thomas Bewick, *A General history of quadrupeds*, 5th ed. p.292).

(very lately brought over) that ever made its appearance on this Island; so that I expect to have the opportunity of doing such of them as I want, from the Life. Our *Natural History* will be put to press in a little time'.[14]

In return, Bewick made four wood engravings for Pidcock to use in his advertisements, of an elephant, a lion, a tiger and a zebra, in 1799.

To this dual role of touring menagerie owner and static collection in London (see Chapter 10), Gilbert Pidcock added a third, that of dealer in birds and mammals (see Chapter 14). This combination of roles was followed by several of the menagerie owners throughout the next century.

Chapter 9

'The Camels were being towed by the Caravans'

The first travelling menagerie of any size or importance was advertised in the *Nottingham Journal* 28 September 1805,

> 'During the Fair Only – The largest travelling collection in the known world to be seen in six safe and commodious caravans, built for the purpose and all united . . . in the Market-place Polito's grand and pleasing assemblage of most rare and beautiful living birds and beasts from the remotest parts of the known world; among which are a noble lion from the Tower of London; a striped Bengal tiger and tigress, commonly called Royal Tigers, acknowledged to be the finest ever seen in the kingdom; four of those most singular of all quadrupeds, the large kangaroos from Botany Bay, males and females; noble male and female panthers, from the river La Plata, South America; that most industrious of all animals, the beaver; remarkably handsome leopard and leopardess, the finest ever seen in this kingdom; male and female wolves from the Alps; the wolverine or glutton; the Civet and Tibet, commonly called muscovy cats; a large satyr or Ethiopian Savage; the ichneumon, the wanderoo and upwards of 50 other quadrupeds. Admittance (being Fair Time) ladies and gentlemen one shilling – working people, servants and children sixpence only Birds and Beasts bought, sold, or exchanged by the proprietor'.

Another bill advertising the menagerie, 1808, was headed, 'S. Polito's Grand Exhibition of Living Curiosities of Foreign Animals, Birds etc. in six caravans, admission 1s. 2s extra to see the animals fed'.[1]

Stephen Polito, an Italian by birth, was also proprietor of the Exeter 'Change menagerie until 1814 when he died and Edward Cross took over at the 'Change, while Stephen's son, John (who married Elizabeth Cross, Edward's daughter, in 1814), continued touring. This touring menagerie, which was taken on the continent of Europe in the 1830s,

121

was on its way to Ireland in 1836 when it was lost with the ship transporting it.

Showmen nearly always gave their animals names exaggerating their characteristics to make them sound more exotic and exciting. The 'Wild Man of the Woods' was also an 'Ethiopian Savage', that we know as the orang-utan, a reddish-brown ape brought from Java and known from c.1631. From the earliest pictures of this species, it was shown seated on a bench with a walking stick in its right hand. The *Daily Advertiser* 4 June 1778 offered an 'Ethiopian Savage' to view saying, 'This astonishing Animal is of a different species from any other seen in Europe, and seems to be a link between the rational and Brute creation as he is a striking resemblance to the Human Species and is allowed to be the greatest curiosity ever exhibited in England . . . also the Orang Outang or real Wild Man of the Woods'.

A 'Wonderful Hog in Armour' was any armadillo. Bewick said this nine-banded armadillo had been brought to England from 'the Musquito shore and lived some time. It was fed on raw beef and milk, but refused to eat our fruits and grain'. Finding out how to feed each species was a matter of trial and error if no notes as to its diet in its native land were sent with the animal.

The black and white monkey, a lion-tailed macaque, was called a 'Child of the Sun' by showmen. It was first recorded and illustrated by Captain Robert Knox (who was held captive in Ceylon for 20 years) in his *History of Ceylon and East India*, 1681, as a Wanderoo. He said that some were 'so large as our English Spaniel Dogs, of a darkish gray colour, and black faces with great white beards round from ear to ear, which makes them shew just like old men'.

The 'Tiger-Wolf' was a spotted hyena of Cross the showman and Bewick, who drew it when exhibited in Newcastle in the spring and summer of 1799. Perhaps one would have thought that the striped hyena would more appropriately have earned the name 'Tiger-Wolf'. Bennett, in *Tower Menagerie*, noted that the striped hyaena, when carried from fair to fair in close confinement, turned sour and vicious. The Tower animal was quite tame, however, and shared a cage with one of the American bears.

There is a shadow of doubt over many of the reports of animals present in the menageries. Apart from showmen's

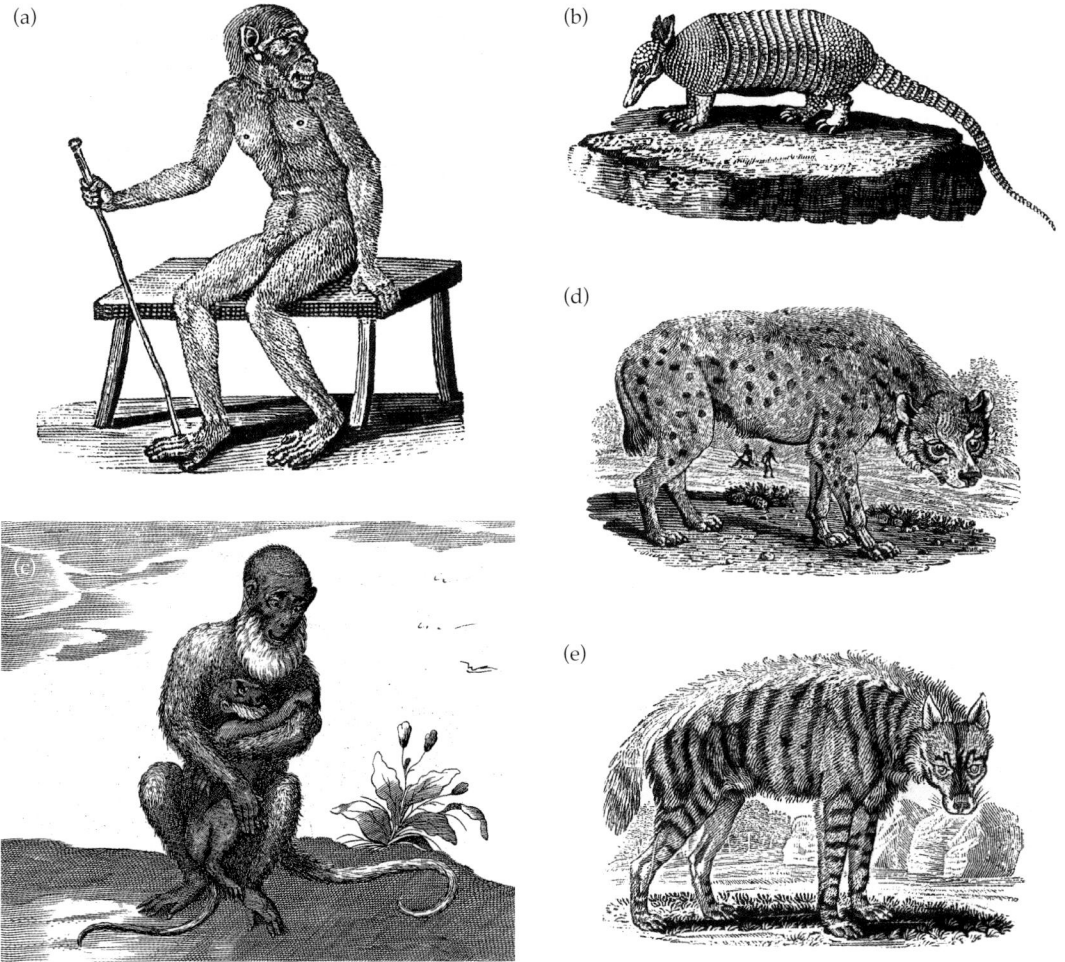

(a) The 'Wild Man of the Woods' was also an 'Ethiopian Savage', now orang-utan. (T. Bewick, *History of quadrupeds*, 1807)
(b) The 'Wonderful Hog in Armour' was any armadillo. Nine-banded armadillo, (T. Bewick, *History of quadrupeds*, 1807). Known in 1607 when London merchants and citizens fed them on garden worms.
(c) Wanderoo, i.e. a lion-tailed Macaque, called a 'Child of the Sun' by showmen. (R. Knox, *History of Ceylon and East India*, 1681).
(d) 'Tiger-Wolf' was a spotted hyaena. 'It was called tiger-wolf at the Cape of Good Hope'.
(e) The striped hyena was more likely to be the 'Tiger-wolf', but is of east and north Africa. A typical confusion by showmen of names and origins of their exhibits.

strange use of language, there are some curious inaccuracies in naming animals, incorporating the name of the place from which they were thought to have been brought originally. Turkeys were imported from North America, but the word 'turkey' was used for all Moslem countries in the 15th and 16th centuries and later came to vaguely indicate somewhere 'foreign'. Guinea pigs did not come from an African country 'Guinea' but Guyana in South America, nor was the little cavy a pig, despite having the flavour and eyes like that of a pig. Sometimes a specimen was thought to have originated in Africa, having been picked up in an African port, but it had merely been trans-shipped there and originated from much further east. Old names for parts of Africa, such as Barbary, the country of the Berbers in North Africa, so called by Arab geographers, were the root of the term Barbary being attached to an ape, sheep and a hen. These are traceable misnomers and historical archaic uses , but there was no knowing what lay behind the mental aberrations of sailors who, anxious to sell a new animal and asked where he had got it from, either tried unsuccessfully to remember in which country he had acquired it, or made up a locality on the spur of the moment. Some Australian species that natives took to the East Indies ports to barter with, also came to England before Australia was discovered at the end of the 1760s. However, there is a strong suspicion that the similar ostrich of Africa and the South American rhea, might have been confused with the emu by some menagerie owners. The names used by early importers and menagerie owners alike need to be treated with caution.

One of the next menageries on the scene was that of George Ballard. This gained considerable publicity on a dark night, 20 October 1816, while travelling from London to Salisbury for the Michaelmas Fair. The caravans containing

Ballard's lioness attacking the lead horse, Pomegranate, of the Exeter Mail coach.

the animals were standing in a line by the side of the road, near the Winterslow Hut, seven miles from Salisbury. A lioness escaped from her enclosure and ran alongside one of the leaders of the Exeter to London mail coach that passed at the moment she got free. On reaching Winterslow Hut, the coachman stopped the coach to deliver letters at the inn. When he stopped, the lioness attacked the lead horse, Pomegranate. He was just about to fire his blunderbuss at the lioness when Ballard and his men ran up with a mastiff dog. Ballard shouted, 'For God's sake, don't kill her! She cost me five hundred pounds, and she will be as quiet as a lamb if not irritated'.[2] The lioness turned on the dog and killed it about forty yards from the coach, then fled to a farmyard and hid under a granary. The keepers enticed her out and took her back to her cage. A Salisbury newspaper reported this incident and concluded, 'This was a very fortunate incident for Ballard, as everyone went to see the lioness that had attacked the horse belonging to the mail coach, and the price of admission was raised to the menagerie'. At the fair, the lioness quite outshone the other animals, even a royal tiger, large white bear, 'tiger owls' and the usual monkeys. Normally, Ballard only charged 1d to view this collection, but the advertisement shows the price had been increased twelve-fold to one shilling!

The advertisement of 1816 states that Ballard exhibited a recovered Pomegrante and the dog now 'in perfect amity', but it is difficult to imagine the horse sufficiently recovered and Thomas Frost said the dog had been killed. Thomas Frost, writing in 1874, also said the horse was fatally lacerated about the neck from the lioness's fore feet on each side of the throat, and his chest from the hind feet. Another account stated that, after making a lot of money for Ballard, the horse was sold to work again harnessed to a coach, this time on the Brighton and Petworth Road. Showmen's and observers' accounts do not always agree.

It is not in dispute that nine years later, when shown at Bartholomew's Fair, Ballard's lioness who attacked the mail-coach was still a great attraction. Ballard's menagerie charged one penny entrance fee at Bartholomew's Fair and took £90 in receipts in the good year of 1828. In 1830 he exhibited a seal floundering round in a tub of water, but it does not appear again in the comments on shows at this or other fairs.

Ballard's advertisement for his Wild Beast show after the lioness attacked the horse Pomegranate. After making a lot of money for Ballard, Pomegranate was sold to work again on the Brighton and Petworth coach, according to one version of the story.

Three menageries took to the road in quick succession. Wombwell's, Atkins's, both in 1805 and Isaac Van Ambrugh's shortly afterwards. Van Ambrugh's animals were trained to perform certain tricks with him. Queen Victoria loved his show and saw it five times in the first two months of 1839. Lady Sarah Spencer, who was Lady in Waiting and accompanied the Queen, wrote, 'The man's courage is very fine to see. I suppose some day the familiarity will go a step too far, & he will *leave* his head in the lion's mouth by mistake'.[3] Sir Edwin Landseer painted a picture of Van Ambrugh in the lion's cage with a lamb and a tiger and leopard, a frightening combination, and exhibited it at the Royal Academy the same year. Queen Victoria saw the painting and thought it was 'just as exactly as I saw him' and bought it.

Thomas Atkins was a menagerie owner in partnership with Gillman in 1817, then by himself in 1825, when he attended Bartholomew Fair. His advertisement was blazed in lamps on one of the largest shows in the whole fair. The display of show-cloths, with pictures of his animals exhibited within, reached about forty feet in height and extended to approximately the same width. Admission was six pence. Accounts of Atkins's collection of animals stress their cleanliness and the animals' good health.

Less is known of Atkins than Wombwell, but he had considerable success in breeding the large cats. In 1824 he announced 'a wonderful phenomenon' which was

The lion-tiger cubs born at Windsor in 1824 while Atkins was exhibiting his animals there. Engraved by John Henry Barlow, after a painting by Thomas Landseer for *Characteristic sketches of animals*, 1830.

ATKINS's Royal Menagerie

A GREAT NOVELTY !!!

THE NOBLE YOUNG

British Male Lion

AND BEAUTIFUL ROYAL

BENGAL TIGRESS,

IN THE SAME DEN, A CIRCUMSTANCE UNPARALLELED IN THE ANNALS OF HISTORY.

They are both so Tame that they will suffer the Keeper to enter their Den, which he will do in Presence of the Company, and is indisputably th only instance of a Lion and a Tiger being known to agree together. The Lion was brought forth at Beverly in Yorkshire, in Feb. 1821, (the Sir and Dam are now in this Collection), and the Tigress was landed at Liverpool the 24th of April, 1822, brought over in the Clydesdale East India man, Capt. M'Killow, and presented to him by the Marquiss of Hastings, Governor General of Bengal, from his Collection of Tigers at Calcutta A singular instance of Savage Ferocity, tranquillised into Animal Discipline.   Next to the Lion, the Tiger is the most tremendous of the carnivorous class, and whil he possesses all the bad qualities of the former, seems to be a stranger to the good ones—to Pride, to Strength, to Courage, the Lion adds greatness, and sometimes perhap Clemency, while the Tiger, without provocation is Fierce, without necessity is cruel.   Instead of instinct, he hath nothing but an uniform rage, a blind fury, so blin indeed, so indistinguishing, that he frequently devours his own progeny, and if the Tigress offers to defend them, he tears in pieces the Dam herself.

A   NOBLE   LIONESS,

Which Whelped at WOOLWICH *FOUR CUBS,* April 17th, 1822,
A PRODUCTION UNPRECEDENTED IN ANY MENAGERIE HITHERTO EXHIBITED,

The Cubs, which are now living, and in perfect health, are so extremely tame and inoffensive, that they may be taken from their Dam, and handled and caressed with th same Ease and security as a Lap Dog, not having the least symptoms of their natural savage Ferocity, and need only be seen to be pronounced
The most surprising and contemplative Wonder of their own Noble Species ever presented to the British Public

A PRODIGIOUS FULL-GROWN MAJESTIC

MALE LION,

TWENTY YEARS OLD !!

Which instantly impresses every Beholder with that magnificent ide no generally conceived of the King of the Brute Creation.   His form is strikingly bold and majestic having a large Shaggy Mane, which he can erect at pleasure, and whilst roaring like Thunder, exhibits
A PICTURE OF GRANDEUR, WHICH NO WORDS CAN DESCRIBE.

The printed bill advertising Atkins' Menagerie at Bartholomew Fair, 8 September 1825. Holding hands with a lion and tiger, the superscription explained his attitude to his animals.

no less than the birth, while the show was at Windsor, of three fine lion-tiger cubs. George IV saw them at the Royal Lodge, Windsor Great Park and was 'pleased to observe that they were the greatest curiosity of the beast creation he had ever witnessed'.[4] Agasse painted the three whelps when they were six months old. These were called ligers, being the offspring of a male lion and a tigress. If the male were a tiger and the female a lion, the cubs were called tigons.

Atkins had extraordinary success in cross-breeding lions and tigers. He was the first to succeed in this, in his

Wombwell's Menagerie at Greenwich Fair competing with other attractions.

travelling menagerie and later in the Liverpool Zoological Gardens. Frost said,

> 'The cubs so produced united some of the external characteristics of both parents, their colour being tawny, marked while they were young with darker stripes, such as may be observed in black kittens, the progeny of a tabby cat. These markings disappeared, however, as the lion-tigers approached maturity, at which time the males had the mane entirely deficient, or very little developed. I remember seeing a male puma and a leopardess in the same cage in this menagerie, but I am unable to state whether the union was fruitful'.[5]

Atkins also showed an elephant which he described as being, 'upwards of ten feet high! Five tons weight! His consumption of hay, corn, straw, carrots, water, etc exceeds 800*lbs* daily'. This animal was trained to use his trunk to unbolt the door of his cage, admit his keeper and then bolt it again. He could pick up a sixpence with his trunk and then lift the lid of a box fastened to the wall and drop the coin inside. The elephant also fired a blunderbuss.

With his eight-man brass band playing alongside, Atkins stood outside the entrance and called out, 'The great performing elephant is *here*; also the only lion and tigress in one den to be seen in the fair, or I'll forfeit a thousand guineas! Walk up! Walk up!'[6]

The author William Hone said that the number of animals shown by Atkins was 'surprising and they were clean and in good condition. Their variety and beauty, with the unusual accessory of monkeys, made a splendid picture. The birds were equally admirable, especially the pelicans, and the emeu'.

On the road, Atkins and Wombwell were great rivals, touring the provinces and making sure they both attended Bartholomew Fair where they tried to upstage one another on every possible occasion. Atkins's rivalry with Wombwell reached an amusing pitch about the time that Atkins had the unique lion-crossed-with-tigress cubs. Wombwell's menagerie was up in Newcastle a fortnight before Bartholomew Fair was due to open, though Wombwell himself was in London. He heard that Atkins, having presumed that Wombwell could not get his menagerie back south in time, was boasting that this year the Atkins' Menagerie would be the only one on view at Bartholomew Fair. Wombwell shot up to Newcastle, packed up the tent, got the wagons and caravans rolling and by forced marches day after day, arrived in London on the morning the fair opened. His triumph was great, until he was informed that the strenuous journey in the large van had been too much for his elephant, and it had died. Atkins soon heard about this disaster and cheerfully announced that he was exhibiting the only live elephant at the fair. Wombwell retaliated by declaring that he was exhibiting the only dead elephant at the show. As for the public, they piled into Wombwell's Menagerie.[6]

George Wombwell (1777–1850) was never at a loss in emergencies and had a good eye for the main chance, that he promptly seized and turned to good account. His career started in this way and he never forgot the lesson. He was born in Essex and was in business in Soho as a shoemaker and cobbler at the turn of the century, though he was not interested in his trade. He had always kept pets, dogs, rabbits, birds and any other creatures a small boy could obtain

Wombwell's Menagerie, a Staffordshire pottery figure with overglaze enamel decoration, c.1830, c. 14½" high, showing the animals, the band of wind instrument players and drummer and the proprietor inviting the public to come and see his show.

in London. In 1804 he strolled down to the London docks one day and saw some very large boa constrictors for sale. The other showmen present were wary of them, not having seen many and being unused to handling them, so Wombwell got them at a reasonable price. He paid £75 for a pair, proceeded to exhibit them, and in three weeks not only recouped his original outlay, but made a profit. This gave him the idea of buying other animals for exhibition purposes, so he secured some premises in Commercial Road, an office and a yard, where he could keep and sell animals and also build cages and wagons for them.

When he was ready, he issued a business card bearing a wood engraving of a tiger and the words 'WOMBWELL, Wild Beast Merchant. All sorts of foreign animals, birds etc bought, sold, or exchanged, at the Repository or Travelling Menagerie'. He began touring with his caravans, frequently going to small towns and villages where no collection of foreign wild animals had previously been seen. The sight of the yellow caravans decorated with oil paintings of boa-constrictors swallowing negro families and Bengal tigers eating British officers and natives was sufficient to set any small village agog with excitement and curiosity, and villagers flocked to see the show.[7]

Wombwell obtained his animals from ships returning to port after long sea voyages and was alerted as to their arrival by the pilots on the Thames (and later on other rivers) with whom he kept in close touch. He thus got the first chance to buy animals brought home. He paid £1000 for a giraffe. Thomas Hood the poet, went to see the 'Cameleopard', as the giraffe was then called, for it looked like a cross between a spotted leopard and a camel. *His Ode to the Cameleopard*, published at this time included the lines,

> 'Welcome to Freedom's birthplace – and a den!
> Great Anti-climax hail!
> So very lofty in thy front – but then,
> So dwindling at the tail!
> In truth, thou hast the most unequal legs!
> Has one pair galloped, whilst the other trotted . . .'[8]

The giraffe died after only three weeks' residence at Commercial Road.

Wombwell totted up the losses through the deaths of his animals and reckoned that, from start to finish, he lost between twelve and fifteen thousand pounds. With tigers costing between one and two hundred pounds, panthers one hundred, zebras one-fifty to two hundred, only a few deaths cut into the profits drastically. Monkeys were the most susceptible to travelling conditions, quickly succumbing to cold, wet conditions. Ostriches were another high risk, from their habit of sticking their necks through bars and breaking them.

Despite such losses and setbacks, Wombwell was remarkably successful as a businessman. The prices he could afford to give for new animals was enormous. He paid Monsieur Reboulet £2000 for five giraffes in the 1840s. He bought his animals from William Cross of Liverpool, Carl Jamrach in London and anyone else who wanted to sell off an unusual specimen. He also traded from his Commercial Road address as a 'Bird and live animal dealer'. His income varied considerably. At the Bartholomew Fair in 1828 his was the largest menagerie on show and his receipts were £1,700, but in the muddy conditions of 1831 he only just cleared his expenses. This was despite having recently acquired

Engraving of Queen Victoria taking some of her children to see Wombwell's Menagerie in 1847.

Lion Queens and King
(a) Nellie Chapman, a Lion Queen who retired unscathed. (Staffordshire figure 11¾" high, c.1847)
(b) Death of the Lion Queen at Chatham 11 January 1850, when a tiger killed Ellen Bright. (Staffordshire earthenware figure 15" high, 1850)
(c) Staffordshire pottery figure c. 12½" high, 1860, of the Lion King, Jack Manchester, Wombwell's Lion tamer who retired to keep a pub in Taunton and died in his bed in 1865. He was the first lion tamer, c.1835, appearing astride a lion called Nero and opening Nero's mouth.

Morgan's smaller menagerie, which he kept separate from his own and for which he charged 6 pence admission. Morgan's menagerie had a few big cats, but one of his leopards had been trained to be carried by his keeper 'pick-a-back' and the show had earned him the modest sum of £150 at Bartholomew Fair in 1828. With Morgan having sold out to Wombwell, by 1833 Wombwell's was the only show of any size or importance at Bartholomew Fair.

Wombwell developed into a showman. In 1825, in the Midlands, he heard some gentlemen discussing the lion fights in the Tower of London in James I's time, and promptly took the cue and organised a lion versus dogs fight. When it was time to stage this lion-baiting, a lion called Nero had a number of dogs placed in his cage. Nero was a gentle, lazy old lion who allowed his keeper 'Manchester Jack' to sit on his back and open his mouth. Nero merely pushed the irritating dogs out of his way. He got a few bites and maimed a few dogs when he used his huge paws to brush them aside, but it wasn't much of a spectacle. The dogs were removed and Wombwell made up for the lack of excitement by entering the cage of the bleeding Nero himself, confident of Nero's tameness, and as usual his judgement was correct. He was equally sure that his other lion Wallace was quite a different proposition and the dogs put into Wallace's cage soon howled to come out again and had to be pulled through the bars of the cage in a very undignified manner, the last being carried about in Wallace's mouth as a rat is by a terrier.

Wallace was born at Edinburgh in 1819, so was six years old when he fought off the dogs for Wombwell and lived in the menagerie until he died in 1838. His body was sent by stage coach to Saffron Walden Museum in Essex, where the skin was mounted on a framework of wooden struts and stuffed with wood shavings. He had a dog under his front paw, but this has since been removed and Wallace stands, baring his teeth aggressively, in the museum where he may still be seen.

At Bartholomew's Fair in 1830, Wombwell's special attraction was his elephant from Siam who could uncork bottles. Elephants and lions with other big cats were always the main draw for the public. Wombwell took great care of his animals and had outstanding success in breeding from them, even difficult lions.

One of his lionesses had a litter of two white cubs and he was breeding lions when the Zoological Society keepers were having a barren score of years as far as lion cubs were concerned. He finally increased his stock to twenty lions, besides many more unusual animals, for example, a hyena in 1829 (previously exhibited by William Bullock at the Egyptian Hall) and Croydon Fair visitors were induced to pay for a peep at a 'bonassus' which turned out to be a bison. 'Satyrs' and 'Tiger-men' were monkeys, usually part of a showman's stock, though they were prone to shivering and contracting a variety of diseases. Monkeys in red jackets, blue trousers and wearing a sailor's hat might be despised now, but then at least the clothes kept them warmer than they would otherwise have been. When two of his monkeys died while Wombwell was at Shrewsbury in January 1836, their corpses were enthusiastically collected by the amateur anatomist and local squire Thomas Campbell Eyton of Eyton who dissected them. He published a description of these green monkeys and said that their lungs were much diseased. A gorilla, that lived only seven months in Wombwell's Menagerie, was mounted as a specimen for the collection of Charles Waterton and on display in 1861. The dead menagerie animals contributed to our growing zoological knowledge of animals, when carefully examined, before being preserved for another audience in museums.

MR WOMBWELL.

A portrait of George Wombwell engraved for Robert Chambers, *Book of days* 1838 vol. 2: 586.

An employee of Wombwell's, D. P. Miller, said that his employer spared no expense to render his exhibits attractive and novel and no other proprietor could boast of such a collection of rare and valuable animals. From modest beginnings with a small caravan, the menagerie grew to the stage when the caravans and wagons numbered 40 and a stud of 120 dray horses was maintained to pull them. The menagerie was split into three parts eventually and it cost over £35 a day to keep the three on the road. The turnpike tolls alone formed a high proportion of the costs and the bands providing the musical enticement to 'step up and see the show' cost about £40 per week to maintain.

Inevitably, with so many people, animals and vehicles on the road, there were accidents. The worst usually involved the unpredictable big cats and the Wombwell tragedy involved a tiger which attacked his niece, Ellen Eliza Bright, known as the 'Lion Queen', whom Sir Robert Heron described as being,

> 'very handsome, of modest and graceful demeanour, such as to attract the favorable notice of the Queen. She was very fond of animals, and I have seen her apparently on the best of terms with them. One day, entering a den in which were a lion and a tiger, she either excited the jealousy of the tiger, or unknowingly offended him; he flew at her, and mortally wounded her'.[9]

This was at Chatham in 1850.

Wombwell was so famous that he was granted the right, by Royal Decree of George IV, to erect and exhibit his menagerie in any market place in Great Britain for any consecutive three days free of cost. He was invited to take his menagerie to Windsor for William IV and Queen Adelaide in 1834, again in 1840 for Queen Victoria. His reputation as an excellent vet was put to the test by Prince Albert, whose hounds kept dying from an apparently incurable disease. Wombwell diagnosed the trouble as being a lack of clean drinking water. As soon as this was put right, the hounds suffered no more loss. The Prince was delighted at this result and asked in what way he could be of service to Mr Wombwell. The old showman, after a little consideration, replied that he wanted no reward, but if the Prince liked, he might present him with a plank of wood cut from the timbers of the lately recovered *Royal George*, to make him a coffin. The strange request was granted and shortly after, a prominent piece of furniture at Wombwell's private residence in Commercial Road was a splendid polished oak coffin.

Wombwell was exhibiting his animals in Northallerton in November 1850 when he died of bronchitis. He was described by Hone as 'undersized in mind as well as in form, a weazen, sharp-faced man, with a skin reddened by more than natural spirits'. *The Times* was more polite and observed that 'No one probably did more to forward practically the study of natural history among the masses'. His grave in Highgate Cemetery, London, is marked by a stone lion on the top.[10]

Wombwell left a will disposing of his three menageries. First to be named was, 'Ann Morgan now living with me' to whom he left,

> 'all that my menagerie or collection of Animals (No.1) now managed and conducted by her together with the horses caravans furniture fittings up and all other appendages by the same belonging or relating and used therewith unto her the said Ann Morgan for her own absolute use and benefit'.

The second menagerie was bequeathed to, 'my niece Harriott Edmunds wife of James Edmunds . . . now conducted by her' and her husband, with the condition that £100 from the takings from this menagerie were to be paid to Ann Morgan per annum. The third menagerie was left to his nephew George Wombwell, who was managing it in 1850. He signed his will with a cross, an illiterate man who could not write his name.[11]

Ann Morgan (1788–1876) continued to manage the fourteen wagons of Menagerie 1 until 1865 when it was handed over to Harriott Edmunds. The Edmonds family had been menagerists for some years, having shown in 1839 a fine group of lions, tigers and leopards and enticed a young woman named Chapman (later to become Mrs George Sanger) to perform with them as a rival to the first 'Lion Queen', Miss Hilton. The Edmonds only kept the enlarged menagerie until 1872 when it was sold in Edinburgh by Mrs Fairgrieve, their niece. A local newspaper reported that Jamrach bought at this sale and William Cross the Liverpool dealer and zoo representatives from Manchester,

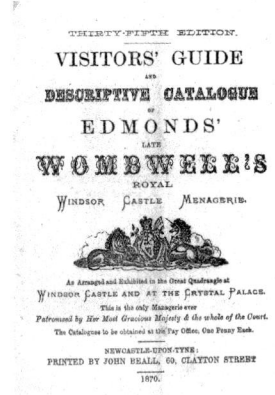

The Edmonds continued to trade on Wombwell's name when they showed their animals to Queen Victoria in 1870.

Bristol and Paris. Van Ambrugh, with three menageries in America, sent a buyer who purchased sufficient animals to fill twenty-two cages, including the first black African rhinoceros to be seen in America. The price the animals at this sale realised was just under £3,000. A 'Mr Rice' bought the most animals, then Jamrach purchased a mandrill for five guineas a pair of pelicans 'bought at the sale of the Knowsley collection, and which had been trained to run races,' for £13, a Tibetan bear for five guineas, three leopards for £60, a fine lion for £200 and a magnificent tigress for £155.[12]

At this 1872 sale, two other menagerists, of the Day family, made some remarkable purchases. John Day had gradually built up a small menagerie of four wagons to eight and now purchased another wagon, the living wagon in which George Wombwell had died at Northallerton in 1850, along with a further animal wagon. Mrs Day purchased the Tasmanian devil which the auctioneer assured his hearers was as strong in the jaw as a hyena, but not to be recommended for purchase as a domestic pet. She paid £3 and five shillings for it and then paid another £7 for an emu. John Day died in 1888, but another Day, James, also had a menagerie and continued showing into the 20th century.

The Wombwell Menagerie No 2 was toured by the Edmonds until about 1888 when the greater part was taken over by the Bostock family (Mrs Bostock and Mrs Edmonds being sisters). It was later purchased by E. H. Bostock. The third menagerie, left to the nephew George (c.1822–1909), declined rapidly and was sold off.

All three new owners tried to benefit from the name Wombwell and the Edmonds' was advertised, 'This Menagerie is the 'Real Wombwell's', in the 35th edition of the *Visitors' Guide and descriptive catalogue of Edmonds' late Wombwell's Royal Windsor Castle Menagerie,* continuing, *as arranged and exhibited in the great quadrangle at Windsor Castle and at the Crystal Palace. This is the only Menagerie ever patronized by Her Most Gracious Majesty & the whole of the Court,* 1870. James Edmond, a big Irishman, had taken over from his wife, and was assisted by Bostock by this date. Special features of this collection were a 'double humped camel' with a calf, Burmese elephant, 'The Giant sacred white camel of India', hyenas, 'Boomah Kangaroos' and Bennet's, sloth bear, an alpaca given by the Queen, one-horned Indian rhinoceros (Mr Edmonds, 'is the only menagerist travelling

Bostock and Wombwell's
Menagerie set up for business.
Postcard.

who ever possessed a Rhinceros'), wombat, boas, a yak, nylghau, porcupines, and coatimundis. The birds included many parrots, cockatoo, owls, Australian quails, laughing jackasses, pelicans, among others.[13]

During this period, the Reverend Francis Kilvert, curate at Langley Burrell, Clyro and vicar at Saint Harmon, went to Wombwell's Menagerie. Perhaps the inclement weather, or a deterioration in the quality of the menagerie after Wombwell's death, had something to do with it, but his diary entry makes dismal reading for Tuesday 7 May 1872,

'Wombwell's Menagerie came into Hay from Brecon Fair today and the elephant was advertized to ride upon a bicycle. This elephant is said to have killed a boy at the Potteries, but whether he did it by driving the bicycle over him or not did not appear . . . I went to see the show but it was very late coming into Hay. Some one said the elephant had turned rusty on the road. Toddy Bevan and I went out to meet the caravans which were looming in the distance along the Brecon road between the trees. The elephant, a very small one, and three camels or drome- daries came shuffling along the muddy road in heavy rain looking cold and miserable and shivering as if they were wet through. The camels were being towed by the caravans.

The elephant walked very fast by the side. I noticed that the camels as well as the elephant moved both legs on one side at once. The camels were immediately put into the stable at the Blue Boar and I heard the owner or manager of the menagerie say to the ostler, "Get a wisp of straw and rub those camels down, they won't hurt you, they are as quiet as sheep." The show was advertized to take place at 3.30, but the beasts did not arrive till 4 and could not be shown till 6 . . .

At 6 o'clock the wild beasts were ready and we all went to the show. There was a fair lion and a decent wolf, which looked as if it had been just freshly caught, his coat was so thick and good and he was so strong and restless. A laughing hyena set us all off laughing in chorus. A black sheep in the pangs of hunger was bleating piteously and had forced his body half through the bars of his cage to get at the biscuits the children were offering him. The exhibition was small and poor. A dwarf three feet nothing pointed out to us "groups of wolves", stirred the beasts up with a long pole and made them roar. There was no bicycle forthcoming. The elephant did not get upon it or seem likely to do so. The camels were coming but not come. The ground was in a swamp with pools of water and huge gaps in the canvas overhead let in the pouring rain. I soon went away'.[14]

Times were happier in Wombwell's day, it seems, and the author of *The Trip to Tiptree* wrote a poem to the celebrated menagerist while he was exhibiting at Weldon Fair in 1838, beginning,

> 'Hail! Hail! to thee, famed Wombwell! Of Menagerists the
>   prince,

Thomas Stevens's Royal Menagerie, Friday 6 May 1863, advertising its eleven caravans and Infant Lion Queen. Stevens was, 'late of Liverpool Zoological Gardens' (opened 1832–63). He toured in Ireland.

> When'er again you visit us all must their joy evince;
> And such the fame of him whose Show all love to set their
>   eyes on
> If once "an Essex *calf*," Great Sir, you've long become a
>   "*lion*"'.

There were seven more verses of equally awful poetry, but the sentiment was sincere and appreciative of the animals he had taken to the public.[15]

The second menagerie was advertised as the Bostock & Wombwell Royal Menageries from c. 1869–88. The proprietess was Mrs James Bostock niece of Wombwell and her husband, James, who had been an assistant to George Wombwell. They were the parents of two other showmen and menagerie proprietors, Edward Henry Bostock (1858–1940) and Frank Charles Bostock (1866–1912). Edward Henry succeeded his mother as owner of 'Bostock & Wombwell Royal Menageries' in 1888 . He transferred his business to his son (John Reginald Wombwell Bostock) in 1919, but had to take it back when his son died a few years later and finally disposed of it, mostly to Whipsnade Zoo in 1931.This menagerie had travelled with a large number of cats, often six to eight leopards, lynx, approximately ten lions, two tigers, a puma and a jaguar.

Frank Charles Bostock travelled in Europe, America, Australia and South Africa, advertising himself as the 'Animal King'. The two menageries of the Bostock brothers carried the tradition on from the Wombwell years (beginning in 1805) through to 1931.[16]

There were a few smaller menageries than Wombwell's. James Chipperfield (born 1824) based his menagerie at Norwich in the winter months and travelled in the summer months. His son, James Francis Chipperfield, added wire-walkers, tumblers and clowns to the menagerie and his nine children were trained to perform so that this menagerie became a circus before 1890.

Earl James had a small show and was also an animal dealer. The only other menagerie of any size belonged to William Hilton, recorded as attending Greenwich Fair in 1839, but was bought out by his keeper, William Manders, in 1852, who then toured under the name 'Manders' Menagerie'. He added to Hilton's eight wagons until he had acquired sixteen. His animals included five elephants and seven camels, two pairs of jaguars which bred and some clouded tigers and several lions. When he died in 1871 his wife Sarah carried on the business, but sold up in 1875. A second James Manders also toured with a menagerie until his death in 1907, when his widow continued to tour until her death in 1912.

Even when travelling the menageries were a sight worth seeing, apart from the painted wagons containing the animals, there was a menagerie owner's caravan, the band wagon and a hundred and more horses pulling them. Manders's show entrance was folded down for travelling, but still measured 30' long and 8'6" wide, requiring nine horses to pull it over the rough roads. It folded out to 60' wide and 35' high. Elephant wagons were the next largest and measured anything up to 30' long and 8' wide. The effect was dramatised by using elephants and camels to draw these huge wagons as they neared their venues. With tolls being paid according to width of wheels (the largest vans required iron-tyred wheels up to 11" wide) and the number of horses and wagons, the large sums expended on tolls became a major item in the menageries' account books.

It was William Hilton who first introduced a circus performance into the domain of menageries. Hilton's menagerie is first noted in 1839 at Greenwich Fair, where the season commenced with most of the shows that made London their winter headquarters. His manager, James Lee, suggested to him the idea of having a 'Lion Queen' to show off his lions as an added attraction. 'Lion Kings' had proved lucrative attractions for circus owners, but a young woman would be an even greater draw. The young lady chosen was familiar with Hilton's lions. She was the daughter of his brother Joseph and made her first appearance with the lions at Stepney Green Fair in 1850. It was such a success that the Edmunds promptly trained a rival, Miss Nelly Chapman, to show their big cats. George Wombwell's Ellen Bright was the third 'Lion Queen', and first fatality.[17]

All these menageries and then circuses, were family businesses, with the wives and sons carrying on and often marrying into other families in the same business. Few remained, however, at the end of the century to continue into the 20th century past World War I.

Chapter 10

'To see the tigers sup'

The earliest notable commercial menagerie to be housed permanently in a building in London was at the Exeter 'Change. c.1785 until 1829. Before that, a shop in the New Road owned first by Baily, then Brookes and then Herring, was often referred to as a menagerie because of the number of animals to be seen there, but this was a dealer's shop, not a permanent display, to which the public was admitted for a small sum to see the animals.

Exeter 'Change was built 1680–81 and contained two walks below stairs and as many above, with shops on each side for sempsters, milliners, hosiers, etc, the builders judging, 'it would come in great request'. It was not as popular as the builders hoped and the large rooms upstairs were used for all kinds of purposes, such as temporary exhibitions, hiring for offices by the Land Bank, and in January 1772, the remains of Lord Baltimore, who had died abroad, lay in state until removed for interment in the family vault at Epsom. After 1772 it was used as a warehouse for storing and printing volumes of the Rolls and Journals of the House of Lords for about a decade.

The first hint that a menagerie was at Exeter 'Change occurs in John Thomas Smith's book of reminiscences, *A Book for a rainy day*, under the year 1785. He and a friend, Mr Baker, were walking home after a night out and, as they approached Temple Bar, about one o'clock,

> 'A most unaccountable appearance claimed our attention, – it was no less an object than an elephant, whose keepers were coaxing it to pass through the gateway. He had been accompanied by several persons from the Tower Wharf with tall poles, but was principally guided by two men with ropes, each walking on either side of the street, to keep him as much as possible in the middle on his way to the menagerie, Exeter Change; to which destination, after passing St. Clement's Church, he steadily trudged on with strict obedience to the commands of his keepers. I had the honour afterwards of partaking of a pot of Barclay's Entire with this same elephant,

143

which high mark of his condescension was bestowed when I accompanied my friend the late Sir James Winter Lake, Bart. to view the rare animals in Exeter Change – that gentleman being assured by the elephant's keeper that if he would offer the beast a shilling, he would see the noble animal nod his head and drink a pot of porter. The elephant no sooner had taken the shilling, which he did in the mildest manner from the palm of Sir James's hand, than he gave it to the keeper, and eagerly watched his return with the beer. The elephant then, after placing his proboscis to the top of the tankard, drew up nearly the whole of the then good beverage. The keeper observed, "You will hardly believe, gentleman, but the little he has left is quite warm"; upon this we were tempted to taste it, and it really was so'.[1]

This animal was afterwards disposed of for the sum of one thousand guineas.

The menagerie was owned by Thomas Clark in 1790 and probably prior to that date, when this elephant arrived. We have a good account of the animals present in 1790–91 from N. Burt, a student at the Naval & Drawing Academy in Tottenham Court Road, who frequently dropped in to see the animals, to draw their portraits and ask Mr Clark questions about where he had procured the animals, how he fed them and where they came from, before noting down the information about each. Burt then published an attractive small book, in parts at fortnightly intervals, for each of which he charged one shilling. The book could be purchased at the Academy, or from Mrs Russell who was currently exhibiting some 'birds over Exeter 'Change' and Mr Pidcock at the Lyceum in the Strand'.

Among the animals, he figured a rhinoceros that was bought by Clark for a large sum. It arrived on 5 June 1790 and Burt hastened to the 'Change to inspect and draw the new arrival. He also drew a zebra, a 'Royal Lincolnshire Ox or Heifer with 2 heads', a young royal tiger and a black bear. The birds included some interesting species with notes as to their place of origin. The usual eagles, macaws, cockatoos were present, and a pelican, secretary bird and an 'Imperial Vulture brought from Vienna', with a 'silver-headed eagle of North America'. Of the cassowary he said, 'Never seen in Europe till 1597 when Hollanders brought

Engraving of portrait of Thomas Clark, owner of the Exeter 'Change building, who dealt in wild animals before Pidcock bought his animals in 1793 to add to his own stock. *European Magazine*, 1816.

it at return of their first voyage from India. Given to them as a rarity by a Prince of the Isle of Java from whence this specimen also had come'. The 'Eagle of the Sun' was represented and Burt said there was another at the Tower of London. This royal menagerie specimen had been taken in a French prize by Admiral Boscawen and presented to the King, but the bird drawn by Burt had been a present from General O'Hara to H. R. H. the Prince of Wales. Burt did not say where his picture of a rattlesnake had been drawn, but that Pidcock had purchased two ostriches to exhibit at the Lyceum and the condor also belonged to him, it was depicted standing over a mutilated lamb. Burt appears to have visited all the menageries in town at that time, for he spoke of a pair of mandarin ducks, 'Those birds were by the late Duke of Northumberland purchased of Mr Brooks, at his menagerie in the New Road and the first pair to have bred in a menagerie in England'. He then refers to George Edwards's account of mandarin ducks from whom he got this information. However, 'The Royal Crown' bird, i.e. Balearian crowned crane, did belong to Mr Clark and could be seen at Exeter 'Change. Some other curious species have strayed into this small book, a 'black and white negro', 'a white negro woman' and on the last two plates, of 'Patrick O'Brien the Irish Giant 7'4" alongside a dwarf, and a 'Double-headed Ox'.

After Mr Clark (who is only shown in the directories 1790–99 as a partner of Willatts and both were 'Hardwaremen at Ex. Ch. Strand') the menagerie proprietor was Pidcock, who bought Clark's animals in 1793 to add to his own stock. John Pidcock and Son were 'Bottlewarehousemen' at Exeter 'Change in 1791, but Gilbert, the son, who was an animal enthusiast and importer of animals at Exeter 'Change took over the menagerie in 1793. Gilbert had been noted as at the Lyceum, by Burt in 1790. This was a room for concerts and exhibitions, built in 1771 in the grounds of Exeter House, and was converted into a theatre in 1794 after Pidcock moved out.

Gilbert Pidcock was an excellent businessman and devised a good advertisement stunt when he placed a sham Yeoman of the Guard outside Exeter 'Change to invite passers-by to step inside to see the lions, tigers, elephant and monkeys. The animals were confined in cages and dens in rooms of varying size, the walls being painted with exotic scenery to

Read, See, and Believe!
The largeft Collection of Living Rarities ever feen in Europe
is now exhibiting, in the Great Room over

**EXETER
CHANGE,**

IN THE STRAND.

In one Apartment are

Three ftupendous ELEPHANTS,

TWO MALES AND A FEMALE;

Which are not only the largeft and ftrongeft Animals in the World, but in Under-
ftanding are inferior only to Man ; as they can naturally do many Things, and are alfo
taught others, which might feem impoffible.   In Asia, they are trained to War, and
have Caftles on their Backs, which contain upwards of Twenty People.   They are faid
to live till between Two and Three Hundred Years.

Admittance, ONE SHILLING *each.*

Likewife is added to

The Grand Menagerie,

Which confifts of near THREE HUNDRED Foreign Birds and Beafts,

Three Bengal Striped Royal Tygers,

TWO MALES AND A FEMALE;

Three Royal CROWN BIRDS,

Which are the greateft Variety of the Feathered Tribe, &c.

AD MITTANCE, One Shilling each Perfon.

Alfo, in an Apartment under the Great Room, is to be Seen from Obfcurity,

BY A CURIOUS APPARATUS,

A great Variety of pleafing Perfpectives and public Animation,

Far excelling any Thing of the Kind yet invented.

Admittance One Shilling, or the Three Exhibitions for 2s. 6d.

N. B. Foreign Birds and Beafts bought, fold, or exchanged, by G. PIDCOCK, as above.

Hancock, Printer, No. 61, Barbican.

Gilbert Pidcock's advertisement of his menagerie at Exeter 'Change.

create an illusion of viewing them in their natural habitats. The roar of the lions and tigers could be heard in the street below and horses passing up and down the Strand were not infrequently terrified by the din.

Pidcock also obtained valuable publicity in the little magazine, *Picture of London,* where a list of the animals he was displaying was printed in the volume for 1808. The collection was housed on two floors now, one apartment on the first floor and two apartments on the second floor. Visitors could pay 2 shillings to see the animals on floor 2 and another 6 pence was charged for the third apartment. Sixteen special 'inhabitants' were listed, but Mr Pidcock

Johannes Eckstein painted the 'Camel at Exeter 'Change' in 1798 when Pidcock owned the menagerie.

had 'also a great number of smaller animals and a variety of curious birds'.[2]

The collection was very good, with Pidcock's lions and tigers being noted for their excellent condition. The specimens of which he was most proud were his lions, particularly the one named 'Victory, who whelped in the menagery of the Dey of Algiers, on the memorable 1st of August 1798, the day on which Lord Nelson obtained the glorious victory at the mouth of the Nile'. There was also a 'South American Lion'. Of the nylghaus, Pidcock informed the public that a pair had bred at Blenheim Park a few years before, among others introduced to England, but he claimed that his own three were now the only ones alive. He asserted that the melanistic black wolf from Canada was the only one of that colour ever brought to England and added that the grey wolf in the same room came from the Alps. The large baboon or papio stood 5' high when erect. The 'tapir – an amphibious animal from Buenos Ayres' completed the notes of interest on the animals, except, perhaps, that he had skeletons of an elephant and a whale. The ostriches and condor had both been mentioned by Burt and there were two emus and a grand cassowary whose predecessor had laid four eggs, but failed to hatch them.

It was not uncommon for Pidcock to have a species never before imported of which he was unaware. Natural historians searched his collection for such rarities and two artists were specifically commissioned to draw and paint such species if they suspected they were new. Lord Stanley (the future 13th Earl of Derby, of Knowsley Hall near Liverpool) asked Sydenham Edwards (1768–1819) to search for and draw birds at Pidcock's, and the Exeter 'Change was visited by Samuel Howitt (1765–1822), another artist, who painted many foreign mammals in the early 19th century. These included giant flying squirrels, African civet with the characteristic pose of an arched back, African jackal, Amerindian dogs, Canada lynx with prominent eartufts, a small hog-deer and a honey badger, or ratel, of Asia and Africa. Drawn from life, these artists' representations were superior to those drawn from skins.

Pidcock exchanged animals with other owners. A letter from Sir Charles Blagden (an army physician, 1748–1820) in Paris, October 1802, to Sir Joseph Banks, mentioned that a pair of kangaroos had arrived there 'not as a present from the King, but by an exchange with Pidcock'.[3] The trade in Australian species was beginning to build up. It was now ten years since the first skins had been sent back from the First Fleet sailors in 1789. It was several years after this that live animals were successfully transported to England. Like so many menagerie owners, Pidcock also imported and dealt in wild animals.

The museum owner, William Bullock, noted several animals that had died in Pidcock's menagerie and then been preserved for his museum: a panther and beaver, a 'Palatine Monkey simia roloway from the Slave Coast of Africa', which had died in the winter of 1808, a puma (*Felix concolor*) successfully bred at Exeter 'Change about 1808, but a stuffed specimen by 1816, a non-descript species of jabiru, and a secretary bird that had been fed on eels while alive.[4]

It was while Pidcock was the owner, in 1803, that the Swiss animal artist Jacques Laurent Agasse (1767–1849) began to paint the menagerie animals. That year he worked on a 'curious African antelope tribe', the first of some seventy accurate animal portraits, including leopards and cheetahs, a sloth, other antelopes and zebra.

Pidcock was succeeded at Exeter 'Change in 1811 by another 'Wild Beast Showman' named Stephen Polito, who was in all probability previously employed in the menagerie. Polito died in 1814 and the only memorable event of

Obadiah Sherratt's Staffordshire earthenware figure of Polito's Menagerie, probably dating from 1808 when the menagerie visited Wolverhampton, close to Burslem where Sherratt worked. The figure is 11½" high and the elephant with its howdah and castle, two monkeys, two parakeets with rollerskates at the sides, tiger and lion, with a monkey on a hurdy-gurdy and cornet players and drummer, are all beautifully portrayed surrounding Polito's wagon. The delightful spelling over the top of the figure reads POLITO'S ROYAL MENAGERIE OF THE WONDERFULL BURDS AND BEASTS FROM MOST PARTS OF THE WORLDS LIONS EC.

The interior of Polito's menagerie, Exeter 'Change. Aquatint no 43. in R. Ackermann's, *Repository of arts*, published 1 July 1812.

his three years' tenure of Exeter 'Change was when Thomas Landseer, the brother of the famous Victorian painter Edwin, etched a print of 'Nero', one of Stephen Polito's lions in 1814. The print was very popular, many copies being sold, and Nero's portrait was used as the model for the sculptures of the lions in Trafalgar Square.

The menagerie was taken over by Edward Cross, Polito's principal assistant. Thereafter it was sometimes referred to

EXETER CHANGE.

From the original Picture in the possession of Ja.ᵐ Northcote Esq.ʳ R.A.

Two boys with the tigers of Exeter 'Change, by James Northcote, 1817. The cage bars are dangerously wide apart, the younger boy is reacting rather more sensibly than the older one.

as Cross's Royal Menagerie. He was a 'wildbeastman' for thirty years and a successful showman, but he had other aspirations. A pamphlet by him, issued in 1820, describing the animals at Exeter 'Change, explained, 'The most anxious wish of my mind is to attract the attention of the youthful visitor to this most pleasing and important branch of natural history'. To this end he added comments on the animals' diet and habits as well as provenance. His elephant, which in its youth had been exhibited on the stage at Covent Garden Theatre, over the last ten years had doubled in size. It was then consuming 800 pounds of food every day, made up of hay, corn, straw, carrots, mangel worzel and biscuits, besides gallons of water.

Cross had the usual teething troubles with lion cubs and though there had been eleven cubs in two years at four births, only one little animal had been safely weaned. The other cats represented were cheetah, panther, a lynx and an unusual white tiger. The Indian jackals and hyaenas had a horrid fascination for the public and Cross kept a striped hyaena from Abyssinia as well as a laughing hyaena which 'entertains visitors at feeding time, by the gesticulations

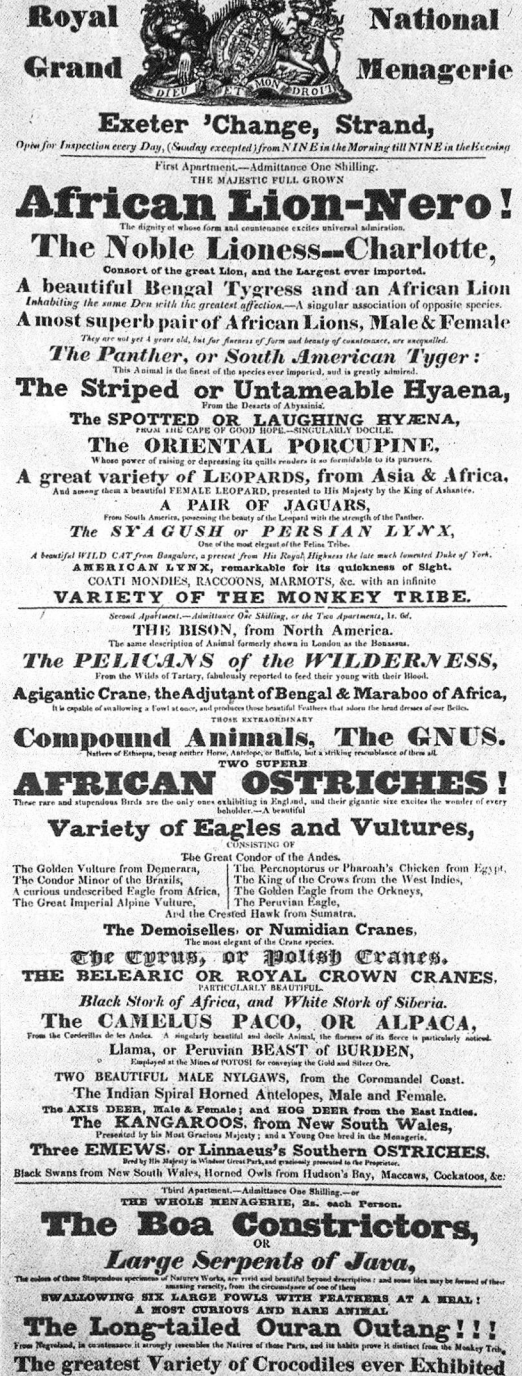

Handbill advertising Exeter 'Change menagerie c.1826. The lion cub, named Charlotte, was picked up in Africa by some sailors and suckled by a dog bitch c.1822. The pair became inseparable and formed one of the main attractions of Cross's collection of animals. They were sketched by Edwin Landseer for his painting called 'Lioness and Bitch'.

Lioness and bitch, drawn
by Edwin Landseer and
engraved by his brother
Thomas in 1823.

of delight he manifests at the moment, and by the curious imitations of the human voice, resembling laughter'. This species was a native of the Cape of Good Hope and, from being spotted, sometimes toured in other menageries in England under the misleading name of 'Tiger Wolf'. Cross's spotted hyaena lived for twenty-five years until a goitre finally put an end to him, then his skin and skeleton were preserved at the College of Surgeons.

Feeding time was a daily attraction for the public and occurred at eight in the evening at the menagerie.

Coatimundis were not common in captivity, but both Atkins and Cross owned some. Other South American animals imported about this time were an agouti, the little rodent with a hare-lip that looks a bit like a guinea-pig, a capybara which Cross believed to be the only one seen in England and a llama from Peru. More rare species at this period were a quagga, a gnu, a 'samboo' or sambar (a large Indian deer) and a nylghau from India, the first of which Cross informed his readers, 'was that introduced into this country, were sent to Lord Clive from Bombay in the year 1767; a male and a female bred several times'. His Australian species included several kangaroos and some emus from Van Dieman's Land (now Tasmania) and a black swan.

The birds were more numerous and some of them hitherto undescribed, among these a beautiful small eagle from the coast of Guinea with greyish plumage and a 'new species of

The outside of the Exeter 'Change was newly painted with animals and a large hoarding at the top of the building when Cross was advertising the ROYAL MENAGERIE there. This detail shows the building shortly before its was demolished in 1829. (Thornbury & Walford, *Old and new London,* vol.III: 109).

vulture sent me from Egypt' which was 'unusually small' and though the second description is slight, it is sufficient to identify it as the Egyptian vulture. His marabou stork from Africa could 'swallow a fowl entire, and with ease', but his crowned cranes were 'nicer' in their habits and he was most enthusiastic about his rose-coloured pelican, an elegant bird from the lakes of Tartary, now called a Dalmatian pelican. There were so many different kinds of parrot that he refrained from listing them all and the smaller monkeys of the 'simia genus' also received only a passing reference. The extremely rare baboon, however, was described in detail, under the name of 'Dog-faced Baboon Simia hamadryas'. It had very long hair at the sides of its head, a grey tail and 'callosities behind'. Happy Jerry was his nickname and it is no wonder that he was a merry character because he drank grog, smoked a short clay pipe and on one occasion dined off hashed venison with George IV at Windsor Castle. This was a rib-nosed baboon, according to the naturalist author Sir William Jardine, who saw the animal drink its gin and said, 'the relish and expression with which it was taken, would have done honour to the most accomplished taster'.[5]

Another very famous naturalist, the American bird artist, John James Audubon, also went to see Cross while he was in London in January and February 1828. He received a 'perpetual ticket of admission to Mr Cross's exhibition of quadrupeds, live birds etc,' which pleased him greatly 'for there I can look upon Nature, even if confined in iron cage'. He went to the menagerie on 26 January and 'had the honor of riding on a very fine and gentle elephant; I say 'honor' because the immense animal was so well trained and so obedient as to be an example to many human beings who are neither'. On 1 February he went to dine at the menagerie with Mr Cross who 'by no means deserves his name, for he is a pleasant man, and we dined with his wife and himself and the keepers of the BEASTS (name given by <u>men</u> to quadrupeds). None of the company were very polished, but all behaved with propriety and good humor, and I liked it on many accounts. Mr Cross conversed very entertainingly'. When Audubon wished to paint an eagle for an 'Eagle and Lamb' painting, he 'bought a superb Golden eagle from Mr Cross'.[6]

Cross was a friend of several animal painters and a particular, life-long friend of Jacques-Laurent Agasse, (1767–1849, an excellent Swiss painter residing in London) who went to the menagerie to paint not only his orang-utan, elephant, large lion, lioness and her whelps, a tiger and hyenas (in 1819), but also three portraits of Edward Cross and his wife and of Miss Polito who was Cross's sister-in-law. Cross was a supplier of animals to the Windsor menageries and George IV also commissioned pictures from Agasse of his Nubian giraffe and white-tailed gnus.

Not all visitors were impressed by Cross's caged animals and Thomas Hood wrote a long poem about a philanthropic monkey called Pug who escaped from the menagerie, joined a crowd at a nearby pub and heard the drinkers 'putting the world to rights'. He returned to the menagerie inspired to give his fellow inmates their freedom. 'Monkey Martyr' was written between 1826 and 1829 and reading the puns and stanzas seems endless while Pug toured cages and dens until he came to Nero the lion and determined to let 'the monarch of the forest' loose. His plan went awry at this point 'For Pug had only half unbolted Nero, When Nero <u>bolted</u> him'.[7]

(a)

(b)

Two dog-faced baboons (a) Thomas Bewick said that a dog-faced baboon was shewn in London under the name of Persian Savage, but figured it in his *History of quadrupeds* under the heading 'The Dog-faced Baboon, *Simia Hamadryas*'. (b) This engraving of 1829 showed a second 'dog-faced baboon' in the Tower of London that enjoyed smoking a pipe.

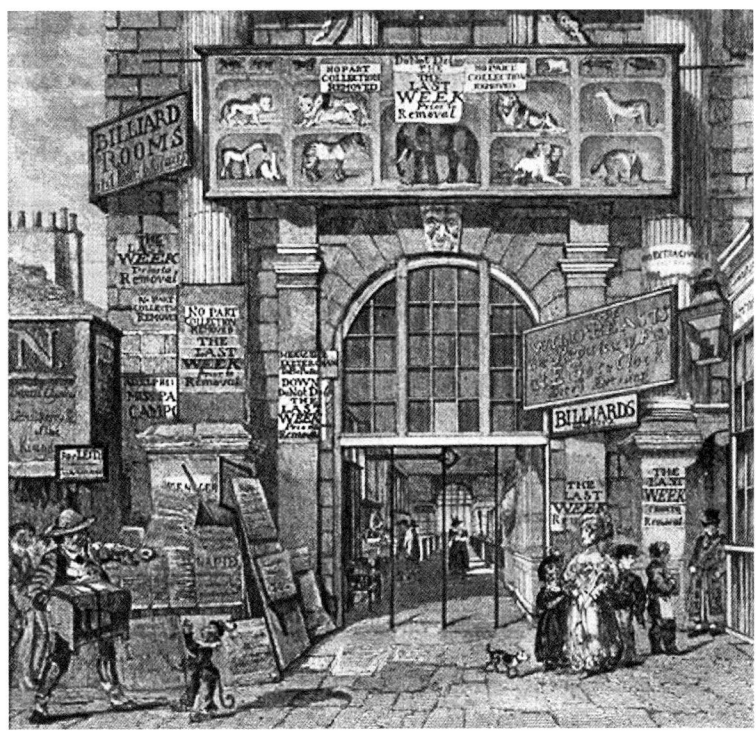

The last week of Edward Cross's menagerie at Exeter 'Change in 1828 before its removal to The King's Mews. A notice says the animals were regularly fed at 8pm every evening, a favourite visiting time. An organ grinder and his monkey have set up a pitch to take advantage of visitors going to the menagerie.

Another famous visitor, Lord Byron, also dropped in to see the tigers sup and noticed that there was a hippopotamus which looked, 'like Lord Liverpool in the face; and the ursine sloth had the very voice and manner of my valet'. When there was a golden eagle in the menagerie, Byron wrote scathingly about one of the keepers who was wont to say of this species, 'This gentlemen, is the eagle of the sun, from Archangel in Russia; the 'otterer it is the 'igherer 'e flies'.[8]

Latterly, Cross's success at the menagerie was due mainly to his elephant, Chunee who had lived in the menagerie since 1809 in a solid oak den that had cost £350 to build. Chunee had had a long career, having originally been purchased for 900 guineas in 1801 to appear in processions on the Covent Garden Theatre stage. Like many mature male elephants, when in must he became ungovernable and in 1826 Cross had to make the decision whether to keep risking his keeper's life or destroy the elephant. The manner of disposing of Chunee was so bungled that it caused great anger and distress. The firearms were then insufficiently

AN UPROAR ON CHANGE OR A TRIP FROM EXETER TO CHARING CROSS.

'An uproar on Change or a trip from Exeter to Charing Cross'. An aquatint by Sparks, 1828, imagining some of the menagerie animals moving from Exeter 'Change to the King's Mews in Charing Cross.

powerful for a clean kill and it took one hundred and fifty-two shots by inexpert marksmen to dispatch him. Chunee's skin was sold for £50 to a tanner and his skeleton for £100 to be preserved at the College of Surgeons. The skin was so punctured with shot holes that the tanner probably found it useless for his trade and may have decided to recoup his £50 by selling bits of the skin as souvenirs. Pieces of labelled elephant hide still appear at sales around the country today, giving rise to queries in newspapers and magazines as to their origin. Thomas Hood wrote another poem, *An address to Mr Cross on the Death of the Elephant*.[9]

From 1826, after the departure of Chunee, the menagerie was not so attractive to the public. Cross was then faced with notice to quit Exeter 'Change three years later when development plans were announced for the buildings in the Strand. Cross had been anxious to quit the menagerie business for some time before these two events. Scherren, who wrote of the formation of the new Zoological Society of London, revealed that on 7 April 1825, upon hearing of the proposals to form the society, Cross had got in touch with the founders. He offered 'his llamas and birds and such parts of his collection as we may choose, to the Society, with a tender of his services in promoting our views'. Sir Stamford Raffles, the founder of the Zoological Society, was already acquainted with Cross, having sent a clouded leopard, which he had brought home in 1816 from Java, to Cross's menagerie at Exeter 'Change. Cross's offer was

The King's Mews, Charing Cross, c.1830 housing the National Repository and Edward Cross's menagerie from 1828 until this building was demolished in 1831 to make way for the National Gallery.

An admission ticket, costing 1/- to the Surrey Zoological Gardens which flourished from 1831 to 1877 when they were sold for redevelopment. Cross sold the menagerie to the Scientific and Zoological Institution and was the manager until handing over to Mr Tyler. The animals were auctioned in 1855.

rejected and Cross repeated it a year later, more specifically. In May 1826 he 'offered his services for the management of the Menagerie, at the same time proposing that the Society should purchase his collection', but though the offer was renewed yet again in 1829, it was refused. Cross knew a great deal about the care of animals and this knowledge would have been of value to the new society, but his attitude to the animals was that of a showman and thus diametrically opposed to the aims of the founders of the new society.

In January 1829, Cross was getting desperate to dispose of the animals, for he was under a month's notice to quit Exeter 'Change. He finally gave up hope of disposing of his entire stock to the Zoological Society and took some rooms in the King's Mews, Charing Cross and removed his animals there. That proved to be a temporary move, however, and his final site was the Surrey Zoological Gardens to which he took his animals in 1831, along with a few specimens from the Tower Menagerie then being disbanded at the command of William IV.

Although he did not know it at the time, Cross was laying the foundations for furthering his influence at the Zoological Society when he kindly let a small boy of five years old, with a passion for animals, free access to run round the menagerie. That small boy grew up to be a greatly revered and much loved superintendent of the Zoological Society Gardens in Regent's Park from 1859 until his death in 1897. Abraham D. Bartlett later recalled that Cross allowed him 'to crawl about the beast-room in that menagerie' so that he could not recall the first time he saw lions, tigers, elephants or any other wild beasts, for the reason that he spent his early years among them. Cross also gave him the bodies of any birds that died and this gave young Bartlett practice in dissecting and mounting specimens. Bartlett went on to become an animal dealer, before taking up employment at the Zoo.[10]

Edward Cross had more liberal ideas over housing the animals than usually prevailed in the early 19th century. A writer in the *Zoological Magazine* in 1833 suggested that his plans be followed for exhibiting monkeys, because Cross's monkeys 'instead of being confined by twos and threes in close cages, are preserved in a large space, well ventilated and heated, and defended by a glass frame; and here they can disport and exercise themselves throughout the winter'.[11] It took decades for the Zoological Society to stop over-heating their animals and to give them access to fresh air. It is a pity they did not use Cross's services and tailor his experience to their own needs.

After the removal of Cross's Menagerie, Exeter 'Change was taken down during the 1829 Strand improvements and the Mews, to which he had transferred the animals at that time, were also demolished in 1830–31.

Cross's menagerie gained a new lease of life when he removed to the Surrey Zoological Gardens in 1831 and remained there until 1855. These formed but a small part of the site of the demesne that had been attached to the Manor House at Walworth. The fifteen-acre garden formed a separate enclosure between the Kennington and Walworth Roads in Penton Place. The grounds included an ornamental lake of nearly three acres, an area for outdoor concerts and for setting off fireworks, staging of flower shows (that had recently come into fashion), displaying large picture models of volcanoes or the city of Rome, Edinburgh Castle and other passing fancies.

A glazed, circular building 100' in diameter was built for the cages of the carnivorous mammals. It had nearly six thousand feet of glass and was then the largest glasshouse in existence. In this unpromising environment Edward Cross

Surrey Zoological Gardens showing the giraffes, deer, peacocks, pelican, a camel with a mock-up of Edinburgh Castle in the background. (A Baxter print from *Child's companion and juvenile instructor*, published by the Religious Tract Society in 1846).

placed his animals in 1831. The lions, tigers and leopards were put in separate cages toward the centre; exterior to them was a colonnade which supported the glazed roof and also cages for the birds. Within the colonnade the hot-water pipes for heating the glasshouse were situated and beyond them was an open paved area for spectators. There was next a 'channel for a stream of water intended for gold, silver and other exotic fishes and round the outer perimeter a border under the front wall for climbing plants to be trained on wires under the roof'. This account, paying particular attention to the plants, was given by John Claudius Loudon, a Scottish horticulturalist, in the *Gardener's Magazine*. Cross's collection had been acquired by the Surrey Zoological and Botanic Society when Queen Adelaide gave her patronage to the new project of having a zoological garden on the south side of the Thames. She stipulated that it was not to be 'in opposition, but only in a true spirit of rivalry for the establishment in Regent's Park'. Apparently, the Queen was ignorant of the attempts by Cross to get himself and his animals accepted as part of the new Zoological Society establishment, otherwise she would have known that the Surrey Zoological Gardens were being set up in opposition to the attractions at Regent's Park. A little further investigation would have shown how inappropriate was the setting for the new menagerie, in the middle of a fun-fair with startling fireworks and noisy bands playing. The animals in the Surrey Zoological Gardens were there purely for the entertainment of the masses, while those in Regent's Park

Another way of advertising the giraffes at Surrey Zoological Gardens upon their arrival in 1836.

were for the scientific observation and study by Fellows and students. Whatever the purpose of the display, inevitably, there would be rivalry to obtain new and exotic species.[12]

The public's attitude to the Surrey Zoological Gardens was described in a ditty of 1843,

'At the Surrey menagerie everyone knows
(Because it's a place to which everyone goes)
There's a model of Rome: and as round it one struts
One sinks the remembrance of Newington Butts;
And having one's shilling laid down at the portal
One fancies oneself in the City Immortal!'

Season tickets were one guinea, or the visitor could pay one shilling at the gate. In 1836 it was possible to see some giraffes in the menagerie, an orang-utan, a young Indian rhinoceros, for which Cross paid £800 in 1834 and Nero the lion. The children had rides on giant tortoises. Balloon ascents became very popular and when a monkey called Signor Jacopo, dressed in a scarlet coat, was lifted in a balloon and then released by parachute on to Walworth Common, there was a tremendous scramble to return the animal safely and claim the offered £2 reward. A Baxter print, published in 1846, shows deer, peacocks, a pelican and a camel, in company with some of those famous giraffes.

When Edward Cross heard, early in 1836, that the Zoological Society had arranged for a shipment of giraffes, he applied to the Secretary requesting to buy one. The Council of the Society naturally refused to part with a

Tallis said of Surrey Zoological Gardens, 'The carnivorous animals are contained in a curvilinear glazed building 300 feet in diameter. Elephants, giraffes, bisons, ostriches, eagles, pelicans, foreign birds of varied and glittering plumage, boas, and numerous other animals, are domiciled in these gardens, to which their present proprietor, Mr Tyler, has added several features which have much increased their popularity'. (John Tallis, *Illustrated London* 1851).

Edward Cross holding a lion cub, painted by his friend Jacque Laurent Agasse in 1838. Agasse painted several portraits of Cross, his wife and his sister-in-law Miss Polito, besides the animals in Cross's charge at Exeter 'Change and then the Surrey Zoological Gardens. This portrait was lithographed by G. Gauci in 1838. Cross retired on 7 March 1844.

specimen, for the giraffes were going to be their chief draw-ing-power and gate asset and they were not going to share them with rivals across the river. Cross therefore sent an urgent message to his agent, Mr Warwick, who had been sent out to bring the giraffes to England, to procure more giraffes for him at all costs. The *Shrewsbury Chronicle* of Friday 15 July 1836 reported,

> 'Mr Warwick has arrived, and brought with him the especial object of his expedition to the plains of Africa. The giraffes reached the gardens at 3 o'clock Wednesday week, and apparently without having suffered much, if

at all, by their journey from their native wilderness. The tallest of the 3 specimens though an animal which has obviously not reached its maturity is upwards of 15 feet from the ground to the top of its head. They are in excellent condition. Their coats are in fine order, dotted with large fawn-coloured spots on a white ground. The eyes of these animals are remarkably fine, something similar to those of the antelope, but projecting further from the head, and capable of taking in an extraordinary scope of vision. They are tame and gentle in their manners'.

This was a much healthier consignment than the one Cross had brought in nine years before for George IV.

Cross retired in 1844 and his secretary and assistant, Mr Tyler, continued at Surrey Zoological Gardens for several years until the property became vested in a limited liability company. In 1855 the animals were sold and a music hall was built on the site of the menagerie buildings. *Punch*, on 17 November 1855, poked fun at the prospect of Mr J. C. Stevens the auctioneer conducting the sale of the animals in the gardens, observing,

> 'We do not quite understand how the sale is to be managed, or how Mr Stevens of King St., Covent Garden, proposes to knock down the elephant . . . We should not be surprised if, while the auctioneer is soliciting "an advance upon the tiger" the tiger were to make a sudden and unexpected advance upon the audience, and there are some lots that will hardly be under sufficient restraint to enable the porters to display them . . . it is possible that while he described a lot of monkeys as "going, going" one or more of the mischievous brutes may be "gone" before he is aware of it'.

However, Mr Stevens had experience of this kind of sale, having sold the Earl of Derby's animals 'on the ground' in 1851 and he not only managed this sale with greater decorum than *Punch* expected, but made very good prices for some of the animals, for example, £150 for a lioness and £225 for a lion, £336 for an elephant, £300 for a male giraffe, £35 for an ostrich, camels made £65.2.0 and £50.8.0, a tigress fetched £82.19.10 and a pelican £18.10.0.

After the sale, the Zoological Society of London, with its collection growing apace, was without rival in the capital.

In 1847 the public had been admitted without any other requirement (such as previously having to get the written permission of a Fellow), than paying one shilling. The need for public funds had caused this and other modifications, in the founders' original charter.

In 1826, Sir Stamford Raffles and a small group of naturalists, had formed the Zoological Society for the advancement of zoology and animal physiology and the introduction of new and curious subjects of the animal kingdom. Its principal object was to 'present as many types of form as possible with the view of illustrating the general variations of the Animal Kingdom'. A prospectus defined the Society's aims further, saying it would feature 'animals brought from every part of the globe to be applied to some useful purpose, or as objects of scientific research, not of vulgar admiration'. The Society was confident of accomplishing this, because Britain was the centre of a huge empire and could obtain animals from her colonies in all parts of the globe. Its acquisitions could be more organised than the haphazard gathering of whatever came in by accident on foreign ships, on which the showmen and other menageries depended. The Society sent out collectors with specific instructions regarding the species that were required.

At a time when Londoners could see captive wild animals in the Tower and at Exeter 'Change, the new zoo had little impact for many years. It was not intended for all Londoners, but for Fellows of the Zoological Society and their friends. By November 1827 nearly 200 animals were exhibited in paddocks, dens and aviaries. When it was opened to the guests of Fellows on 27 April 1828 there were 430 animals on view and this collection was augmented in 1831, when George IV's menagerie was removed from Sandpit Gate to the gardens, followed in 1834 by the last of the Tower menagerie. The Society also had a museum and a library and a place for dissections to enable them to discover what diseases ailed their charges for preventive measures to be taken.

It was not long before other places in Britain wanted to have zoos for their citizens to enjoy. Within two decades of the London Zoological Gardens being created, similar institutions at Leeds, Manchester, Liverpool, Bristol, Dublin and Rosherville in Kent were opening their new gardens with animal collections to enlighten and educate the public.

The 19th century menageries were primarily for entertainment and only secondly of educational value. The London Zoo was designed to be a scientific institution, but had to admit the public in 1847 because of financial duress. Throughout the remainder of the 19th century there was still a place for the travelling menageries to instruct the labouring classes, who had not the advantage of zoological gardens, about living animals, which many knew only by pictures. In the 20th century, these differing purposes were to be catered for by different kinds of zoos, safari parks, and conservation trusts.

PRIVATE MENAGERIES AND AVIARIES

Chapter 11

'Many close averys of birds'

Throughout the Middle Ages birds were kept as pets in cages or allowed the freedom of the house. The largest of these were the hawks and falcons used for falconry, that were perched in the bedchambers of their owners. The cage-birds were more often our own native song birds such as nightingales, linnets and goldfinches. Very rarely a foreign bird is mentioned, or depicted in a painting, and it is not until the 16th century that they are at all common.

From the 16th century, we have evidence of the presence of an increasing variety of bird and mammal species. Some small monkeys were imported and a few seed-eating birds were brought home by sailors from the coasts of Africa, South America and the West Indies. A family portrait group, painted by Hans Holbein in 1530 of Sir Thomas More when Lord Chancellor, shows his wife, Lady Alice, with a chained monkey by her feet. Sir Thomas is known to have kept other monkeys, foxes, ferrets, weasels and many birds at his house in Chelsea.

The family of birds that travelled most successfully, and thus more of them reached an English port alive, was the Psittacidae or parrots. They were greatly admired for their colourful plumage and talking ability. They were so highly prized as valuable objects that one was the subject of a bequest in a will. The Duchess of Northumberland died in 1555 and left her green parrot to the Duchess of Alva saying she had 'nothing more worthy of her'.[1]

Sometimes South American birds were bought by our sailors in Portugal and Spain and brought to England on the last stage of their long journey from their native forests. Others were not so innocently acquired, having been taken as part of prizes by English privateers who had captured Spanish galleons. In the early 16th century English traders challenged Portugal's monopoly of West African trade in ivory and gold, with incidental occurrences of one or two birds and mammals being included in their cargoes. The few specimens that reached English shores were sold for high prices. The combination of their rarity, owing to difficulties in transport, and costliness, resulted in there being very few notable collections of animals outside the royal menageries until the late 16th century. Even then birds predominated, since they tolerated being confined in the small space available on board ship better than mammals, and were generally easier to feed in transit with seeds and hard tack.

For those who could afford to buy foreign birds, there followed the problem of keeping them alive and in good health in safe enclosures. The wire cages that were constructed were either called aviaries, volaries, or vivaries. Some confusion then occurred when the word 'aviary' was used to describe both the wired enclosure and the birds it contained. Later, a similar conflation occurred when the word 'menagerie' was used for the building as well as the mammals, or mammals and birds, or even just birds, which were housed in it.

The earliest records of aviaries are to be found in descriptions of Tudor gardens. Harrison makes mention of, 'our costlie and curious aviaries', in 1577.[2] The occupants might well have been some peacocks which, complained Thomas Tusser in his *Five hundred points of good husbandry*, published in 1573, scratched up the seedlings when allowed to roam freely in a garden. Tudor gardens also had dove cotes and 'may be a poole or two for fysshel yf the pooles be clene kept as necessary and pleasant'.

The Italian influence on the structure and adornment of English gardens at this period was strong. Lorenzo de Medici had a famous collection of animals in a menagerie, and an aviary and these were considered normal features in the large Italian gardens of the mid-16th century. It was a lay-out with which the educated young Englishman, while on his cultural visit to Italy, would become familiar. The Earl of Leicester adopted a number of these ideas when he made improvements at his home, Kenilworth. When he entertained Queen Elizabeth I at Kenilworth Castle in 1575, a courtier called Robert Laneham wrote to a friend describing the beauty of its garden, saying that its arbors were 'redolent by sweet trees and flowers', decorated with carved 'white bears of stone, obelisks and spheres'. He added, 'In the middle of the wall furthest from the terrace was a great aviary 30 feet long, 14 broad and 20 high, and in the centre of the garden a fountain in an octagonal basin wherein pleasantly playing to and fro carp, tench, bream and for varietie pearch and eel'. Laneham was more of a fisherman than ornithologist so he did not name the birds, but he added that there were also 'plenty of deer'.[3] Few of Queen Elizabeth's subjects could match the Earl of Leicester either for wealth, glamour, or his garden and its exotic embellishments.

Francis Bacon described the manner in which, in 1626, the enclosures of contemporary gardens were not always stone walls, but preferably were formed by 'stately arched hedges' which could be cut to shape with small turrets and spaces for cages of birds.[4] Imports were increasing at this time. The term 'volary', first recorded in 1630 by Ben Jonson in a play, indicated an aviary and in this sense Thévénot repeated the term in his account of his *Travels in England in 1687* to describe 'a volary full of rare fowl, as Estridges, Peacocks & others'.[5] Mrs Margaret Calderwood, in 1756, was a little more explicit for she said she had seen 'a volary which is a little place with the face of it wire'.[6]

Both the diarists, Evelyn and Pepys, recorded visits to houses where there were aviaries. John Evelyn gives us some tantalising glimpses of them from the 1650s onwards, but he was singularly unfortunate to arrive at the wrong moment to view them, usually just as the building was completed, but still unoccupied. Such was the state of the aviary, 'a poore business' at Sir Thomas Fowler's house at Islington and though Sir John Shaw (M.P. for Lyme Regis 1661–78) had an 'aviarie handsome' in the grounds of his new house at Eltham in Kent in July 1664, we are no wiser about his birds either. Evelyn was a great connoisseur of other people's houses and gardens and an indefatigable visitor to the more splendid mansions. One which drew him often was Ham House. He described it approvingly, after a visit one August day in 1678, as being 'indeed inferiour to few of the best villas in Italy itselfe, the House furnished like a great Princes; the Parterre, flo: Gardens, Orangeries, Groves, Avenues, Courts, Statues, Perspectives, fountains, Aviaries, and all this at the banks of the sweetest river in the world must need be surprizing'.[7]

Ham House on the south bank of the Thames opposite Twickenham came into the ownership of John Maitland, Duke of Lauderdale, through his marriage to Elizabeth, Countess of Dysart. Her father, William Murray, had bought it a few years after its erection in 1610. The Countess of Dysart was a bird-fancier and she ordered John Vanderbank to include her pet sulphur-crested cockatoo when he painted her portrait. In the 1670s she had one of the bed chambers converted into an aviary, so that she had easy access for the purpose of feeding her foreign birds. This special room inside was called the 'volary'. The smaller bird cages that were hung on the branches of trees in the garden throughout the summer, were carried indoors to the volary room where their occupants could be kept warm during the bleak winter months. There are two interesting over-door paintings by Francis Barlow in the volary room. Appropriately, Barlow filled the areas with birds: snipe, kingfishers, lapwing, grey lag goose, wheatears and ducks in one and an owl mobbed by chaffinch, jay, great spotted woodpecker, goldfinch, great and blue titmice, a pair of magpies, swallows, a redstart, greenfinch and white wagtail in the other; all of them are still clearly identifiable three hundred years after they were painted.

Evelyn had a beautiful house himself at Sayes Court, Deptford, which had an aviary in the grounds. His home was visited in turn by other sight-seers. As was customary in those days, if a party arrived to look over the house, the owner invited the visitors in and provided the running commentary himself. When the 'old Marquis of Argyle, the Lord Lothian and some other Scotch noblemen all strangers to me' arrived on 14 June 1656, Evelyn showed them over the house and grounds. He later wrote about this visit and was still chortling over the solecism of the 'old Marquis (since executed)' who 'tooke the Turtle-Doves in the Aviary for Owels!'[7]

Samuel Pepys was another close observer of the fashion for keeping birds and at one time or another he owned canaries, one of which lived for four years, and a fine singing blackbird which woke him up early in the morning when it shared his bedchamber. Each of the three references in his diary to the starling that he owned, proudly stated that it had once belonged to the King 'which he kept in his bedchamber, and doth whistle and talk the most and best that ever I heard in my life'. Pepys admired a mynah bird in the possession of the Duke of York and a parrot owned by his friend Sir J. Minnes which 'talked, laughed and cried'. Mr Creed, another navy office employee, also had a parrot that he carried about on his shoulder, but this misbehaved (on 9 March 1665) and 'struck Mr Povey, coming by, just by the eye, very deep; which had it hit the eye, had put it out. This a while troubled us; but not proving very bad – we to our business'.[8] Mr Povey, fortunately, had some sympathy with birds for he had constructed a volary at his house in Lincoln's Inn Fields two years before this accident. These birds had been brought by naval captains and proved useful presents, or bribes, for navy officials.

Charles II had his own volary for which Pepys, in his official capacity as a servant of the navy, may well have supplied 'some old sails for the closing of the windows this winter' i.e. in September 1667.

The dismissal of the Earl of Clarendon from his office as Lord Chancellor by Charles II was viewed by the King's favourite, Lady Castlemaine, from her volary, or from her outside aviary. Pepys tells the story of her involvement in this affair, in his diary on 27 August 1667,

> 'this business of my Lord Chancellors was certainly designed in my Lady Castlemaine's chamber, & that when he went from the King on Monday morning, she was in bed (though about 12 a-clock) & ran out in her smock into her Aviary looking into White-hall garden, & thither her woman brought her her nightgown, & stood joying herself at the old man's going away. And several of the gallants of White-hall (of which there was many staying to see the Chancellor return) did talk to her in her Bird cage; among other, Blanckford, telling her she was the Bird of Paradise'.[9]

Another sprightly lady, Celia Fiennes, toured England on a horse (riding side-saddle) during William and Mary's reign. In her journals she frequently mentioned the gardens that she visited and she took great pleasure in their decorative features such as fountains, imposing gate-ways, summer-houses and bowling-greens. Occasionally there are details of aviaries, such as that belonging to the Earl of Chesterfield at Bretby near Burton on Trent (demolished 1780). In May 1698 she said that one aviary, 'stood like a 'summer house open' and there, were many close averys of birds'.[10] The Earl collected rare trees and his birds were housed among such exotics as a cedar of Lebanon and a tulip tree. At another house, Patshull Park belonging to Sir John Astley, the large

aviary had 'branches of trees stuck into the ground'.[11] Celia kept her best and most detailed description for the Duke of Devonshire's aviaries at Chatsworth, and no wonder, for these were outstanding at that date.

The account which she wrote for her *Journey into Derbyshire and Back in 1689* took note of the manner in which the aviary had been designed as an integral part of the house. William Cavendish, the 4th Earl of Devonshire, had begun rebuilding Chatsworth in 1687, as an excuse, so it was rumoured, for staying away from James II's court. Celia reported that,

> 'the house is built all of stone that is dugg out of the hills, its like free stone; a flatt Roofe with bannisters and flower potts; in the front is 7 large windows the glass is diamond cutt and all off large looking-glass, the panes bigg 4 in a breadth 7 in a height; to the garden ward is 12 windows of the same glass 4 panes broad 8 long; the lowest windows are made with Grates before them and are for birds an Averye and so looking glass behind . . '.[12]

The little windows may be seen in Buckler's watercolour of the south front, though only some of the bottom row of

J. C. Buckler's watercolour drawing, 1812, of the south and east fronts of Chatsworth House as originally built. The rooms set aside for birds (of which the first Duke was 'passionately fond') had bars with glass behind them. They were situated at ground level, to the right of the steps.

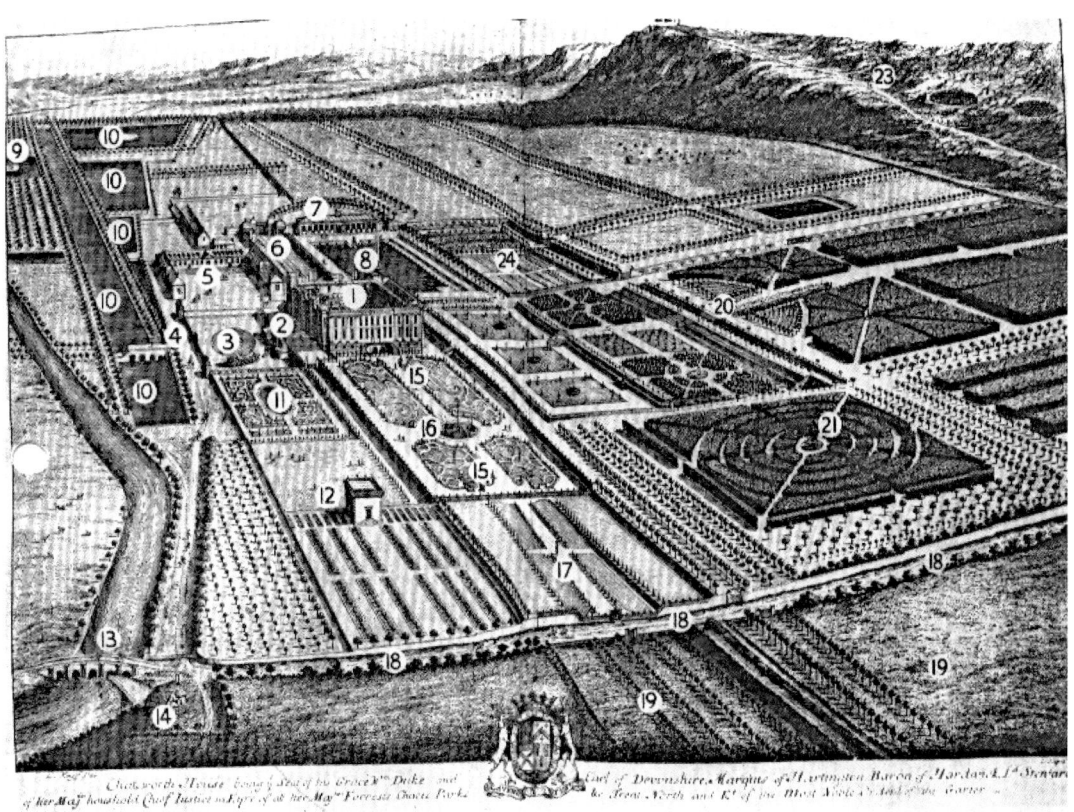

Chatsworth House being y Seat of his Grace y[e] Duke and ... Earl of Devonshire, Marquis of Hartington Baron of Hardan & Ld Steward of her Ma[ty] houshold Cheif Iustice in Eyre of all her Ma[ty] Forrests Chaces Parks. &c. from North and K[t] of y[e] most Noble Order of the Garter

Chatsworth bird houses 1699.
L Kniff's drawing (engraved
and published by Kip in
*Nouveau théâtre de la Grande
Bretagne,* 1718, plate 17) shows
the bird houses, number 6,
built of stone with a group
of four domed gazebos with
grass in the centre, number 7.

small windows gave light to the aviaries. Glass, inciden-
tally, was still an exceedingly expensive novelty, hence
Celia's astonishment at the number and size of the panes of
glass in the many windows.

The Earl (created a Duke in 1694 by William III) subsequently recognised that this indoor provision for his birds
was gloomy and unattractive. Instead, he ordered some
very handsome 'Bird Houses' to be built in the North
Forecourt in 1697–98 when Kniff was commissioned by
the Earl to prepare a detailed drawing of his improvements to both the house and grounds at Chatsworth. This
drawing shows the bird houses to be extensive and imposing buildings, suitable for the many pheasants, ducks,
pigeons, macaw and other species in the Earl's splendid
collection.

The Earl might have purchased his canaries as early as
1685, in answer to an advertisement in the *London Gazette*
which gave notice that 'There is lately come over from

Canary, 700 Canary birds'.[13] This was an unusually large consignment and they would have been grey-brown birds streaked with dark brown and only a little green and yellow colouring then, as still found in the wild state in Madeira today. Only many years later did breeders produce the yellow birds with which we are now familiar. The attraction for buyers in 1685 was primarily the singing abilities of canaries.

Admiral George Churchill (a younger brother of John, Duke of Marlborough), retired from the navy in October 1708 to his house, Ranger's Lodge, in the Little Park at Windsor. He constructed an aviary which he filled with a very valuable collection of rare and colourful birds, situated in his equally pleasant and famous garden. He passed his short retirement in caring for his birds and plants and, on his death (8 May 1710), bequeathed the birds to his two friends James Butler, 2nd Duke of Ormonde, and Arthur Herbert, the Earl of Torrington and a fellow Admiral of the Fleet.

Were it not for the beautiful canvases of the Hungarian artist Jakob Bogdani depicting the inhabitants of this aviary, we should know little more about it. Queen Anne bought one series of canvases in 1710 and they are now preserved in the Royal Collection. Bogdani (1660–1720/4) specialised in drawing birds, flowers and fruit, as he himself explained in 1691 in his strange English, 'he paint in the Spring flowers & in the Somer flowers & fruits when they are out Lobsters and oyster pieces. In the Winter pieces of Fowell & plate'.[14] Queen Mary II had employed Bogdani at Hampton Court where his bird paintings were greatly admired.

Eleven canvases purchased by Queen Anne, including seven from the Admiral's estate, may be described as paintings of birds, or birds and fruit in landscapes. Bogdani also frequently included birds in his flower pieces and some of these flower paintings were also purchased by the Queen. From Bogdani's work an astonishing list of species may be compiled, the most interesting ones being those from South America. One canvas had distinctly South American characteristics from both the background and the bird species, troupials, chachalaca, guan, curassows and a toucan. Others included flamingos, pigeons and doves, small passerines, many macaws and cockatoos with other parrots, peacocks, guineafowl and pheasants.

Jakob Bogdani, a Hungarian artist living in England, painted birds in Admiral Churchill's aviary, among them many parrots.

Some of the species are first or very early records of foreign species seen in this country and one can only conclude that Churchill's fellow seamen brought them home for him. Bogdani also delighted in painting British species and among our native waterfowl may be found ruffs and reeves, lapwings, oystercatcher, stone curlew, black-headed gull, stork, moorhen, coot, kingfisher and lots of geese and ducks, the latter often shown with their ducklings. Common farmyard inhabitants are to be seen scratching in the earth alongside splendidly plumaged turkeys and pheasants and both the common and the then rare red-legged partridge. A woodcock is another game bird present and two unusual British birds, a chough and a two-barred crossbill.

Mammals occur less frequently in these early paintings, but one can be identified as a chital, another as a gazelle (Guinea deer) with a small antelope and a Capuchin monkey. Bogdani's paintings are delightful and full of interest and movement. As a result of the patronage, first of William III and then of Queen Anne, we now have a good number of his pictures of great botanical and zoological interest, both in the Royal Collection and other private and public collections in England.

Leaving the aviculturalists, we must note Cannons, at Little Stanmore in Middlesex, a collection that may well have been the first 'safari park' in England. It was created by James Brydges, 1st Duke of Chandos, who was exceedingly wealthy and also in an unique position to import animals from many different places in his capacity as director and shareholder in the South Sea, East India and Royal African, or Guinea, Companies. His contacts with the merchants and sailors employed by those companies gave him the opportunity to place orders for all kinds of foreign creatures to be transported to England.

James Brydges was born in 1674 and his dukedom was granted in 1719, after his business acumen had netted him a fortune in various government departments. Ten years before this he had purchased a splendid mansion called Cannons from his first wife's uncle, Warwick Lake. In the spacious grounds he created his menagerie of wild mammals and birds. His interest in animals was long-standing and his collection had been growing for some years. His journals record his awareness of the imported animals on show in London over a long period. In the winter months of December 1698 and January 1699 he had been to see a 'tyger and leopard' and 'the porcupine in Longacre'. On another occasion he saw an armless man and a 'crockadore' or cockatoo at Tower Hill, and in February 1702, while walking from the City to Westminster, he turned aside to view an elephant. He was so taken with the crockadore that at the first opportunity to acquire one, he exchanged both a monkey and a parakeet for it. He also made a point of visiting the Tower Menagerie whenever he was in town.

Shortly after acquiring Cannons the Duke lost his first wife. In 1713 he made a happy choice for his second wife, Cassandra Willughby, his cousin and the daughter of the famous naturalist Francis Willughby. Cassandra had inherited her father's love of natural history, so the Chandos couple were united in their interest in animals and the enjoyment of their menagerie at Cannons. Their house was the wonder of the day for it was so palatial and richly furnished, while the gardens were the envy of many. There were nineteen gardeners to look after the extensive grounds with the added responsibility of taking charge of some of the birds that freely roamed the park. In between tending rice plants, newly imported kidney beans, pineapples, cinnamon and coffee-trees, they cared for flamingoes from Antigua and parakeets from Barbados. Plants and animals frequently arrived together in a cargo for the Duke. Captain Massey sent plants, more flamingoes and a 'Mexican squash' from Carolina. The 'squash', perhaps a beaver or muskrat, was 'rough coated, very tame, and charming to play with'. Another mixed package arrived from Pennsylvania whence Major Gordon had transmitted some singing birds with some wax and a bill for £84 attached. Unfortunately the present of hams accompanying this parcel acquired additional fauna while in transit and, on opening the packet, the Duke discovered the hams to be full of maggots.

The Duke's animals included a tiger, which became angry when prodded by a servant and nearly killed the foolish man, and a small deer of Whydah (in Dahomey) that was literally scared to death by some visitors who crowded too closely round its coop. Some bucks and does were sent from Virginia in 1725 and, when thanking the sender, the Duke asked if some waterfowl and singing-birds could be sent. A mocking-bird had already arrived from the same state. The Duke may well have been one of the earliest owners of tortoises when some were sent to him from Minorca.

The Barbary hens were brought over via Portugal and storks, quails, pheasants and partridges arrived from Holland. The waterfowl were supplemented from time to time from Holland and also from different parts of the British Isles. Muscovy ducks shared a pen with some 'barrow ducks' i.e. shelducks, from Llandwarn and Bridgwater, wild geese from Barbados and some powises or helmeted curassows.

Whistling ducks and a red bird of particular prettiness from the Gold Coast survived well, but a crown bird or crowned crane fell foul of a Gambia gander and was killed by the belligerent bird. Wherever the visitor chose to walk in the 83 acres of garden, along avenues leading to the villages of Edgeware, Whitchurch and Stanmore, there were

Archbishop Laud (died 1647) placed a tortoise in the gardens of Lambeth Palace. When it died, in 1751, it was claimed to be 110 years old and only succumbed then through the carelessness of a gardener. The tortoises at Cannons had come from Minorca c.1719.

interesting birds and mammals to be seen. Near the house, in the Office Court, there were two Portland stone basins where eagles bathed and drank.

The Duke's last years were not so happy. He lost a lot of money in 1730, when George Robinson the banker absconded with ten thousand Africa bonds which he held as security for the Duke's account and he lost a fortune in the African Company, estimated at £125,000. A further loss, this time of £300,000 as a result of speculation at the time of the South Sea Bubble, made another enormous hole in the Duke's fortune. The glory of Cannons endured for little more than twenty years and the house was demolished soon after 1747.[15]

The 2nd Earl of Oxford (1689–1741) had a menagerie at Wimpole Hall, Cambridgeshire, in the 1720s, but little is known of animals inhabiting it.

At Longleat a novel assemblage of mammals was brought together by Thomas, Viscount Weymouth, in 1733–34. The estate carpenters, Benjamin and Robert, were kept busy making suitable dens and homes for the new purchases,

'For Benjamin, three days up at the live creatures in ye grove	5/-
Robert, five days a making a house for ye leopard	8/4d
Robert, one day for making a perch for ye parrot	1/8d
Benjamin, one day for making a house for ye bear	1/8d
Benjamin three days for making a house for ye wolves	5/-'.

The two carpenters also renovated a building for two vultures and an eagle and were occupied for a while in the cellars of the house, building a cage for the bear down there so that it was conveniently situated near to the great hall. The bear was led into the great hall to entertain the household in the evenings.

An elephant, which caused a sensation when it appeared in the great hall with two men balanced on its trunk and eleven sitting on its back, was hired for an evening's entertainment at Longleat. It obligingly waved coloured flags with its trunk and delicately picked up a sixpence, but it also caused damage when twenty one flagstones cracked under its weight as it walked into the house. All told, this proved to be an expensive evening's entertainment.[16]

Sir Hans Sloane's interest in animal specimens, both alive and dead, was more scientific. He acquired a vast number of stuffed specimens, an herbarium and a collection of coins, that formed the nucleus of the British Museum after his death. When a newly qualified doctor, Sloane was appointed to accompany the Duke and Duchess of Albemarle on their journey to Jamaica in the capacity of physician to the Governor and his wife. Albemarle died after only 18 months, but Sloane, despite losing his patient, remained in favour. He had been very active in the short time available and collected many plants and animals, which he brought home in 1689. These specimens were the beginnings of the famous collection that was to grow over the next sixty years to enormous proportions. His interest became widely known and his collections were visited by many foreigners to study his cabinets and see the rare species he owned. His interests were wide and he sent artists to visit exhibitions of wild birds and mammals, whether in inns, coffee houses, menageries, or at fairs and other travelling shows, and he stored their drawings and paintings of new or rare species.

In his capacity as President of both the College of Physicians and the Royal Society, his correspondence was voluminous and his correspondents widely dispersed. They sent him specimens to add to his museum and Sloane employed his artist George Edwards, who was the librarian and beadle of the College of Physicians, to describe them. Some of Edwards's drawings were made from living specimens in Sloane's house in London, or at his country home, the Manor House, Chelsea, after he purchased it in 1712.[17]

In his celebrated volary, at one time or another, Sloane kept an eared grebe caught at Hampstead that was then considered a great rarity, though we now know that black-necked grebes occur regularly on the coast in winter. The Arabian bustard, kept in his house for many years, had been brought from 'Mocha in Arabia Felix and presented to Sir Hans Sloane by Charles Dubois treasurer to the India company'. Edwards said that it had not previously been described and proceeded to make good this omission calling it *Otis arabs* (now known as the great Arabian bustard *Ardeotis arabs*). Another species, which we think quite

A male and female Reindeer (Greenland Buck) were presented to Sir Hans Sloane in 1738 by Captain Craycott. Sloane later sent them to the Duke of Richmond for his park at Goodwood, but they failed to breed. (Thomas Bewick wood engraving, *History of quadrupeds*).

common now, though it was regarded as unusual three hundred years ago, was the 'spotted Greenland Dove' or black guillemot, which Captain Craycott brought home alive from Greenland. Rather more extraordinary was the large 'King of the Vultures' that lived many years with Sloane. There were three or four other king vultures in England at this time, the 1740s, but the little 'Padda or rice-bird' that Edwards said had come from China was a solitary specimen. Its scientific name reflected its food *Padda oryzivora* i.e. rice-eater, but it is now known in England, where it is still a popular cage-bird, as a Java sparrow. The purple swamphens survived for some time, as did the hardier pheasants. Golden pheasants were being imported in some numbers and Edwards reported that 'I have seen several of them in possession of our nobility'. Silver pheasants were not quite so numerous, but those in Sloane's garden hatched young ones and brought them to maturity.[18]

Sloane's house in Bloomsbury stood in seven and a half acres of garden, with shrubberies and aviaries and cages, enough to house these and other birds, as well as a small, select menagerie of mammals. Captain Craycott's visit to Greenland in 1738 had produced a pair of 'Greenland Buck' or reindeer, as well as the black guillemot. Sloane later sent the pair to the Duke of Richmond for his park, Goodwood in Sussex, hoping they would breed in the more spacious paddocks there, but they died without any increase. Three other mammals were brought from the New World. From Hudson Bay he received a porcupine that he dispatched to live at Chelsea, and a 'Quick-hatch or wolverine' which remained in London with some opossums, where they were all spoilt and admired by visitors. The third specimen was a little 'monax or marmotte from Maryland' that thrived on soft meats. Americans call this stout, burrowing rodent a woodchuck. Peter Collinson had sent this 'cross between a rat and a squirrel, called a monac . . '. with the instructions, 'he requires to be kept very warm and fed with all sorts of greens, apples, carrots, chestnuts, etc. If he is put in a large squirrel box filled with hay, for as he grows naked he grows very tender'. Collinson added, 'I hope you have received from Lady Wager a she possum with 3 young ones'. Later Collinson sent a male possum advising that it be kept by the kitchen fire until the weather should break. He also sent a curious 'hermaphrodite goat' that he had discovered on a West Indies ship.[19]

A number of Sloane's acquaintances kept one or more foreign birds in their houses and Edwards was invited to see them and draw them. He said he had seen living birds in the homes of Sir Charles Wager, lst Lord of the Admiralty, a Captain Chandler and Charles du Bois, treasurer to the India Company. Their links with sailing ships visiting foreign countries explains the number of foreign birds in their possession.

The 2nd Duke of Richmond (1701–50), a keen aviculturalist and friend of Sir Hans Sloane, collected living specimens whenever possible. He also had mounted specimens in glass cases, including birds from Surinam, in his cabinets. Most notable among the birds in his aviary were a black parrot and a speckled pigeon. Both were drawn by Edwards in May 1742, the black parrot being thought to have 'not yet been described'. The Duke's pair of 'Triangular Spotted Pigeons from Guinea' were accurately described by Edwards and then named *Columba guinea*, the scientifc name used today for these unusually marked birds with triangular white spots on the wings.[20]

In 1725 the Duke had a menagerie in the High Wood at Goodwood, where wild animals were kept in dens with

iron barred gates. He, too, was visited by many people curious to see his animals. Among the Goodwood household
books is a list of some of his pets and the amount of food
they consumed daily,

	'Pounds a day	
	Horse	Beef
5 Woulves	10	10
2 Tygers	4	4
1 Lyon	3	3
2 Lepers	4	4
1 Sived Cat	1	2
A Tyger Cat	1	1
3 foxes	1	2
A Jack all	½	½
2 Greenland Dogs	3	3
3 Vulturs 2 Eagles	5	5
1 Kite	0	1
2 Owls	1	1
That is all yt Eat flesh	70 lbs	

3 bears	2	loafs
1 Large Monkey	¼	"
A Woman Tygerr	1	"
3 Racoons	¼	"
3 small monkeys	¼	"
Armadilla)	¼	"
1 pacaverre)		
7 Casawarris	½	"

That is all ye annimalls that eat Bread'.

The civet was sent by Sir Thomas Robinson, Governor of
Barbados c.1744, some twelve years after the Duke 'had
great augmentation of the menagerie of late'. Sloane sent
a small animal to the Duke who wrote back, 'I wish indeed
that it had been the sloth that had been sent to me for that
is the most curious animal I know; but this is nothing but
a common young black bear which I do not now what to
do with, for I have five of them already'. He added that he
hoped Sloane would tell the agent that sent the bear 'not
to send me any Bears, Eagles, Leopards or Tygers for I am
overstocked with them already'.[21]

   The Duke allowed the public to view his menagerie, but
the collection became so famous that his steward, Henry

Charles Lennox (1701–50), 2nd Duke of Richmond, from 1723 maintained one of the largest collections of animals during the early 18th century on his estate at Goodwood in Sussex.

Foster, wrote to him in 1730, 'we are very much troubled with Rude Company to see ye animals. Sunday last we had 4–5 hundred good and bad'. Because the duke was frequently abroad, Henry Foster, sent him regular accounts of the menagerie.[22]

The Duke's successor, the 3rd Duke, Charles Lennox, inherited the menagerie in 1750 and added to it. His contribution to the growing knowledge of animals in the second half of the 18th century was to acclimatise species at

Goodwood and breed them with a view to their being useful as an additional food source.[23]

A new awareness of the value of these specimens
being brought to England in steadily increasing numbers
impressed itself on Sir Hans Sloane and his artist and
author, George Edwards. They realised that many of these
species had not previously been seen in England, even in
Europe. They set about recording every new species even
if, as Edwards wrote, 'I knew not so much on many Birds,
as to what Country they came from, which is very material
in Natural History'. He went on to justify the recording of
such species despite this lack of knowledge, 'as . . . the like
Birds might never be met with again it was better to preserve the Figures without knowing their Countries than not
at all'.[24] This very modest beginning at the awakening of
scientific interest was to gather momentum during the last
half of the century, especially after Carl Linnaeus had visited Sloane and subsequently published his list of all known
species, with binomials, in the 10th edition of his *Systema
Naturae*, 1758.

Chapter 12

'Charming to play with'

In the second half of the 18th century greater attention was paid to the grounds surrounding country houses, for this was the era of the great landscape gardeners. The formal garden was cleared away to be replaced by a naturalized landscape. First came the introduction of the ha-ha or invisible ditch which made the lawn in front of the house appear to be contiguous with the park beyond and then the architect and landscape gardener William Kent (1684–1748) harmonised the park features into a natural-looking garden with groves and views. Lancelot Brown (1716–83) followed with further improvements and by 1787 the fashion for landscape gardening was being satirized. 'If you should have purchased a good old Family Hall (seated low and warm, encircled by woods, and near a running stream)' advised the author of 'Modern taste' (in *The World* 26 October 1787) then 'pull it down & sell all the materials, cut down all the trees ... grub up all the hedges ... make the approach to your house as meandering as possible ... keep numbers of Peacocks and Guinea fowls, who will make delightful serenades, adding to the cheerful sounds of geese and poultry'.

Where the properties were newly designed, the service buildings were placed out of sight at the back. The only buildings seen from the main windows of the house were ornamental structures placed at focal points at the end of long vistas, or avenues of trees, or on hill-tops. They were sometimes follies, ruins, or temples and occasionally a building that acquired the name of menagerie or aviary from its use. These buildings were in situations away from the house, in a wood or dell like Knole's pseudo-gothic aviary of 1761 and the ionic menagerie of the 1750s made for Horton in Northamptonshire, or on the edge of the park by lakes, like the Georgian menagerie at Osterley Park. They were solid structures, built mostly in stone, which is why they have survived to the present day and some are now

185

The sham gothic Bird House at Knole. The first Lady Amherst's pheasants, brought from China by Lord Amherst where he had been on an embassy in 1816, were kept in this Bird House.

converted into houses, for example, the Osterley and Horton menageries and the Audley End aviary. The latter was built as a chapel in 1776, modelled after designs by Robert Adam, then used as an aviary for rare birds. Bills and accounts from the 1770s onwards, for the Menagerie, Bird Room and Aviary are in the Essex County Record Office, along with a poem describing it.

A third notable landscape gardener, Humphrey Repton (1752–1818), recognised that the garden buildings, dairy, pheasantry, etc., had, 'become so many detached establishments' at an inconvenient distance from the main house, and in the 19th century purpose-built aviaries were erected much closer to the house. These 19th century aviaries were light, airy structures with a metal frame and wire-mesh in-fill, like conservatories with wire instead of glass. Because of their light structure, many have perished and disappeared. The Waddesdon Manor aviary is an exception, it survived partly because it was constructed so much later, in the 1880s. In addition, the 19th century aviaries were more frequently attached to the house and when they became old they were not allowed to remain to become unsightly and were removed.

The owners of the new or modernised 18th century houses, with their landscaped parks, were very self-conscious about their improvements and the literature of the period abounds with references to the grounds with their lakes, temples, aviaries and similar features. Drawings and

The most magnificent 19th century aviary was designed by a French landscape gardener who was employed to provide accommodation for exotic birds at Waddesdon. It was built in stone, brick and elaborate wrought and cast iron for Baron Ferdinand de Rothschild in 1889 and restored in 1960–66. It is capable of housing more than 300 birds in the flight and glass-fronted cages.

An etching of a young moose (Oliver Goldsmith, *A History of the earth and animated nature*, 1774) that catches the profile of the animal with its spindly legs. Thomas Pennant saw the first imported moose, a female, in the menagerie of Charles Watson Wentworth (1730–82), Marquis of Rockingham.

paintings of stately homes and gardens were carefully preserved and sometimes also the architects' plans and drawings of the garden buildings, for example, those of Knole and Horton, including details of the aviaries and menageries. Adam's plans of 1768 for the grounds of Bowood in Wiltshire, was for dens which subsequently housed a lion, wild boar in 1769, a white fox, an orang-utan and a tiger in 1781.

Apart from this architectural interest in the menageries, their owners and visitors recorded their delight in the increasing variety of new species with which they were stocked.

The first moose to be sent to England, arriving from the St Lawrence river, Canada, was received by the 2nd Marquess of Rockingham, Charles Watson Wentworth (1730–82, Prime Minister in 1766 and 1782) for his menagerie on his estate in Yorkshire. Another moose was housed at Ampthill Park, Bedfordshire, where the 2nd Earl of Ossory received it in 1767. A third one (the first bull) went to the Duke of Richmond and was painted, at Goodwood, by Stubbs in 1770. A painting of a newly acquired mammal was on a par with a painting of a racehorse, the house and grounds and portraits of the family; all signs of wealth and pride of ownership that were so much an accepted part of high society living at this time.[1]

Early in the second half of the 18th century Horace Walpole commenced his visits to country seats and recorded them in his journals. He started near home, at Twickenham, and then gradually went further afield. Usually, permission to see neighbours' houses and gardens was given freely, but occasionally a small fee was charged. Farington said that Arundel Castle, the seat of the Duke of Norfolk, was shown on Mondays only and the profits were given to the poor. Walpole received a number of visitors himself at Strawberry Hill and enjoyed demonstrating its beauty and novel ideas in furnishing etc. free of charge. He would also show them his own landscaped garden with his 'Turkey sheep and two cows, all studied in their colours for becoming the view'. The pond in Walpole's garden was celebrated for the number of goldfish that bred freely there. The poet Thomas Gray (1716–71) wrote an 'Ode to the death of a favourite cat drowned in a tub of goldfish' in 1742. The cat was Walpole's Selima.[2]

The first menagerie which Walpole mentioned having visited, belonged to Mr Spenser at Wimbledon House where, in 1751, he was delighted to find, 'an eagle with white head and tail. A Toucan, a bird almost as large as a pheasant, black body, whitish tail, the bill yellow, red, blue and salmon colour most beautiful . . . two blackbirds, quite brown . . . a green maccaw'. Travelling through Wiltshire to Dorset, he paused to visit two seats belonging to Stephen Fox Strangways, Earl of Ilchester. First he went to Redlynch House, where he was impressed by a handsome menagerie, but was even more astonished at the sight of the 'park filled with a particular breed of cows which have a pretty effect – Their whole fore and hinder parts are black and brown, & the bodies milk white, divided in such strait lines, that they look as if they had a sheet flung over them, whence they are called, Sheet-Cows'. At Melbury Park, the Dorset seat of the Earl of Ilchester, Walpole observed 'a pretty aviary'.

The best menagerie seen by Walpole was in a Palladian building at Horton or Houghton, Norfolk, in 1763, when it was the seat of George Montagu, 2nd Earl of Halifax. 'In the Menagerie, which is a little Wood, very prettily disposed with many basons of gold fish,' Walpole discovered, 'Several curious birds & beasts. Storks; Raccoons that breed there much, & I believe the first that have bred here; a very large Strong Eagle, another with a white head; two hogs from the Havannah with navels on their backs; two young Tigers; two uncommon Martins; doves from Guadaloupe,

THE SHEETED BREED OF SOMERSETSHIRE.

The Somerset sheet cows may have descended from some Dutch belted cows introduced in the 17th century. They are now extinct. This illustration of three 'Sheeted somersets', bred by John Weir of West Camel, Somerset, was drawn by William Shiels and lithographed by Thomas Fairland for David Low's *The Breeds of domestic animals of the British Isles*, 1842.

brown with blue heads, & a milk white streak crossing their cheeks; a kind of Ermine, sandy with many spots all over the body and tail'.[3]

The menagerie of the 2nd Earl Tylney, John Child, in the very formal gardens at Wanstead, Essex, apparently housed some parrots and a beautiful pigeon from the 'Isle of Nicobar'. This, along with a 'Lesser white cockatoo with a yellow crest' was drawn by George Edwards on a visit to Essex (his home county) to see the house and gardens. These were as yet unchanged by the new fashion for landscaping, though when Cannons in Middlesex was pulled down, the Ionic columns from that great house were used to embellish the garden front at Wanstead. Perhaps some of the remaining menagerie was transferred at the same time.[4]

A menagerie containing mammals was kept by Lord Shelburne at his villa on Hounslow Heath. His fierce lion (painted by Stubbs in 1760) would have acted as a strong deterrent to any highwayman with thoughts of making good his escape by a short cut through the grounds.

Knole had a small aviary from 1761, the period when Lionel Sackville, 7th Earl and 1st Duke of Dorset (1687–1765), was spending considerable sums on Knole, including heating for one of the aviaries where the exotic birds were kept.

The decade of the 1760s was a prolific period for the erection of aviaries and establishment of menageries. Castle Ashby's classical menagerie by Capability Brown and Robert Adam was erected c.1764–67. The 7th Earl of Northampton was interested initially, but his brother and successor, the 8th Earl, had to sell the birds and mammals to pay off debts. There were many cocks and hens, geese and swans, pheasants and turkeys, a few parrots and a collection of British song-birds. A Newfoundland dog and Angola goats appear to have been the sum total of quadrupeds.

When Warren Hastings returned from India in 1783 on the *Barrington*, a fast sailing-ship, he brought home goods insured for £20,000, including a fine Arab horse. Among other animals that he hoped to introduce and acclimatise in England was the Kashmir goat. Its hair was used to spin a fine wool for the shawls then becoming popular in Europe. His black tiger proved too much of a handful and was sent to the Tower of London. Hastings had previously sent home a yak from India and commissioned George Stubbs to paint it for him.

Having arrived home, Hastings looked for a suitable property to purchase, which had some land round it for his collection of animals. Eventually, he found, 'a very pleasant little estate of 91 acres in Old Windsor, called Beaumont park' in 1785 and said of it, 'I see nothing in England that I like so much'.[5] Sophie La Roche visited Mr and Mrs Hastings at Beaumont Lodge on Thursday 5 October 1786. She set out from London in the morning and enjoyed,

'A charming, delightful journey past the loveliest villages and villas along the winding banks of the Thames . . . The road winds quite imperceptibly uphill, and the magnificent river, with swans to give it life, its tortuous bed, bordered by a myriad plantations, shimmers along through the fertile valley. Beaumont Lodge . . . an old English residence surrounded by tall trees, likewise a pretty house quite large enough to accommodate hosts and guests . . . Fine views of Windsor and the entire park'.[6]

Walpole saw the menagerie at Horton in 1765 and said there were 'two hogs from the Havannah with navels on their backs'. Bewick engraved (*History of quadrupeds*) the Peccary or Mexican hog *Sus tajuca* and noted that it 'differs most essentially from the Hog, in having a small orifice on the lower part of the back, from which a thin watery humour, of a most disagreeable smell, flows very copiously'. He also stated that it inhabits the 'hottest parts of South America'.

Jacob's or piebald sheep. one of the 'useful' breeds acclimatized in England after their introduction by George Hammond Lucy of Charlecote, Glocs., in 1759. 'Piebald' came from spots of black on white; 'Jacob's' from the Biblical reference to Jacob in Genesis chapters 30, 31. Stubbs painted a portrait of this breed at Wentworth about 1760.

Sophie greatly admired Warren Hastings who, she said, 'combines those two excellent qualities – intelligence and gift of language' and his wife (Marian Imhoff whom he married in 1777) she found to be, 'modest and unassuming yet of very fine character'. They both talked of their time in India while they showed Sophie a fine grey Tibetan cow, with both her young, and several other Eastern animals. They had also brought home two Indian boys, aged thirteen to fourteen years, as servants.

Warren Hastings's introduction of the goats and cows was no isolated instance of the importation of 'useful' animals. Serious attempts were being made by other landowners to breed herds of foreign deer for food and to increase the number of species in Britain. The 3rd Duke of Richmond had a herd of axis deer, then called Ganges deer, since this animal inhabited the immense plains of India watered by the river Ganges. Some of his axis deer cross-bred with his fallow deer. The Duke of Portland also had a herd of axis deer on his estate at Welbeck.

Robert Clive (1725–74), 1st Baron Clive of Plassey, was another great servant of the Crown in India, between 1743 and 1767. When he retired, he had Claremont House built in 1772 in the Palladian style by Capability Brown. He lived only two years to enjoy it before he was succeeded by his eldest son Edward (1754–1839). The 1774 inventory of the menagerie listed a zebra with a foal, spotted and hog deer, antelopes, an African bull, and some goats. Among the birds were geese, ducks, turkeys, guinea fowls, pheasants, peacocks and curassows. Clive helped John Hunter with breeding nylghau and obtained a cross between a zebra and a donkey. Clive gave a tiger to the 4th Duke of Marlborough, in the 1760s, for his menagerie at Blenheim. George Stubbs painted it three times.[7]

The Royal Park and Medieval Palace of Woodstock, founded by Henry I, which was the site of the first royal menagerie, was granted by Queen Anne to the Duke of Marlborough in 1705 and re-named Blenheim. In the gardens at Blenheim there was a menagerie building, described by John Byng (later 5th Viscount Torrington) as being, 'a dirty shabby place' in 1787. He mentioned a fine Spanish ass, 'from whom all the fine mules who work in the park are descended', two blue cow deer from the East Indies and two moose from America, 'the oddest shapen, and ugliest animals I ever saw, with the heads of asses, bodies of every ill shape, and with legs so thin and long, that they appear like spiders of fifteen feet high'. All the animals were closely confined, which was probably the reason for Byng's disapproval. Apart from the mammals at Blenheim, Byng discovered, 'In various parts of the park are clusters of faggots around a coop, where are hatch'd and rear'd such quantities of pheasants that I almost trod upon them in the grass'.[8]

Pheasants were being turned down on a number of estates in this period. Loisel refers to the Duke of Northumberland (Hugh Smithson, 1715–86) 'qui introduisit le premier, en Europe, le faison à collier'.[9] He was followed by Lord Carnarvon at Highclere and the Duchess of Portland at Bulstrode. Our earlier imported pheasants had no white collar, but they interbred with the collared pheasants, introduced before 1768 when it was first noted by Thomas Pennant, until today the collared variety is predominant. Pennant said, 'Mr Brooks the bird merchant in Holborn, shewed us a variety of the common pheasant which he thought came from China, the male of which had a white

Ring-necked pheasants were first noted as present in England by Thomas Pennant in 1768. They were followed by the green pheasant imported in 1840 by the 13th Earl of Derby and the Mongolian imported c.1898–1900 by Lord Rothschild. Finally the Prince of Wales's pheasant was introduced in 1902 by Colonel M. Sunderland. The interbreeding that followed has given us the infinite variety of plumage in our present day feral pheasants. (Thomas Bewick, *History of quadrupeds*).

4   The Pheasant

ring round its neck'. By 1783 John Latham said it was 'not uncommon'. Mrs Delany mentioned another attempt to acclimatise foreign pheasants being carried out at Longleat by Thomas, Viscount Weymouth. He had married the daughter of Mrs Delany's close friend, the Duchess of Portland, and Lady Elizabeth (Bentinck) had thus become the mistress of an extensive menagerie at Longleat. Mrs Delany said that, 'Lady Weymouth showed us her menagerie. I never saw such a quantity of gold pheasants; they turn them wild into the woods in hopes of their breeding there, for they are as hardy as other pheasant'.[10]

A contemporary of Mrs Delany and Lady Weymouth, who was another society lady diarist, Mrs Powys, has left an account of her own effort making an aviary. Before she started work on it in 1762, she visited the seat of George Pitt, afterwards Lord Rivers, at Stratfield Saye and reported, 'Tis an ancient white house, habitably good, the park, the shrubbery, and grounds laid out prettily, and a menagery exceedingly so, one of the first that was made in England, shows the pheasants &c to great advantage, being of a circular form with pens all round it'.[11] This evidently inspired her to construct one herself, with the help of her brother-in-law Captain Richard Powys, at her girlhood home, Hardwick, Oxon. 'In 1766 my brother . . . and myself began the Menagerie; 'twas where before was called the Wilderness Walk'. They also had a little summer house which they called the bird-house 'or place for canary birds', but that lost favour and was pulled down in 1782 to make room for glasshouses or greenhouses that were then becoming fashionable. Two years later, they 'new fenc'd round the Menagerie this year', but that too was doomed to destruction because it had some choice trees within its enclosure and the wood from these trees was required to make chairs for the house at Hardwick. The chairs cost four and a half guineas (£4–14-6d) each to make, so it was prudent to use the free wood.

A much more interesting collection was that owned by William Murray, Earl of Mansfield, at Kenwood. After a rewarding visit on 22 July 1773, Mrs Delany recalled that in his aviaries was,

> 'the finest louri I ever saw, and very tame and good-humoured, and an extra-ordinary bird they call a

"secretary", an odd creature of the eagle kind, and about that size – a mixture of brown and black. The feathers at *each ear* it has the power of setting up like rays about his head; but generally speaking they are pendant. I took a rough sketch and sent it enclosed to my brother wch gives a little notion of its uncouth shape; I think it came from the Cape of Good Hope'.

An engraving of the portrait of Lady Margaret Cavendish-Holles, Duchess of Portland (1715–86), who married William Bentinck, 2nd Duke of Portland (1709–62). She lived at Bulstrode Park in Buckinghamshire. (A. S. Turberville, *A History of Welbeck and its owners*).

Mrs Delany's descriptions were usually accurate, and this is no exception. We can quibble only with the colouring of the secretary bird, more grey than brown. The crest of long plumes suggested a bunch of quill pens stuck behind the ear of a lawyer's clerk, hence the name 'secretary bird'.

Mrs Delany was a woman of taste and education, a member of the Granville family, and enjoyed connections with members of the aristocracy that gave her free entrance to their houses and gardens. That she was the intimate friend of Lady Margaret Cavendish Harley, who became the wife of William Bentinck, 2nd Duke of Portland, in 1734, was an added recommendation. The Duchess had aviaries and a menagerie pavilion that was really the dairy 'adorned with a Chinese front, as a sort of open Summer house' at Bulstrode Park near Beaconsfield, Buckinghamshire. Most of our information about the Duchess and her wonderful collections comes from Mrs Delany's letters.[12]

The Duchess, like Mrs Delany, was a charming, intelligent woman and had inherited her Harley family passion for collecting. She took a great interest in art and natural science, besides being an accomplished turner of wood, jet,

Bulstrode House, Buckinghamshire. (A. S. Turberville, *A History of Welbeck and its owners*).

Mouflon or musmon, a breed of goat which it was hoped would become acclimatized in the Welsh mountains. (Thomas Bewick, *History of quadrupeds*).

ivory and amber. She collected pictures, snuff-boxes, precious stones and gems, shells and curiosities of all kinds. She was also keenly interested in botany, mammals and birds, especially those living creatures that were unusual in appearance or habit, or were rare. At Bulstrode she took her guests, and there was a constant stream of people going there to visit including George III and his family, learned foreigners such as Rousseau and scientists such as Pennant and Banks, for an after-breakfast stroll around the gardens to introduce them to her livestock. They first inspected her bantams, guinea fowls, pheasants, peacocks and ducks, then moved on to admire her enclosures containing at one time or another, java hares (i.e. long-nosed cavies), 'beautiful deer, oxen, cows, sheep of all countrys, bufalos, mouflons, horses, asses; all in their proper places. Then hares and squirrels at every step you take so confident of their security that they hardly run away!' The mouflons (the smallest wild sheep) bred and produced two young, one of which died, but a male survived. There was an idea of naturalizing the mouflon in Wales and the Hon. Mrs Boscawen reported to Mrs Delany on her visit to Bulstrode in June 1779 that, 'Mad^e Mouflon is better perhaps with one son than two, tho' it should retard a little the *peopling* of the Welsh mountains'.

After November 1753 there was a new bull to be admired, 'a beautiful little bull from the East Indies', as Mrs Delany described him, 'as round as a ball, and looks as if it was bursting with fat'. It was quite small, 'not so high as some dogs I have seen, the colour a pretty grey, between its shoulders rises a hump, in camel fashion, much higher than its head, it looks dark and soft like a sable, it is as tame as a lamb and has a very good-humoured countenance; his horns were broken off in a duel with an animal of his own kind'. By October 1754 the Indian bull had a companion 'who it is hoped will bring him an heir'. This was a zebu.

Bewick's engraving of a zebu (*History of quadrupeds*, 1807: 44). He said, 'it was docile and gentle, covered with fine glossy hair. The hump varied in weight from 40 to 50 lbs', adding 'That part is in general considered as a great delicacy; and when dressed, has much the appearance and taste of udder'.

Just outside the windows of the house, on the lawn, a small mixed group of fifteen or sixteen hares, peacocks and guinea fowl could be seen feeding together. The screams of the peacocks and guinea fowl formed a constant background noise in which the cackling bantams joined. Cranes and gold and silver pheasants were less noisy garden inhabitants most of the year. In August 1774 the Duchess, 'added to her usual assemblage on the lawn under the windows of sheep, hares &c about 50 little pheasants of this year, part of which she hopes will be so familiar as to attend her in her garden, and make her amends for the loss of ye two past years'. By 1777 there were 'never less than 30 hares sup with us every evening'.

Pets which were allowed indoors included Caton the Jonquil parroquet, who breakfasted with the family as usual on 6 September 1768 and then had his portrait drawn by Mrs Delany. She worked the portrait in chenille, amid sprays of purple china asters, 'which set off his golden plumage to admiration'. Lady Mary Coke (4 May 1768) said that the Duchess 'has just now purchased a yellow Perroquet which likewise has never before been seen in this country, and may have come from Brazil'. The Duchess had many foreign birds in her outdoor aviaries, but she infinitely preferred to have them flying free about the garden. She once had a cage with eight nightingales in it brought to her, in mid-June, and promptly set them all at liberty. In the early years of her marriage, while the collection had been put together, they had trouble keeping birds because of the cold, some predators, also thieves. Consequently, some birds had to be kept in aviaries for their protection.

In the outside aviaries, positioned in front of the greenhouse which formed one wing of the house, many beautiful birds were enclosed. Two Numidian cranes that lived there had been kept, 'upwards of 30 *years* – they are so tame that they come hopping to us, and eat bread out of our hands', this was written in 1783. There was also a scarlet ibis, Mrs Delany's remarkable, 'Curlew whose feathers are the brightest scarlet, a long slender neck like a crane, and a very long slender bill, this bird is about the size of a large pigeon'. But whether at large in the house or garden, or in enclosures, the one remarkable factor which evoked comment from all visitors was that, 'every bird and animal in this place, of which there are a great variety, are tame and sociable'.

Goldfish were still rare and in great demand, so that they made welcome presents from the Duchess to her friends. They were kept in 'basons' though it is not clear whether these were outside or inside the house.

The Duchess had inherited £8,000 per annum from her mother, the Countess of Oxford, and she laid out a great part of this sum every year in her flower-garden and menagerie at Bulstrode. Despite this large inheritance, the Duchess ran into debt, though she remained blissfully ignorant of the fact right up to her death on 17 July 1785. Her son, the 3rd Duke of Portland, then took over the care and management of Bulstrode, as well as the other Portland property, Welbeck Abbey. When his own son married, in 1795, the 3rd Duke quitted Welbeck in his favour and went to reside at Bulstrode where he died in 1809. The 4th Duke re-established the family's finances and repaired the damage to their fortunes to such good effect that he became a very wealthy man. He was aided partly in this recovery by the sale in 1810 of Bulstrode to the Duke of Somerset. The house no longer exists having been demolished in 1869.

Mrs Philip Lybbe Powys saw Bulstrode in 1769 and wrote,

'The menagerie, I had heard, was the finest in England, but in that I was disappointed, as the spot is by no means calculated to show off the many beautiful birds it contains, of which there was great variety, as a curassoa, goon, crown-bird, stork, black and red game, bustards, red-legg'd partridges, silver, gold, pied pheasants, one, what is reckon'd exceedingly curious, the peacock-pheasant. The aviary, too, is a most beautiful collection of smaller birds – tumblers, waxbills, yellow and bloom paraquets, Java sparrows, horetta blue birds, Virginia nightingales, and two widow-birds, or as Edwards calles them "red-breasted long'twit'd finches". Besides all above mention'd, her Grace is exceedingly fond of gardening, is a very learned botanist, and has every English plant in a separate garden by themselves. Upon the whole, I never was more entertain'd than at Bulstrode'.[13]

Had Mrs Powys been invited to visit John Hunter and been allowed to see all his bird-cages and dens for quadrupeds, she would have been equally entertained as at Bulstrode, but probably also more than a little shocked. Dr John Hunter was an anatomist and a man with a great urge to experiment. He had an extensive anatomical museum with about 500 different species of mammals, birds, fishes, etc. He also kept a wide variety of live species for his own observation and experiments. Many of these, in due course, ended up in his museum and the species mentioned below would in all probability later be exhibited, either dissected, stuffed, or pickled, in his museum.[14]

John Hunter, an engraving after the portrait painted by Sir Joshua Reynolds.

Hunter had a house built at Brompton, called Earl's Court House, and moved there in 1772. In the spacious grounds he kept all the rare animals that came his way, purchasing them mainly from London dealers. Sometimes he placed unwanted animals in charge of travelling menagerie proprietors, thereby gaining their cooperation in letting him have their difficult subjects, surplus stock, and any dead animals for him to dissect.

Animals in Hunter's ownership did not lead the life of pampered ease which their counterparts enjoyed on the large estates in the country. They were made to earn their keep, scientifically. He obtained a she-wolf from Gough the dealer and mated it with his own dog in order to find out if cubs would result and of what kind. He performed a similar experiment with a jackal and the results were given in a paper that he read before the Royal Society on 26 April 1787, *Observations tending to show that the wolf the jackal and dog are of the same species.*

He petted the animals a great deal and walked among them as though they were tame. The little bull that the Queen gave him was a sparring partner for wrestling matches, but it objected to the treatment one day and would have killed him had not a bystander intervened. On another occasion he was alerted by his dog chasing two leopards which had slipped their chains in the yard. He dashed after them, grabbed hold of them and marched them back to their dens. Having calmed down he suddenly realised the enormity of the risks he had just run and almost fainted on the spot.

Hunter kept bees in the conservatory for the intense interest they afforded him as much as for their honey and a flock of geese in order that he might have a never-ending supply of eggs to investigate the development of a chick within the egg.

For his more unsavoury experiments, such as the preservation of the skeletons of human dwarves and giants, he had an underground laboratory which was reached by a subterranean passage entered by a sunken way five feet deep. Close to this area were dens of various sizes. The dens were formed by the earth being raised to a considerable height, surmounted by a castellated brick wall. Whatever he did down there, remained 'out of sight, out of mind' as far as his wife was concerned, but should any unpleasant smells drift upwards and come to her notice, the learned doctor soon heard about it. Some of the experiments involved the use of rabbits, vipers, bats, hedgehogs, snakes and snails. Even the little pigs did not escape for they were fed on madder to turn their bones red. Two ducks were similarly forced to exist on strange diets, one exclusively on sprats and the other on barley for a month. When they were killed, Hunter discovered, not surprisingly, that one tasted very fishy and was 'hardly eatable'. The pigeons in the house above the stables had their milk glands investigated and other birds, cocks and hens, turkeys, geese, eagles, owls and hawks in the hayloft, plus the ostrich in the cowshed, were all the subjects of experiments to prove that the air cells in their bones and feathers were directly linked to their lungs.

Among the animals around the estate were wolves and jackals chained up in the stable yard, a dingo in a kennel, opossums, donkeys and mules and a famous free-roving marten. The zebra and his mare were not allowed to live and mate in peace, but the mare was crossed with a quagga to see if the offspring would produce a different pattern of markings and coloration, and they did. For some years prior to 1792 the curious sight of Hunter's buffaloes in harness could be seen trotting through the streets of London.[15]

Hunter's scientific achievements were many and well-known to all students of anatomy and medicine. He was a cultured man too and quickly recognised the talent of the artist George Stubbs. He commissioned Stubbs to paint the 'Baboon and Albino Macaque' from his own specimens, and later acquired Stubbs's magnificent painting of Warren Hastings's yak. The 'Indian rhinoceros' was a painting commissioned by Hunter from Stubbs, who studied the live animal at Pidcock's menagerie at Exeter 'Change in the Strand while it was being exhibited in 1792. It was Hunter's custom to obtain paintings or drawings of species which he could not obtain alive in order to study their anatomical structure. Since Stubbs was also a student of animal anatomy, his paintings were sufficiently correct anatomically, besides being beautiful artistic compositions, to satisfy Hunter.[16]

There is a reference to Hunter's great variety of species in Middleton's book on *Middlesex*, published 1793, the year of Hunter's death. Middleton said how amazing it was, 'to find so many living animals in one herd from the most opposite parts of the habitable globe'. It would appear to have been yet another successful experiment, this time in peaceful co-existence, and how fortunate those animals were in comparison with so many others in the collection of this 18th century scientist of such insatiable curiosity.[17]

Following his death, John Hunter's anatomical museum formed the nucleus of the Royal College of Surgeons Museum in London. Another very famous museum of the same date, brought together by Sir Ashton Lever, was housed in Leicester Fields from 1775–86. This huge collection of natural history specimens, ethnographic objects including costumes, weapons and domestic implements from all parts of the world, was arranged in sixteen rooms in Leicester House, where Sir Ashton also lived. He kept some living mammals in a field behind the museum. He owned a gentle nylghau 'fond of being caressed' which 'always licked the hand by which it was either stroked or fed. Its sense of smelling appeared to be exquisite, as it always applied to it for information when any new object presented itself, particularly when either food or drink was offered it'. John Church, who described it in his book on quadrupeds, said it was also known as a white-footed antelope and had 'been frequently imported from India, particularly in the year 1767, when several of them were brought to this country' and bred for several years thereafter.

Sir Ashton Lever also had a young female orang utan as a pet. During the six months that it lived with him it 'was very much attached to him, imitated human actions, fed itself with a spoon, and lay in bed, with its head on a pillow, and its body and limbs covered with bed clothes'. In a large cage, Sir Ashton kept a leopard which 'always seemed pleased and grateful by the attention paid it' when anyone admired and patted it. It responded by 'purring and rubbing itself against the cage like a cat'. This tame leopard was allowed to play with a porcupine and a large Newfoundland dog when all three were set free on the grass behind Leicester House. 'As soon as they were let loose, the leopard and dog began to pursue the porcupine, who at first endeavoured to escape by flight; but finding that ineffectual, he thrust his nose in some corner, making a snoring noise, and erected his spines, with which his pursuers pricked their noses, till they quarrelled between themselves, and gave him an opportunity to make his escape; we have frequently been eye-witness to this diverting scene'.[18] Sir Ashton eventually presented the leopard to the Royal Menagerie in the Tower of London.

The first book published in Britain to record and illustrate the contents of a private menagerie was *Rare and curious birds accurately drawn and coloured from specimens in the Menagerie at Osterley Park*, 1782. It appeared because an impecunious bird artist, William Hayes (1735–1802), lived at the post office in nearby Southall and was given permission to visit the elegant Georgian aviary, called 'The Menagery' to paint the exotic species. There were two lakes adjoining the aviary, with an assortment of waterfowl, looked after in 1776 by two gardeners, Isaiah Smith and Edward Wildcock, who were paid eight shillings each for a six-day week for work in the menageries.[19]

Osterley Park belonged to the wealthy banker Robert Child (1739–82). It was visited by people who went to admire the house, remodelled by Adam with its magnificent decoration and furnishings. Horace Walpole called it 'the palace of palaces'. By 1773 the menagerie housed some truly rare and beautiful birds, though Walpole exaggerated, in his whimsical manner, when he said that it was 'full of birds that came from a 1000 islands, which Mr Banks has not yet discovered'.[20]

There is a charming portrait of Sarah Anne Child, the daughter of Robert and his wife Sarah, with some of her pet doves in the house at Osterley. It is one of Sir Joshua Reynolds's masterpieces. Sarah Anne was involved in one of the most celebrated runaway matches of the century when she eloped to Gretna with the handsome 10th Earl of Westmorland in 1782. She greatly distressed her father,

The Georgian menagerie building at Osterley Park was built in the late 1760s. William Hayes included this picture of the birds' house in 1794 as the frontispiece to *Portrait of rare and curious birds . . . in the menagery of Child the banker at Osterley Park.*

Pencilled or silver pheasant, etched and hand-coloured by William Hayes and family, 1794, for *Portraits of rare and curious birds with their descriptions. Accurately drawn and beautifully coloured from species in the menagery of Child the banker at Osterley Park near London.* Silver pheasants were introduced to England in 1740 and soon became naturalized.

who died a few months later, leaving the estates first to his wife, Sarah, and then to Sarah Anne's second, unborn, child. Sarah Child, his widow, managed the bank and the Osterley estate by herself until she married the 3rd Baron Ducie in 1791. Throughout this time, she allowed William Hayes to continue to visit the menagerie and paint. He published his paintings, now supplemented with new ones, a second time in two volumes, 1794 and 1799 and called it *Portraits of rare and curious birds with their description accurately drawn and beautifully coloured from species in the menagery of Child the Banker at Osterley Park near London.* Hayes's wife and children assisted him in drawing and painting the birds. These included crowned cranes among several kinds of cranes, a pair of bustards that had been an appropriate gift to Robert Child from the Marquis of Bath, for they roamed Salisbury Plain at this time. A pair of king vultures had been sent to Hayes himself by the Marquis of Stafford. Hayes evidently visited other collections too, for he mentioned that Lady James and Lady Ducie both had black-capped lories; the Duchess of Portland had a helmeted curassow which, with Lady Ducie's specimen, he believed to be the only specimens having been met with so far in England. He said that the Countess of Essex had golden pheasants in her menagerie, but there were many of these birds, some being feral in England by this date. The Childs also had silver pheasants (then going under the more charming name of 'pencilled pheasants').

Although Lady Ducie thought the best bird in her aviary was an Indian pigeon, but having drawn and observed so many unusual and beautiful species, any one of which could have been regarded as outstanding, Hayes chose another to name, quite categorically, as his favourite. Of the Numidian crane, he wrote, 'This is the most pleasing bird in the Osterley collection and received the name of Demoiselle on account of its elegant form, the graceful attitudes, and affected gestures'.[21]

Members of the parrot family were unusually varied in this collection. The rose-headed ring parakeet, nonpareil parrot, also a blue-headed parrot and Alexandrine parakeet, were present with the black-capped lories. Some of the other birds to be seen in contemporary collections were purple gallinule, scarlet ibis, paradise widow bird and a secretary bird. The Osterley collection was of greater interest because of the number of small cage birds, some species not having been listed or mentioned by other collectors: the small red-billed quelea, some grosbeaks, a shaft-tailed whidah, a red-cheeked cordon-bleu, paradise tanager, and the more common red avadavat and waxbill. No other collection was to be so well illustrated and documented until John Edward Gray performed a similar service at Knowsley, the seat of the Earls of Derby, in the middle of the next century.

Mrs Powys visited Osterley on 22 May 1788 and was disappointed. Perhaps this was a natural reaction to a collection that had had such an enormous reputation for many years. 'The menageries,' she wrote, 'which for years I had heard so much of, fell short of my expectation; that of Lady Ailesbury's at Park Place is vastly superior in elegance; nor were there so many different birds as I have seen at others'. But she added an important item of news about the Gobelin tapestry room at Osterley, saying that it was 'done in wreaths of flowers from nature, in the most elegant taste, and numbers of curious birds, formerly in the menagerie'. In the tapestry room the birds are painted in the intervening wall spaces and surrounding the large medallions, after designs by Francois Boucher (1703–70).

The menagerie at Osterley Park is now a privately owned house called 'The Aviary' with 48 acres, including the two large lakes providing sanctuary for flamingoes, crane, black swans and a variety of ducks.

The 'Lady Ailesbury' to whom Mrs Powys referred was the wife of General Henry S. Conway who retained the title she had acquired from her marriage to her first husband, Charles Bruce, Earl of Aylesbury. The Conways lived at Park Place, Henley on Thames, and were very attached to the beautiful house, spending a great deal on it and on the grounds. Lady Aylesbury was a keen naturalist and gave Mrs Powys '14 quires of papers containing plants, sea-weeds, roses etc which she had mounted'. Mrs Powys visited her on many occasions, but though she thought her menagerie at Park Place superior to that at Osterley, she failed to give an account of it.

She made some amends, however, after visiting a Buckinghamshire seat, that of General Owen P. Williams near Marlow, called 'Temple'. She was there in 1796 and thought it most oddly fitted up and furnished so that, 'one cannot help fancying oneself in one of those palaces mention'd in the Arabian Nights' Entertainments; but what surprised us, there is not a picture, but that of Mr Williams himself. Statues of every kind, and at the farther end of a most magnificent greenhouse is an aviary full of all kinds of birds, flying loose in a large octagon of gilt wire, in which is a fountain in the centre, and in the evening 'tis illuminated by wax-lights, while the water falls down some rock-work in form of a cascade. This has a pretty effect, but seems to alarm its beautiful inhabitants, and must be cold for them I should imagine'.[22]

The Earls of Strafford, whose seat was Wentworth Castle, near Barnsley in Yorkshire, had an interest in unusual fauna throughout the 18th century. They had a pet monkey called Jenny Pug who was alive 1705–10 and also a parrot. A new house was built in 1710–11 with enclosures for menagerie animals. Lord Bathurst called on the Earl in 1725 and found a cascade in the court and then proceeded to view the menagerie that he thought was very handsome, but did not comment on the animals. Walpole visited the house in the 1760s when Lady Anne Strafford had an aviary there and was expert at raising peafowl, guinea fowl and pheasants, on a diet of bread rolls. The Countess was epileptic and had no children, but delighted in animals of all kinds, with favourite horses, dogs, cats, squirrels, parakeets and singing-birds. She had been interested since early childhood, having kept some green lizards in a box, which she let loose to catch flies in the garden when the sun shone.[23]

These are the most notable menageries of the 18th century, when aviaries formed part of the garden landscape, and some were suitable for birds, while others were more pleasing to their owners, where some birds could live a long life, loved and tenderly cared for, while others shivered and were frightened. By the end of the century much had been learned about the great variety of species the world had to offer. In 1758 Linnaeus had known of 444 bird species, but by 1799 some 3,000 species were known to exist. The next century was to see this figure more than doubled.

Chapter 13

'Dignified by the presence of an immense elephant'

The earliest notable menagerie of the 19th century was situated in London, at Chiswick House. This was the town house of the 6th Duke of Devonshire, better known for his keen interest in horticulture, but who, nevertheless, had a great love of all natural history subjects. At Chiswick he kept elks, emus, kangaroos, a monkey, Indian bull and cow, goats 'of all colours and dimensions' and some 'pretty sportive death-dealers'. He allowed his mammals and birds to roam in large paddocks at Chiswick arranged on similar principles to those of King George IV at Sandpit Gate.[1]

When Sir Walter Scott visited Chiswick in 1828, he afterwards wrote in his diary for 17 May,

> 'The Duke of Devonshire received me with the best possible manners. The scene was dignified by the presence of an immense elephant, who, under the charge of a groom, wandered up and down, giving an air of Asiatic pageantry to the entertainment. I was never more sensible of the dignity which largeness of size, and freedom of movement give to this otherwise very ugly animal'.

Portrait of the bachelor 6th Duke of Devonshire (1790–1858), owner of Chiswick House in London and Chatsworth in Derbyshire. His conservatory sheltered a fine collection of tropical birds and fishes.

This sagacious elephant had been trained by its keeper to kneel down and allow him to mount her and ride on her neck. Though this is today seen as a most characteristic movement, with which we are all familiar, it was then a novel idea, imported along with the elephant and mahouts from the east.

Another of the Duke's animals, a giraffe, caused a diversion in 1844 when Czar Nicholas visited Chiswick. It escaped and attempted to swim across the lake in a bid for freedom.

It was about this period that the greatest change in accommodation for birds occurred in the design of aviaries. After the 1830s, when there was a dramatic drop in the price of glass, conservatories (sometimes called glasshouses or stove houses) became very fashionable and desirable possessions. Their construction, a light basic structure of

The Volary at Chiswick House, Lord Burlington's Palladian villa later owned by the Dukes of Devonshire. An engraving from a survey of the gardens by John Rocque in 1736.

a metal frame holding panes of glass, was adapted by the Victorians for aviaries. The metal framework was infilled with wire-mesh, and the aviary was often attached, in a similar manner to a conservatory, to one wall of the house. Nesting-boxes or retiring-boxes were fixed to the house wall providing the birds with additional warmth and protection. Sometimes the aviary was constructed as a part of, or inside, the conservatory, as at Syon House and then Chatsworth in 1836.

Chatsworth's conservatory was spectacular and included a fine collection of tropical birds and fishes, flowers, trees, fountains and specimens of minerals. It was built by Sir Joseph Paxton in 1836, 277ft long and 123ft wide, with 75,000 square feet of glass covering one acre. The ridge of the roof was 67ft high and a coach and horses could comfortably be driven through it. Visitors paid 5 shillings to the house-keeper at Chatsworth to see the Duke's art collection and to be allowed to wander round the gardens, marvel at the conservatory and enjoy the quadruped and bird 'curiosities which met every glance'.[2] The conservatory cannot be seen today, it was pulled down in 1920.

Very few examples of elaborate Victorian aviaries still survive, but three outstanding examples are preserved, two in Buckinghamshire, at Dropmore and Waddesdon Manor, and one in Norfolk at Somerleyton Hall. These aviaries allowed a mixed group of birds to be kept within one enclosure. Birds with special requirements were placed in a separate compartment with a barely perceptible wall of netting dividing them from the main enclosure. In the larger compartment, a pool provided sufficient water for waterfowl, ducks and waders, perches high up gave finches, colourful starlings, pigeons and members of the crow family places from which to sing or take short flights, while on the ground brilliantly-plumaged pheasants strutted about. The kind-hearted Victorians also gave sanctuary to any wounded bird brought from the surrounding countryside (provided it was not edible). Feeding stations were provided on different levels, with tree branches, shrubs and rocks to resemble as much as possible the birds' normal habitats. Accommodation for birds was far more enlightened, sensitive and imaginative than for mammals, which still endured unsuitable enclosures.

A much smaller collection belonged to Dante Gabriel Rossetti, the Pre-Raphaelite artist and poet. He had a studio in Chelsea that he shared with a number of tame creatures, which he had either bought, or his friends had given to him. At different times he owned peacocks, one of which lost part of its train when a deer trod on it, owls and a jackass penguin. Among reptiles there were salamanders and a green lizard. These were among his well-behaved companions, but an armadillo burrowed under the garden and surfaced in a neighbour's kitchen and a mischievous raccoon raided his neighbours' hen-coops. The small Indian bull chased its master and successfully treed him for an uncomfortable period of time, after which Rossetti had to dispose of it. Numerous small mammals from the British countryside were joined by a woodchuck and marmots. He also had two kangaroos, but his favourite mammal was a rotund, plush-coated wombat. He had seen the small creature at the Zoological Gardens and while he, Edward Burne-Jones and other members of the Pre-Raphaelite group were decorating the Union at Oxford in 1857, they covered the windows,

Two Pre-Raphaelite wombats. (a) 'A very lively wombat, unaccountably running in front of a pyramid and palm tree!', drawn by Edward Burne-Jones, from *Memorial of Edward Burne-Jones*. (b) Dante Gabriel Rossetti's self-caricature mourning his dead pet wombat in 1869.

(a)

(b)

which they had whitened in order to tone down the light, with sketches, chiefly of wombats drawn by Burne-Jones in endless different postures and situations. Subsequently, Rossetti could not be happy until he too owned a wombat and, eventually, one of these snub-nosed Australian marsupials went to live in his studio at Chelsea.[3]

By the second half of the 19th century when the Zoological Society was well established, such small collections were becoming a thing of the past. The main collections were much more extensive and serious affairs, owned by Sir Robert Heron, the Duke of Bedford, two Earls Fitzwilliam, Lord Stanley (the 13th Earl of Derby) and finally Lords Lilford and Rothschild.

Edward Smith Stanley, 13th Earl of Derby (1775–1851), owner of the large collection of birds and ungulates at Knowsley Hall, 1834–51.

In the second quarter of the 19th century, the largest private menagerie belonged to the Earl of Derby of Knowsley Hall, Prescot, Lancashire, the second largest to Earl Fitzwilliam of Wentworth, Yorkshire and the third to Sir Robert Heron, a Baronet, of Stubton Hall near Newark, Lincolnshire. These three owners exchanged letters and notes regarding their animals in order to facilitate breeding. All were interested in the idea of domesticating and acclimatizing ungulates in particular and hybridizing exotic birds such as the highly colourful pheasants, ducks and pigeons.

The 13th Earl of Derby owned the greatest collection. He began to collect birds in the early years of the century, but it was not until he succeeded his father in 1834 that he was able to fully indulge his passion for birds and then add the ungulates and create aviaries and paddocks at Knowsley Park to accommodate them. Throughout his long life (1775–1851) he was interested in all aspects of natural history and became knowledgeable in several fields. He was also a great patron of naturalists and naturalist-artists. On the death of his birds and mammals, many were transferred to his museum, that he bequeathed to form the basis of the present-day Liverpool Museum.

The Earl sent out collectors to Asia, Africa, Australia and the Americas to collect for him, thereby achieving a more organised approach to collecting with a consequent increase in the accuracy of the records of where the species were found, their habitat, food, and behaviour. He also took an active part in the propagation of zoological knowledge by serving as a Trustee of the British Museum, President of the Zoological Society 1831–51 and President of the Linnean Society 1828–33. He was a generous donor to the Zoological Society and exchanged specimens for breeding purposes. One of his reasons for stocking small groups of the same species was the hope that 'useful' animals, i.e. ones that could be farmed, would breed in this country. For this purpose he always tried to have both a male and female alpaca, llama, guanaco, different species of goats and deer, zebras, quaggas and kangaroos, among other mammals.

Maintenance of the menageries and aviaries, which occupied 100 acres within Knowsley Park, in addition to lakes covering some 70 acres, cost him at least £10,000 a year. In 1851 he left 345 individual mammals of 94 species and 1272 individual birds of 318 species. A more important figure was that 750 of these that had been bred at Knowsley bearing eloquent witness to the good management of his keepers and thoughtful provision made for the animals. The description of the large paddocks and spacious runs under wired covers reads like an account of the way Whipsnade and the more advanced zoos are run today.

Some of the species he owned had been introduced to England for the first time, others were great rarities. The graceful Stanley crane and the first specimens of the Derbyan or Stanley parakeet to reach Europe were named after the Earl, and his six black-necked swans from Valparaiso were the first to reach this country. Other new introductions included some masked parrots from the South Sea Islands and Cape Elands. He had been delighted by the wonderfully rich colours in the plumage of pheasants and had imported the southern green pheasant from Japan in 1840.

In the light of the rescue operation at Slimbridge in the 20th century to preserve the nene, Hawaiian or Sandwich Island goose, from extinction, it is of interest that the Earl obtained some specimens from Hawaii in 1823 and they bred in 1824 and the following years. In 1832 Lady Glengall presented a pair from Hawaii to London Zoo. One of these became the type of the species when described and named by N. A. Vigors, Secretary of the Zoological Society, *Anser sandvicensis* after Lord Sandwich. (The Sandwich Islands, also named after the Earl of Sandwich by Captain Cook in 1778, were later re-named Hawaii.)

In 1830 the American bird artist and author John James Audubon (*The Birds of America*) purchased 350 passenger pigeons at four cents each in a market and conveyed them to England as gifts for the Zoological Society and several noblemen. The Earl had seventy of these which bred and flew freely at Knowsley.

Pursuing a policy of breeding birds for the table the Earl raised young capercaillies from three sent to him in 1838 by the Duchess of Blair and Athol. The animals he hoped to acclimatise included gnu, yak, eland (the only living specimens in England), Indian antelopes *Capra cervicapra* (the only ones brought over), several kinds of foreign goats, sheep and Brahmin cattle. He also had zebus, elk, rodents, lemurs, armadillos and dogs. He successfully bred ten species of deer, llamas, alpacas, guanacos and vicunas, as well as kangaroos.[4]

Some of the animals depicted in the *Illustrated London News* on 4 October 1851, advertising the sale of the Knowsley aviary. (Top, from left), bontebok, gazelles and male and female elands. (Below, left), bara singha deer. (Below, right). Elk with keeper.

Following the Earl's death in October 1851 nearly all the stock was sold and realised £7,000. The exceptions were gifts, under the terms of his will, to Queen Victoria who chose two black-necked swans and five Impeyan pheasants, and the eland antelopes chosen by the Zoological Society. The auctioneer, Mr Stevens, sold the Derby menagerie on the ground. The prices paid for the animals caused many raised eyebrows at the time. Two gnus fetched £283, and the Zoological Society paid £1,000 for 5 elands and £105 for 2 wapiti. A Brahmin bull fetched £50, a yak £100, llamas £25 and £69 and zebras £130, £140 and £150. A quagga, now an extinct species, made £50 and a lot of 3 kangaroos went to £105. Among the birds, a harpy eagle made £25, a masked parrot £21 and a Japanese male pheasant, described as 'the only living specimen in Europe' went for £28. Even ostriches sold for £16 to £70 apiece and 4 black-necked swans made £160. Three Orinoco geese, first introduced to Britain by the Earl and which bred successfully from 1844 onwards, sold for £14.[5]

Jacques-Laurent Agasse, *Guanaco*. Paul Mellon Collection, Yale Center for British Art.

There is a curious interwoven story concerning Polish swans that connects the Derby collection, the St James's Park collection and the dealer D. Castang. 'Polish swan' was a name given to mute swans which produced white-downed cygnets from the egg instead of the usual grey cygnets. In the spring of 1836 the Ornithological Society of London purchased from Mr Castang, the London bird dealer, a pair of Polish swans with one cygnet. The old female and the cygnet died the following winter. The Earl, having only a female or pen Polish swan and the Ornithological Society still possessing their solitary old male, the latter was sent to Knowsley to form a pair. Four white cygnets were produced. At the sale of the Knowsley collection, the two old birds were purchased by Mr Bartlett for the Ornithological Society and placed on the lake in St James's Park. They produced a brood of seven cygnets in the summer of 1854 and another six in 1856, all white from the egg. In the 19th century there was great interest in unusual forms. Melanism in black panthers and leopards or albinism in white peacocks and pheasants was highly prized and sought after by collectors.

The Earl ensured that there would be a permanent record of the outstanding species at Knowsley by employing natural history artists to paint the animals in his collection. He invited the artists Benjamin Waterhouse Hawkins (who drew the ungulates), Edward Lear (who made some wonderful watercolours of birds) and Joseph Wolf (the outstanding Victorian animal artist) to paint at Knowsley. Some of their work was reproduced in two volumes of J. E. Gray's *Gleanings from the Menagerie and Aviary at Knowsley*, printed privately between 1846 and 1850.

The Earl was an indefatigable correspondent and kept in touch with other menagerie owners, frequently passing on management hints and exchanging specimens for breeding purposes. One of his correspondents, the 2nd Earl Fitzwilliam, owned the second largest menagerie to his own.

The menagerie at Wentworth Woodhouse in Yorkshire belonged to William (who took the additional name Wentworth), 2nd Earl Fitzwilliam. Before 1819 the Earl had successfully bred black swans from New Holland and sent a pair, in 1822, to Stubton for Sir Robert Heron. Sir Robert went to visit the menagerie at Wentworth and was singularly unimpressed by the management there. He found nylghaus and llamas (both of which bred) and alpacas housed together, but the kangaroos with a fine pair of rheas, earlier presented by him, had died.

When Charles William became 3rd Earl Fitzwilliam on the death of his father in 1833, Sir Robert Heron thought reviving the menagerie would prove to be a herculean task. The Earl was keen to try, however, and requested from Knowsley some of the Knowsley passenger pigeons and wild cock pigeons, a pair of silver pheasants and collared doves, but he was tired, he said, of wild ducks and guinea pigs which they had had so often that he no longer cared about them. The birds requested from Knowsley were in exchange for two cormorants. The Earl said these were not, 'at all nice about their food – offal meal suits them quite as well as fish'. Other species kept at Wentworth prior to 1857 when the 3rd Earl died, apart from the programme of breeding nylghaus, llamas and alpacas, were zebus, emus and rheas.[6]

The third menagerie owner, who also was active from the early part of the century until the 1850s, was Sir Robert Heron (1765–1854). He was a Whig politician who, through the 2nd Earl Fitzwilliam's interest, was returned as Member of Parliament for Peterborough in December 1819 and remained an MP until 1847. He was born at Newark, the only son of Thomas Heron of Chillham Castle, Kent, but through two uncles he obtained wealth and a title. He succeeded to the baronetcy on the death of Sir Richard Heron in 1805 and to a fortune through the death of Reverend Robert Heron of Grantham in 1813. Side by side with his political career, his extraordinary flair for keeping and breeding exotic mammals, birds and fishes was used to increase his own menagerie from about 1809 onwards, as well as those of the Earls Fitzwilliam and Derby. He served on the Council of the Zoological Society of London and assisted with providing animals to form breeding pairs at their gardens in Regent's Park, occasionally taking one of their animals (e.g.

a black curassow *Crax alector* in 1832) to pair with another of the species at Stubton.[7]

Heron had several of the mammals that were thriving in other collections and some more esoteric creatures; not everyone wanted muskrats or a male tapir. He exchanged specimens of hog deer with the Earl of Derby for breeding purposes and bred porcupines, both hairy and weazleheaded armadilloes, and opossums. He bred alpacas successfully, but had trouble with a guanaco female that killed one of his axis deer in 1849. A male llama killed a female and, when he decided to shear three of them, they died of cold in the following winter, having lost their protective warm wool. Heron purchased some flying squirrels in London in 1844 and a pair of marmots that he got from Canada produced three young. Angora rabbits were in vogue about 1840, having been imported in some numbers and Heron said he had, 'plenty'. A long-tailed lemur was not a common occupant of cages here when he had one in 1848, nor a spotted dasyurus from New Holland, which he bought from the dealer Atkins of Liverpool in 1843. He also had some Syrian jerboas, desert rodents that jump like kangaroos.

His outstanding group of mammals, of which he bred and collected the different species, was the kangaroo family. Despite all the many large grey kangaroos, *Macropus major,* brought over from Australia they had gradually died out and became nearly extinct in Britain. By 1843 Heron thought only three remained in England and commented that, 'Lord Derby and I are trying to recover the breed . . . after mutual exchanges, we have each one male and two females'. He had received a male from Sir Joseph Banks in 1816 and another pair from Lord Bath in July 1815, so had been breeding them for some thirty years. Heron also owned 'Macropus penatus my little kangaroo', and Cuvier's, 'a small & dark species rarely seen here'. He gave a surplus pair of bush kangaroos or wallabies to Knowsley in 1836. In addition he had musk kangaroos in 1839 and Bennet's wallabies. He obtained a jerboa kangaroo from Knowsley in 1832 and then in December 1843 bought, 'a pair of beautiful little jerboas of E[dward] Cross; they are tame and doing well'. He bought a bridled kangaroo, *Macropus fraenatus,* in 1846.

Heron was breeding goldfish by 1809 and continued to have success with them and 'blue fish'. In 1815 he wrote,

George Edwards drew and etched this jerboa (*Gleanings of natural history*, 1758) owned by an optician near St Ann's Church, Westminster, but had to be careful 'as I could not conveniently handle the living animal, which would bite when held fast'.

Chameleons were interesting and attractive reptiles and thrived as pets.

'I have bred gold fish for 6 years in the aquarium and have now about eleven hundred of all ages in a paved pond in the flower garden . . . of my original stock, six came from Burleigh and six from Kendrick's in Piccadilly'.

Things did not always go well in his menagerie. On 28 March 1820,

> 'a chameleon was sent to me – 11" in a wicker basket covered with flannel. From Brazil. Killed on 22 June 1820 when a stupid under gardener destroyed him by hastily closing one of the lights on which he had climbed. During a journey of six months no food was given him, and it was a month longer before he recovered his appetite. His brother who travelled with him is at Exeter Change'.

Heron had purchased, 'three Brazil tortoises two and three quarter inches in the greatest length of the shell; the flesh green and yellow striped, the shell of a dingy green, brown and red. They delight in the warm water of the aquarium, but when the sun shines, sit basking on a post, a stone or gravel . . . in 3 months have grown three-quarters of an inch'. Apart from two Surinam toads, Heron seems to have had few other amphibians.

Heron had black swans from Wentworth. On 13 November 1832 one original female had died, but she was 16 years old. She hatched forty-four black swans and reared forty in those sixteen years. Similar numbers were reared from his emus, although one male killed its female. The Zoological Society asked him to help them breed cereopsis geese and he succeeded.

His attitude to cassowaries followed the same pattern we have witnessed throughout this story of aviculture, delight at first, then anxiety to be rid of them. In October 1843, he wrote, 'Two magnificent cassowaries have been here three years. They are very furious and very powerful. We have introduced them to each other, but, hitherto, they only fight'. By December 1843, it was a case of, 'My cassowaries having killed a kangaroo, wounded a man, and frightened everybody, I sold them to the Zoological Society for forty pounds. The cassowaries were both females, having both laid eggs. I begin to doubt whether there ever was a male in England'.

South American tinamous were more tractable. Heron again assisted the Zoological Society by taking in a black curassow (he had both black-billed and yellow-billed) in order to mate it with a bird he owned. Three years later, in 1835, he could report breeding of this species.

With his rheas, the opposite problem arose. They were far too fertile for their own good.

> 'Ld Fitzwilliam having a solitary young female gave it me in the year 1841 . . . During the last year, 44 eggs were laid, and the male most perseveringly sat on three broods. Nine were hatched, of which we could only rear three; of these I gave a pair to Lord Fitzwilliam. Lord Derby has reared four, and I believe there have been no others brought up in England'. In December 1843 he said, 'My female rhea died, probably from laying the enormous quantity of eighty-eight eggs in two years. She has left me a fine pair of young ones'.

Of Oriental species, only two tiger bitterns were noted as of interest. His Sandwich Island geese had come from Knowsley in 1836, as did some Missouri pigeons and Carolina teal.

Heron's notes on the behaviour and interaction between species, (he penned several species together in large paddocks) make the most interesting reading in his book *Notes*. In 1836 he commented on the strong personality of one of his cranes,

> 'The male Balearic Crane is lord of the menagerie, but does not use his power offensively. An emu had laid the female crane on her back and would presently have demolished her, but hearing her cries, the male ran to her assistance, and drove off the emu. The kangaroos resist the emus with success, but the black swans, when they have young ones, fight an equal and dangerous battle with them'.

Heron was indeed, very successful in breeding birds and mammals. His careful provision of nesting sites would contribute to this. On the islands of his menagerie he provided 'wigwams of earth roofed with weeds' to provide both warmth and shelter. In January 1848 he recorded,

> 'I have reared, during the Spring, the following valuable animals; two nylghaus, two large kangaroos, four rheas, four cereopsis, three Orinoco geese, and one patterson

partridge, with many of less value. Last year, my nyl-ghaus produced twins, males. I have also acquired two long-tailed lemurs, three axis deer, three roe deer, two hog deer, and many birds; also four flying squirrels'.

In August 1849 he again congratulated himself,

'My menagerie has been, lately, greatly increased, and I am believed to be more successful in rearing animals than others: in fact, I know of no other considerable private collections, except Lord Derby's and Lord Fitzwilliam's. I possess at present llamas, alpacas, nylghaus, gua-nacos, Indian antelopes, Virginian deer, long-tailed lemurs, agoutis, common porcupines, hog deer, jerboas, and kangaroos (macropus major), macropus bennetti, bettongia pencillata, armadillos, Angora rabbits, and capybaras'.

Sir Robert Heron died in 1854, three years after the Earl of Derby and three years before Charles William, 3rd Earl Fitzwilliam. Their three very productive collections were dispersed within six years and much zoological knowledge and experience in aviculture died with them. Sir Robert Heron's letters provide the most information on how the animals were housed and treated, and clues as to why he succeeded, or failed.[7]

In the second half of the 19th century another really large private menagerie, with many different species, was brought together for the pleasure of its owner, Thomas Littleton Powys, the 4th Lord Lilford (1833–96) of Lilford Hall, near Oundle in Northamptonshire. As a boy at Harrow he kept a small menagerie and carefully recorded his observations on the behaviour and antics of his pets. At Oxford his col-lection and his knowledge of natural history grew together. His grandmother, Lady Holland, bequeathed to him a large collection of stuffed British birds which formed the nucleus of the museum of specimens which lined many of the walls at Lilford Hall.[8]

The steadily growing collection became of absorbing interest to Lord Lilford who did not enjoy good health. At the end of his life he was confined each winter to his sitting-room where he kept his special favourites, a coal-black bull-finch, blue rock thrush and a brilliantly-coloured troupial from Brazil. Also in this very personal and cosy room, were many beautiful paintings of falcons by Archibald Thorburn and Joseph Wolf, two outstanding animal artists of the late 19th century. Lord Lilford, like the Earl of Derby before him, was a connoisseur of bird art and, like the Earl, sent collectors to different parts of the world to bring back live or preserved specimens for his menagerie, museum and pictorial records.

On warm days Lord Lilford was taken outside, in a bath-chair, to which hereditary gout confined him and visited his menagerie. Barbara Allen, a goshawk from France who took several hundred rabbits in her life-time, was a great favour-ite and was always visited by Lord Lilford. Her perch, alongside three peregrines, was under an old cedar tree at the corner of the terrace gardens. Behind them, in grottoes with ivy-covered sheds were the owls, rare ones such as a Nepal wood owl, Savigny's eagle owl and a chestnut owl, and what were then very rare, but are now common, little owls. Many of the little owls bred at Lilford were allowed to fly freely and spread outwards from Northamptonshire to colonise neighbouring counties. Two more birds of prey, lammergeiers or bearded vultures, soared and circled above the grey stone gables of the hall and the deer park. The twelve species of eagles, including four imperial eagles and a white-breasted Australian sea eagle, shared a sepa-rate area of 20 square yards for vultures, hawks, buzzards and falcons.

There was a nearly complete collection of crane species (monk, wattled, Manchurian, demoiselle, great white from the sandhills of America, sarus, and Chinese sacred) in the Pinetum in an enclosure of about five acres. Their pool was planted with sedge from Norfolk reedbeds.

Many of the birds appear to have been quite tame. A black Japanese kite flew to Lord Lilford's chair to take a small mouse gently from his fingers. Birds in the gallery in the courtyard were similarly fed with dates, grapes, both dried and fresh figs and bananas. These were the more delicate birds from warm climates, such as touracos, golden-winged blackbirds from Palestine, a pied grackle from China, grey coly shrikes from the Persian Gulf, glossy green starlings and small grass finches from Queensland. The variety of ducks and herons, waders and gulls was just as astonishing as other groups in the gardens, round the fountains, and in large aviaries.

Lord Lilford also had mammals in a deer park, where fallow deer, coloured creamy white to almost black and cattle, also variously coloured, grazed. Some white Afghan cattle always walked about the park in single file as though still treading meticulously along narrow mountain tracks.

Jenny, the otter, lived in a round pond in the centre of the kitchen gardens. Morena, an Asturian bear, ate great quantities of buns and cakes brought by the local villagers. Other mammals were a Cape coney, ruffed lemur, golden guinea pigs, ichneumon, genet, prairie dog, all of which received attention to the point that they were relatively tame. The exception to this was the wild cat that proved to be untameable. Lord Lilford was happy to see other people enjoying his grounds and animals and opened the park to camping St John's Ambulance men, clubs and societies on many occasions.

The sight of the elderly Lord Lilford in his bath-chair and two gigantic tortoises from Aldabra being trundled past on a trolley, off for a sunbathe in a warm spot, would have remained in the memory of any visitor to Lilford Hall. The little girl who was lifted onto the back of one 346lb tortoise to take a ride would have remembered it to the end of her life. When Lord Lilford died, his collections were dispersed by sale. Rarely is a passionate interest in natural history inherited by the successors to these magnificent collections.

Of all the aristocratic families who at some time or another owned a remarkable menagerie, the Bedford, or rather Russell family, appears to be the only one in whom there was a recurring interest in natural history sufficient to maintain a collection over a long period of time spanning several generations.[9]

John Russell, the 6th Duke of Bedford (1766–1839), who succeeded his father in 1802, intended to have a collection of birds and beasts 'in a moderate way' at Woburn Abbey in Bedfordshire. As is often the case, this modest beginning burgeoned into an impressively large collection and this one, unlike the other 19th century menageries, has continued to this day.

The menagerie at Woburn was designed by Humphrey Repton and described in James Forbes's *Hortus Woburnensis*, as consisting of 'wired compartments for separating the various birds and mammals. Shrubs form shelter for the pheasants. Lower part of central octagonal building for

canaries and small birds which nest in apertures around the walls. Upper half of the building for the numerous pigeons of many varieties. The wings on either side of the octagons are keepers' apartments. Space occupied by the menagerie covers nearly two acres'.[10]

Woburn Menagerie designed by Humphrey Repton, 1833. (Lithograph by F. Ross in *Hortus Woburnensis, a descriptive catalogue* by James Forbes, 1833: 285).

Lady Sarah Spencer accompanied Queen Victoria and Prince Albert when they went to Woburn on 29 July 1842. She wrote,

'We yesterday had a very noble part of the Duke of Bedford's park to drive through – and then we all walked through menageries & aviaries, and dairy, and farms, & a glorious garden. There never was a place so complete'.[11]

In 1826 Prince Pückler-Muskau visited Woburn, when the

'fourth or fifth attendant awaited us . . . and showed us first several plumed parrots and other rare birds . . . As we walked out upon the open space our papageno whistled, and in an instant the air was literally darkened around us by flights of pigeons, chickens and heaven knows what birds. Out of every bush started gold and silver, pied and common, pheasants; and from the little lake a black swan galloped heavily forward, expressing his strong desire for food in tones like those of a fretful child'.[12]

However, this idyllic setting was the scene of one of the most disastrous successes in acclimatization during the 19th century, when the Duke introduced the grey squirrel at Woburn. More commendable was the breeding of the cereopsis geese. When the Duke's gander died, he wrote to William Yarrell, the Secretary of the Zoological Society on 2 July 1838,

> 'The Duke of Bedford presents his compliments to Mr Yarrell and begs to know whether he can spare him a Cereopsis male goose from the Zoological Gardens. The Duke of Bedford had his originally through the kindness of Lord Derby; but he is now in want of a male, and knows not where they are procured, until the Zool. Soc. should have 1 spare'.[13]

There was great enthusiasm for this goose, *Cereopsis novae-hollandiae*, which is a primitive Southern Australian species and distinctive in appearance. It is predominantly black and grey, but has a peculiar black bill with an extensive lime green cere. It was valued as an Australian exotic, rather than for its appearance. Following John Gould's epic journey to Australia and Tasmania in 1838–40 and the publication of his books on *The Birds of Australia* and *The Mammals of Australia*, all the species illustrated and described became prized commodities among collectors. His earlier *A Monograph of the Macropodidae or Family of Kangaroos*, in 1841–42 with 30 plates, had added to the interest in kangaroos, initially aroused by Sir Joseph Banks on Captain Cook's first voyage some seventy years before.

Herbrand, the 11th Duke of Bedford (1858–1940), collected animals whose descendants are living in the park today. He became a member of the Zoological Society in 1872, early showing his interest in animals. He was elected to the council in 1897 and became President in 1899. This duke built up the herd of European bison, specimens of which had originally been obtained for him by his cousin, Sir Odo Russell, while Secretary at the British Embassy in St Petersburg. They were a present from the Tsar of Russia, who was given two American bison in return. The large herd present in the park today has been nurtured from these modest beginnings.

Of far greater importance than the bison, however, was the extraordinary foresight of the Dukes of Bedford in obtaining Pére David deer, building up stocks and distributing them for safety into other collections in breeding numbers, until the species is now safe from extinction. The 11th Duke laid the foundation of this achievement when he imported five deer from various zoological collections on the Continent. The specimens in those foreign zoos later died out, while those at Woburn continued steadily to increase in number. The same duke was responsible for the great interest generated in the wild Przewalski horses, bred from a small group of five stallions and seven mares captured in Mongolia and the Gobi Desert, before he succeeded to the Dukedom.[14]

Apart from these spectacular species, the Duke imported forty-six species of deer, sixteen of antelope, two of gazelles, four of goats and five of sheep, many of which bred successfully in the beautiful, large grounds at Woburn Abbey.

The 12th Duke (as Lord Tavistock, before he succeeded to the dukedom in 1940) built up a magnificent aviary of rare parrots in part of his father's estate at Woburn. Because he accommodated them in very large enclosures, built over living vegetation, well provided with nesting boxes, even rare and difficult species multiplied satisfactorily.

In the 19th century the motivation changed from making collections of animals purely for entertainment, to keeping and breeding certain species for conservation, acclimatisation and for scientific reasons. In the 20th century, this diversity of purpose would increase even further.

DEALERS AND COLLECTORS

Chapter 14

'Just arrived, a fresh parcel of fine song canary birds'

For centuries, imported mammals and birds were destined only for the King. They were usually part of a gift from a fellow sovereign and brought by an ambassador returning from a tour of duty abroad. Such gifts were rare and we have the briefest of references to them in ancient pipe rolls and documents, otherwise full of important matters relating to the government of lands, armies, taxes and the court, so that the sudden intrusion of an order for a chain for a lion or rope for a bear always creates a surprise. Such ephemeral details among so many weighty matters strike one as bizarre. However, for centuries, leopards and lions were extremely uncommon anywhere in Europe, so were a valuable part of the English kings' possessions.

The first exotic bird species, i.e. non-European, were imported into England, often via European ports, in the 16th century. Christopher Columbus returned from the Canary Islands and Cuba in 1493 with some parrots, and Spanish ships brought the turkey and muscovy duck from central America between 1525 and 1530. The most sought-after species, however, were parrots.

Indian parakeets, Cuban amazons and macaws, and the *Ara ararauna* and *Ara macao*, were all imported before 1600, while the African grey parrot, *Psittacus erithacus*, from the west coast of Africa, became a favourite from the time of its first depiction by Lucas Cranach in a painting of paradise *circa* 1520. A similar story can be told of cockatoos arriving from the east.

By the time the Tudors were on the throne, the captains of merchant and naval vessels brought an increasing number and variety of species home with them. Merchant adventurers, intercepting Spanish vessels, plundered their holds and triumphantly brought into port species hitherto not seen in England. As England gained mastery of the seas, these plundered consignments included birds and a few mammals from the West Indies, Spanish South America and the Dutch East Indies. George Edwards reminds us that this looting was still being carried out as late as the 18th century. A bush-tailed monkey was brought to him, 'by Captain Jn Dobson of Rotherhithe, Capt. of a private ship of war who took it in an enemy's ship returning from the W, Indies in 1759'.[1]

With the establishment of the East India Company in 1600, normally acquired animals could arrive and sixty-five years later many of the colourful birds on board East Indiamen were there at the express wish of Charles II. Trading settlements at Bombay and Fort William were established and the Great Moghul sent an ambassador bearing gifts to the King. The Hudson's Bay Company similarly conveyed exciting new 'products' from Pennsylvania, the Carolinas and New York, as well as the territory up to the shores of Hudson Bay. Treaties with the Turks and Moors allowed Englishmen free access to the riches of the Mediterranean. The Africa Company ships carried home many of the early specimens that subsequently acquired the adjectives 'Barbary' and 'Guinea' in their names.

When these animals reached England, they were put on show, either at the Tower, or by inn-keepers, stall-holders at fairs and later by travelling showmen. Our records of these imports are as scattered as the animals' own final destinations around the country. We are dependant on diarists such as Pepys and Evelyn, letter-writers and the journals of travellers, particularly of foreign visitors to Britain, such as Saussure, Sophie La Roche, Uffenbach and Bielfeld. Even better indications of animals present in this country may be seen in paintings and engravings from the 17th century, when Francis Barlow was active, into the 18th century and onwards.

In the 17th century there had been a gentle stirring of interest in zoology. Topsell's *Historie of four-footed beastes*, 1607, sparked off an interest in mammals, and Ray & Willughby's *Ornithologia*, 1676, in birds. The following century, George Edwards, Thomas Pennant, Thomas Bewick and John Latham recorded and portrayed many new foreign species. Their books contain references to animals in private hands. Only at the end of the 17th century were birds, mammals and reptiles imported in sufficiently large numbers to warrant a few dealers establishing pet-shops.

The Bland family of Tower Dock, London were importing birds in small numbers by 1685. Thomas advertised shipments in the *London Gazette* (1685 No. 2077/4).

> 'These are to give notice, that there is lately come over from Germany, 700 Canary Birds:
> To be sold at reasonable rates at the Sign of the Black Bull on Tower Dock, by Thomas Bland'.

And again in 1692 (No. 2811/4).

> 'There is newly come from Germany a parcel of choice Canary Birds, choice Pidgeons, Turtle-Doves, an East-India Loury, Parrakeet, with several other Out-landish Birds: to be sold by Tho. Bland at the Black Bull at Tower-Dock, London, at reasonable rates'.

Michael Bland, probably another member of the family residing in the parish of St Botolph without Aldgate and trading near the port, inserted an advertisement for a much greater variety of species in the *Daily Post* on Thursday 17 February 1732,

> 'Just arrived, a fresh parcel of fine song canary birds of all colours, both Cocks & Hens, of the sort for breeding as well as singing; fine scarlet nightingales from the West Indies, small green Parroketes with red-Heads, with other sorts of Parroketes; a Scarlet Moccow from India; large Breeding two years old Pheasants; small India Fowls, large Hambourg Fowls, a parcel of large Fowls from Bruges in Flanders, large muscovy Ducks, large muscovy Geese, breeding Turtle-doves, several fine breeding Pigeons, fine Parrots, Peacocks & Peahens, a large Musk Cat from Guinea, with other rarities. To be sold by the Owner of them, Michael Bland, at the sign of the Tiger at Tower-Dock near Great Tower-hill'.

A few more dealers were included now in the London Directories, for example, 'Hare Wild Beast Man' in the 1730s. This decade also saw an increase in the pet trade. The Exeter 'Change menagerie owners acted as dealers, from 1773 to 1831 and William Gough who was dealing in live animals advertised as a 'Live poulterer, 99 Holborn Hill' from 1790 to 1793. Gough sold a macaque to John Hunter to be included, with a baboon from Bailey's shop,

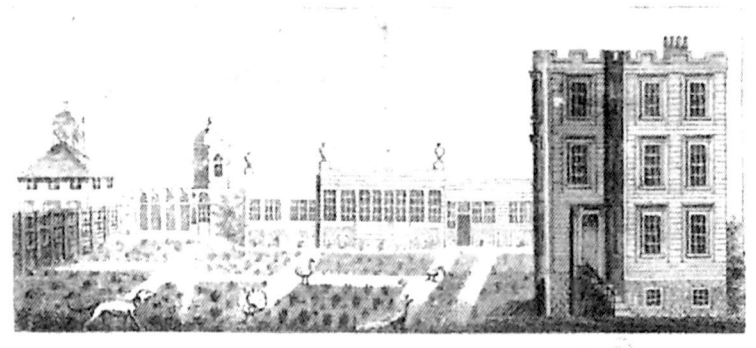

JOSHUA BROOKES,
ZOOLOGIST,
At his MENAGERY, in the New-Road, Tottenham-Court,
(Removed from Gray's-Inn-Gate, Holbourn.)
Buys and Sells and Exchanges all Sorts of FOREIGN BIRDS, QUADRUPEDS, &c. viz.

BUSTARDS.

CRANES.
Crown Bird of Africa
Cyrus from Asia
Numidian, or Demoisel
Whooping American.

CASSAWAYS.
CURACOAS
CUSHUA
COCKTTOOS
Small ditto.

DAWS, (Cornish)

DUCKS.
Aylesbury
Carolina
Dutch Topping
Hook bills
Manderil
Mule
Muscovy
Roan
Schild
Spanish
Turkish
Wild
Whistling

DOVES.
Black Ring
Cinnamon from Carolina
Cream from Barbary
Cuba Bald Pate
Cuba Blue Pate
Ground from Cuba
Nicomber
Oriental Chafer-wing'd
Passage from Carolina
Pea from ditto
Red-Rings from Senegal
Spotted Cape Triangular
White-Wings
White from Barbary
Widow from Senegal

EAGLES.
Carolina
Guinea
Norway
Russia

FLEMINGOS.
Major and Minor

FOWLS.
Algerines

Bantums
Chitagalls
Hampdens
Humborgh
Large Darking white
Poland
Rumpkins
Guinea fowls
Pyde
Purple
White and Black
Shag-Bags
Spanish
Silk Sumatra

FEN FOWLS.
Baldcoots
Danbirds
Easterlings
Golden Eyes
Garganeys
Shovel Bills
Teal
Widgeons
Guinea
Purple
Peele
White
Pyde
Common

GEESE.
Afracan
Brent
Canada
Chinese
Cospian
Cape
Greenland

HERONS.
Blue
Red
White

IBIS, or Secretary.
LOWRYQUETS
LUQUORS
LOWRYS.

MINOS

MACCAOS.
Blue
Deep Red
Green
Scarlet

Small Red from the Main.

OWLS.
Great Horned, from Aunspack
Large ditto, from Hudson's Bay
Small ditto, from Aunspach
Small ditto, from America

OSTRICH.
OLIVES
ORTOLANS.
American
European

PHEASANTS.
Chinese, Gold
Ditto, Silver
Ditto, Ring Necks
English, Py'd
Ditto, White

PEFOWLE.
Japhaneses
Pyde ditto
White ditto
Wild ditto

PEROS.
European
Oriental

PARTRIDGES.
American
Barbary
French }Red Leg'd
Portugal

PARROTS.
American
East India
Guinea
Portugal
Spanish Main.

PARROQUETS.
Large Ring
Necks
Ditto, with }India.
Red Wings
Small ditto,
Spotted
Small ditto,
with Red}Africa.
Heads

All Green
Do. Ring-neck'd
Ditto Grey }Africa
Heads, with
Yellow Breasts

All Yellow
with Orange
Breasts, and
All Green,
with Orange }America
Heads
Large Green,
with Red
Heads

QUAILS.
American
European
Oriental

SPOONBILLS.
SWANS.
STORKS.

SONG BIRDS.
Averduvats
Blue breasted Finches
Brazil Finches
Canaries Junk
Ditto Turn-Crowns
Ditto Mealy
Ditto Fancy
Ditto Brazil
Cardinals
Carolina Robins
Dominican Widow Birds
Ditto Pintail
Ditto Common
Grenadiers
Java Sparrows
Indian ditto
Large Blue Birds
Manakins
Mocking Bird
Mule Bird
Nuns
Purple Birds
Ring Ouzell
Small Blue Birds
Schombargos
Tropial of Cayan
Virginia Nightingale
Wax Bills.

Note, Proper Baskets, Coops, &c. provided for their Conveyance to any Part of the World, Birds, Poultry, curious Quadrupeds of all Sorts exchanged.

The advertisement sheet for Joshua Brookes, dealer in wild birds.

in a dual portrait by George Stubbs, painted c.1770–75. John Hunter also obtained the carcase of a large black bear from Patna, that had been kept alive in Gough's shop for many years, and the she-wolf that Hunter mated with his dog. Gough's shop was on Holborn Hill opposite St Andrew's Church.

George Edwards said that, in 1743, the bird merchants of London had 'grackles of different sorts' and the 'bird merchants in White Hart Yard in the Strand had Indian Sparrows (Loxia Malacca Linn.)'. Some of the dealers who sold live cage-birds and mammals had stalls in markets, such as the famous London meat and poultry market at Leadenhall, which not only sold cages of goldfinches, nightingales and other British species, but some less common birds imported from France and the Low Countries.

A man called Bailey had a shop in Piccadilly, about six doors away from the top of Haymarket, where John Hunter saw a zibet or civet and from whom he bought a baboon. His shop was taken over, prior to 1755, by a dealer who stayed in business longer than most and from his appearance, as well as his trade, was known in London as 'Wild-beast Brookes'. George Edwards called him a 'great dealer in foreign birds and curious poultry,' about 1755, and the author Thomas Pennant went to see him in 1768. Pennant was interested in a bird which Brookes showed him as a 'variety of the common pheasant which he thought came from China, the male of which had a white ring round its neck, the colors ressemble those of the common species but were more brilliant'.[2] A good number of these ring-necked pheasants were imported about this time and appeared on estates in different parts of England.

Another of Joshua Brookes's patrons was the Prince Regent, who bought animals from him from the late 1780s onwards. Brookes ceased trading about 1810 when Herring took over his shop, that Timbs described as 'an old wooden house at the western corner of Brook-street, New-road'. The new road was Euston Road where members of the Herring family were dealers into the 1870s.[3]

Sophie La Roche, in London in 1786, was interested in the variety of advertisements in the morning papers and listed some from the paper published 7 September, which included, 'Two large green tortoises for sale, which can be pond-reared or else fed'. She also enjoyed shopping expeditions and, when writing about the district between Bloomsbury Square and the Monument (to the Great Fire of 1666, built 1671–77, at 202 feet the tallest isolated stone column in the world), she said,

> 'We also passed shops where animals were for sale, which goods were both novel to us and comical. Peacocks were placed on pretty perches, bright cages with song-sters hanging in between; there were cases of monkeys, large bird-cages containing turtledoves, others with fine domestic fowls; lap-dogs of every type followed in nicely padded kennels; pointers lay at the bottom on leads, and by their side baskets of all kinds of game – all grouped so artistically that the whole made a charming picture'.[4]

It sounds as though this pet-shop keeper had little to learn about window-display and the art of attracting customers.

Despite the traders, at the end of the 18th century, as soon as a ship docked, keen aviculturalists and travelling menag-erists were waiting to get on board. Lady Mary Coke went to meet an East India ship that docked at Woolwich in 1769. She wrote,

> 'When we arrived where "The London" lay, we were hoisted aboard in a Chair, which was a very easy convey-ance. I was looking about for east India goods; a number of fine Birds presented themselves before me; an Noble Mino that I wanted to buy but was told the Capt. had brought it as a present for the lady who calles herself the Duchess of Kingston, there were, I think, in two Cages about twenty small birds; two of which the Capt. made me a present of'.

A few days later she wrote again of these 'The two little birds the east India Capt gave me, he said were called black caps, but they seem to me the same as some of the Duchess of Montagu's & I think she calls them wax bills'. Later she referred to them as her 'two little China Birds' and said they were 'in perfect health'. When she went to see her friend and relation, Lady Albemarle, on 12 July 1774, she wrote, somewhat enviously, 'to Lady Albemarle's whose house is a sight from the quantity of foreign birds; all the bird shops in Town cannot produce half the number'. Even allowing for exaggeration, this points to the smallness of the trade in bird shops at this date.[5]

JAMES PILTON's MANUFACTORY,
KING's ROAD, CHELSEA, MIDDLESEX.

THE INTERIOR OF THE MENAGERIE,
Displaying Ornamental Works for Country Residences, and Specimens of the Invisible Fence.

Mercier and Chervet, printers,
32, Little Bartholomew Close.

Wood engraving of the interior of the menagerie, c.1800, of James Pilton and William Pilton, who made 'Pleasure Ground Fences' and wire-work bird cages from 1791–1811. A few of their menagerie birds can be seen surrounded by examples of their wirework.

James and William Pilton catered for aviculturalists by selling birds, as well as advertising as wireworkers at their 'Manufactory, King's Road, Chelsea' from c.1791–c.1812. Faulkner, writing about *Chelsea* in 1810 stated that 'In the King's Road is a grand menagerie for foreign and English birds, the property of Mr James Pilton; as also his manufactory of light fences for inclosing lawns, shrubberies and ornamental walks; which is very properly called *Invisible Fences*: as at a comparatively small distance they vanish from the eye, and leave the prospect free and uninterrupted'. In the 1805–07 London directories, their entry was more specific, 'William Pilton, wireworker and bird cage maker 204 Piccadilly & King's Road, Chelsea'. Pilton's stock was strong on ducks and geese, both wild, including Greenland, laughing, Cape, China, Canada, and domestic varieties then popular, Rouen, Carolina, and hookbill. The Piltons also dealt in foreign songbirds.[6]

In the early years of the 19th century George Wombwell traded in all kinds of animals and, by the time he had accumulated sufficient species to start touring the country with a menagerie, his contacts with the port of London pilots and captains were well established. Wombwell's stock was always changing, as he continually bought and sold, so that his menageries could be visited with interest each time they came to town.

Wombwell would also keep a close watch on the Castang's shop. These East End bird merchants were first a D. Castang of Hampstead Road, dealing in waterfowl, pheasants, doves, songbirds, 'firebirds, lovebirds and Mountain witches, Vulture Pigeons (i.e. Nicobar pigeons) from Africa and the east', in 1807–36, then a Philip Castang c.1836–1920. Philip was a licensed dealer in live game at 3, Ship Tavern Passage and a bird dealer at 158, City Road. He also supplied foxes. The Earl of Derby bought extensively for Knowsley from Castang between 1807 and 1814. Sidney Castang who succeeded another Philip in 1920 was a poulterer, so the Castang family were in the animal importing business for well over a century.[7]

In the early years of the 19th century another prosperous dealer in small seed-eaters and parrots was named G. Kendrick, operating c.1807–19 at the 'Royal Menageries, St James Church, Piccadilly'. He was trading in birds imported from Brazil by the early 1800s. Sydenham Edwards, a bird artist, haunted Kendrick's shop, sometimes buying birds when he could afford them, such as a 'Red-breasted Thrush' from America and a 'Great Crested Grosbeak', other times, when they were as expensive as a 'Pagoda Thrush' which sold for 12 guineas in 1808, drawing them in the shop. Like other bird dealers at that date, G. Kendrick, also sold gold and silver fishes, some imported from Brazil. Sir Robert Heron noted, 17 June 1815, that he had bred gold fish for six years in an aquarium and had about eleven hundred of all ages. Originally six had come from Burleigh and six from Kendrick's, Piccadilly and he had since then purchased what `Kendrick called Braszil fish' from him, but Heron said they did not differ from his others.[8] In 1819 Sir Robert Heron purchased three Brazilian tortoises from Kendrick. At one time Kendrick had nylghaus for sale.

Arthur Harrison's bird shop in 'Parliament-street' was visited c.1810 by George Graves and Dr John Latham, for new birds they wanted to include in their ornithological books.

William Herring took over Joshua Brookes's shop at Euston Road, that had a good collection of animals in the first half of the 19th century. Besides birds and fishes listed on his letterhead, he also dealt in mammals, notably zebus, antelopes, East Indian squirrels, ichneumons and axis deer.

Letter heading of the dealer William Herring who succeeded Joshua Brookes at the 'Menagerie, New Road'.

Drawing of Pidcock, dealer in birds and beasts, pen and ink and watercolour. The thatched hut is on the bank of the Thames with bird cages on the walls. (Yale Center for British Art).

In 1838 he had some rare peacock pheasants and sold some to the Earl of Derby. He allowed the artist J. L. Agasse to study his stock, resulting in paintings of an East India bull and a llama in 1848. Agasse reciprocated by painting a portrait of Mrs Herring, who was related to Edward Cross. William and Ann Herring named their son William Cross Herring when he was born in 1821 and baptised at St. Clement Dane. This was another instance of animal-trade dealers, menagerie owners and circus families frequently intermarrying. William Cross Herring became a naturalist.[9]

Gilbert Pidcock, with a travelling menagerie on the road in the summer and a base in Exeter 'Change, was also a trader. In the early 1800s he was selling monkeys, pheasants, doves, quails and parrots, and in 1807 had a consignment of Java sparrows, avadavats and 'nutmeg spice Cinnamon' birds for sale, besides a small monkey.[10] Edward Cross, from 1817, followed Gilbert Pidcock's example at Exeter 'Change and continued to trade, exchanging and selling live animals, as well as keeping the menagerie. Trading there was an important part of the business for over fifty years. It was also a sizeable part of the business of other travelling menagerie owners. George Wombwell was a frequent visitor on board ships docked at London until he became too preoccupied in travelling with his three menageries in the 1840s, after which he left the business of acquiring animals to his agent in London, Charles Jamrach. The 'Wombwell' listed in the London directories under 'Birds and Live Animals – Dealers' in 1851 and 1871 was George Wombwell's successor, still trading under his name.

In London, in the 19th century, the number of 'Birds and Live Animals – Dealers', under which heading the London directories listed them, grew steadily. In 1842 there were 14 animal dealers, in 1851 there were 32, in 1861 there were 47, in 1882 there were 81 and in 1892 the number had risen to 118.

Liverpool, with its thriving port, also had live animal traders throughout the 19th century. William Bullock (who later became a famous museum owner after he moved to London) not only exhibited his museum in Liverpool at Lord Street, 1800–04, then on the corner of Church Street and Whitechapel, 1804–09, but also did a brisk trade in live birds. The Earl of Derby, who had an aviary at nearby Knowsley Hall, Prescot, bought from Bullock, also from John Smart at the same date. Thomas Atkins (who ran the Liverpool Zoological Gardens in Boaler Street, between 1832 and 1863), James Mather (trading in skins and live birds) and Joseph Hegan (importing alpacas, llamas and vicuna, as well as condors from South America), selling to the Earl of Derby and Sir Titus Salt, who hoped to acclimatise alpacas in the Pennines, traded in Liverpool in the 1820s and 1830s. John Bates of Liverpool traded in the 1840s and was collecting in Central America, based in Belize, from June 1842 to September 1843. George Armstrong, ideally situated at no.2, India Buildings, was procuring animals for the Earl of Derby and skins for the Scottish naturalist Sir William Jardine of Dumfriesshire, who bought birds from India, Java and Sumatra from him c.1837. Armstrong advocated sending out a collector to South America as a solution to the problem of getting specific species brought home alive, rather than depending on *ad hoc* collections.

There were small traders (W. B. Page of Southampton operating c.1834 was one in other ports) taking advantage of sailors wishing to dispose of animals picked up on their travels.

Lovell Augustus Reeve (1814–65) began to trade about 1840 in natural objects and became a publisher of natural history books at his London Emporium, King William Street, Strand. John Baily combined dealing in birds with a poulterer's business,1834–50, but had some nice species for sale in 1834, when he was offering storks, honey buzzards and white peafowl.

Thomas Andrews, c.1850, was a bird merchant, also a cage maker, wire worker, dealer in foreign and British birds, animals, gold and silver fish, birds and a beast preserver, at the Conservatory, Pantheon, Oxford Street. This combination of three trades of dealer in live birds, taxidermist and cage maker was not common when he was dealing c.1850s. The author William Yarrell advised the Reverend J. Dixon to go to Mr Andrews for some *Geopelia cuneata*, but when Dixon got there, the specimens which had been kept at the Pantheon Bazaar were all dead. These diamond doves had come all the way from Australia, surviving the months' long journey, to die unsold in the dealer's hands.[11] Dealers in skins, of course, had fewer losses and they were numerous too in the directories. Andrews, being a taxidermist as well as live bird dealer, could minimise his losses to some extent.

Two major names stand out, among all the scores of dealers in London, representing the two largest families in the pet trade, Leadbeater and Jamrach. The Leadbeaters operated from c.1805 until 1875. Benjamin Leadbeater (1773–1837) opened a shop that was to become the haunt of the most eminent naturalists of the first half of the 19th century. His imports provided birds, previously un-named, for John Gould, Nicholas A. Vigors and Dr T. Horsfield.

Vigors described and named after him *Platycercus leadbeateri*, a rosella, in 1831; Vigors and Horsfield had previously named *Sericulus chrysocephalus,* the Australian regent bowerbird, from a female supplied by Leadbeater in 1827. Benjamin married Elizabeth Almley in 1796 and a son John was born in 1804.[12] The family moved south to London after the birth of John and Benjamin was listed in a directory of 1823–24 as a 'Bird & Beast Stuffer' of 20, Brewer Street, Golden Square. He is known to have supplied skins to collectors at least ten years before this.[12] The American bird artist J. J. Audubon went to see Benjamin in 1828 and saw only stuffed specimens.

Benjamin's son John took over the business from his father in 1837 and in 1841 he appeared twice in the directory, as a bird and beast stuffer, but more importantly, also as a 'Naturalist'. By 1851 John was listed as an 'Ornithologist to H. M. & Royal family', still based at 19, Brewer Street. John (1804–52) did a brisk business in live birds, was highly respected as a knowledgeable 'ornithologist' and was elected a Fellow of the Royal Society.

John had two sons who were also 'Ornithologists', like their father, in the census of 1851, Benjamin, born c.1830, and John, born c.1832, both in the parish of Westminster St James. John went to Melbourne, Australia, where he traded as a taxidermist to c.1875. The London business ended c.1852 with the death of his father.

The Leadbeaters had dominated the London scene in the first half of the 19th century. The Jamrach family took over this position as the most celebrated animal dealers in London in Victorian days. The family was German, established by Jacob Gerhard Gotthold Jamrach (1792–1860) in Germany, before he sent his elder son Anton to establish a branch of the business in London in 1840. Jacob died in 1841 and was succeeded by his younger brother, Carl Johann Christian (1814–91), always known in England as Charles Jamrach. His grandson joined him in the business in 1876 and inherited it on his death, but by then trade was waning and died out with the advent of World War I.[13]

Mr Jamrach's Wild Beast Shop, East London.

In March 1861 Jamrach acquired '6,000 Australian grass parakeets' brought in on the clipper ships *Orient* and *Golden Star*. He said that he called them cockatiels from the name kaketieljes applied by Dutch sailors to the first specimens brought to him c.1850. (John Gould *The birds of Australia*, volume V, plate 45, Cockatoo parrakeet).

Jamrach's shop was in the rough area near the docks, known as Ratcliff Highway. He acquired a near-monopoly of the wild animal trade through the port. Some suggested it was owing to his close resemblance to Prince Albert, which inspired respect, but he built up the business to the point where several of his employees bought from the sailors as ships came in and he had agents on the Continent and in other British ports.

Wheatley and Cunningham in *London past and present* gave a description of Jamrach's operations.

'Nos 179 & 180 Ratcliff Highway (or St George St.) is the remarkable establishment of Charles Jamrach, naturalist – the largest dealer in wild animals in Europe, where you may at any time purchase anything in that line from an elephant, giraffe or rattlesnake to a doormouse or Java sparrow. Here and in his store at Old gravel Lane, close by, you may be supplied with hyaenas by the dozen, lions in neat little lots of twenty to five and twenty each; parcels of giraffes, snakes, or boa-constrictors; and samples of tigers, buffaloes, eagles, monkeys, bears & kangaroos'.[14]

'The wild beast shops in this street [Ratcliff Highway, now St George Street] have often been sketched by modern essayists. The yards in the neighbourhood are crammed with lions, hyenas, pelicans, tigers, and other animals in demand among the proprietors of menageries. As many as ten to fifteen lions are often in stock at one time, and sailors come here to sell their pets and barter curiosities. The ingenious way that animals are stored in these out-of-the-way places is well worth seeing'. (Thornbury & Walford *Old and new London*, 1873, vol. 2: 132, 134).

MR. JAMRACH'S WILD BEAST DEPÔT, RATCLIFF HIGHWAY

Engraving of the interior of Jamrach's shop with its small cages and cramped conditions. (*The Graphic*, 24 July 1875: 92).

An article in *Nature*, January 1870 (p.317), listed all the occupants of his store and one wonders how he managed to keep and feed such a huge number.[15]

Jamrach's shop was in the parish of the Reverend Harry Jones of St George's and the rector wrote an amusing account of his near-neighbour's activities, in 1875,

'I was much struck the other day with the pose and expression of a posse of owls on view. They sat side by side full of thoughtful silent wisdom, with just a twinkle of possible humour in their eyes, like judges <u>in banco</u>' while in an oblong recess within the shop beyond them there were twenty-four large and perfectly white cockatoos standing in two precise rows, shoulder to shoulder, and giving out their best notes, exactly like a surpliced choir. In another room were two thousand parroquets flying loosely about, or clustering like flies upon the window frames in ineffectual attempts to get out. The incessant flutter of this multitude of captives filled the air of the apartment so thickly with tiny floating feathers that they settled on our coats like flakes of snow. We came out powdered . . . There is a great demand for talking parrots. Mr Jamrach always has orders in his books for more than he can supply'.[16]

The Rev. Harry Jones said that Jamrach kept no written list of the cost of his animals and that he had no need to advertise, for he had customers in all the zoological museums in Europe and the Sultan had 'been one of the largest buyers of his tigers and parrots'. He used to announce his consignments in newspapers in London, Paris, Berlin and Vienna with just a plain statement that such animals had arrived 'at Jamrach's', with no address being necessary, so well-known was this dealer everywhere. The Rev. H. Jones added that, 'Beside that of Mr Jamrach's we have divers shops for the sale of birds, especially parrots, and I imagine that many a sailor turns his collection of foreign curiosities into money within the limits of St Georges'.[17]

The sailors were now bringing home a far greater variety of birds and mammals since the length of the voyage had been shortened by the use of steamships and our knowledge of foreign species increased rapidly as a result. In addition, expeditions were being organised by aristocratic collectors, the Zoological and Geographical Societies and others. How Robert Cecil, Earl of Salisbury, would have envied these 19th century earls and dukes. In 1607 when he made application for leave to send out a man in the East India Company ships to bring home, 'parratts, munkies and marmasitts for his lordship', he had received the brusque reply that, 'as the man may die and his things miscarrie', it would be more convenient if the company's servants provided what was required.[18] Officialdom must frequently have stifled enterprise in a similar manner over the intervening centuries.

Sir Joseph Banks showed how to collect in depth while accompanying Captain Cook on his first voyage round the world, 1768–71, from which he returned with quantities of skins, shells, and artefacts. Collecting live animals was an entirely different proposition. The simplest way to achieve a supply of live animals was to employ the services of a relation, diplomat, missionary, doctor or similar professional acquaintance living in a foreign country, who sent out natives to collect fauna. Such persons would have gardens, or sufficient space to build holding pens to rest the animals after journeys from the interior, sometimes four hundred miles and more to the coast, until a ship arrived to transport them to Britain. Few men wanted the toil and responsibility for feeding and watering a collection of wild creatures in their gardens for weeks at a time, but there were some. One of the most successful was the Reverend John Fry in South Africa, who supplied the Earl of Derby with some remarkable animals for Knowsley.

The London dealer, G. H. Garnett of 29, Queen Anne's Street, Cavendish Square, negotiated between the Earl of Derby and the Reverend John Fry in South Africa. Garnett not only dealt with collectors directly in the field, but he also notified the Earl of Derby when ships entered port with cargoes likely to be of interest to him.

Garnett listed such imports, with their likely cost, to Knowsley. Even with a willing helper such as John Fry, the costs were prohibitive. Shipping, with accompanying fodder, cost pounds sterling per mammal. The number of deaths *en-route* caused much loss and argument. Though unfair, it was the supplier who stood the loss, despite careless ships' personnel being to blame on occasion.

It was not until the mid-19th century that collectors with contracts giving specific instructions as to which species were to be collected, how they were to be transported and an agreed salary, were sent on expeditions. To send a man to Africa, India or South America cost a great sum to keep him in the field supplied with a gun and ammunition and the means to construct cages, purchase baskets for birds, and pay natives. It cost over £400 per annum, plus shipping costs, to finance Louis Fraser's expedition to Africa and even more for Devereux Fuller to collect in India and Singapore in 1846. The Earl of Derby and Lord Rothschild had the means at their disposal, hardly anyone else. Even they balked at financing a collector singly and would join another menagerie owner in sending out a man. The Earl of Derby joined with William Hooker of Kew to send Joseph Burke to collect plants, mammals and birds in North America. Burke had been highly successful in Africa, but the frozen lands round Hudson's Bay in winter defeated him and he was called back in disgrace, having done little or no collecting in three years. He was one of the very few failures, but others got little back safely through no fault of their own, due to adverse weather conditions, unexpected outbreaks of war, recalcitrant natives, shipwreck, floods, over optimistic reports of fauna in the area to which they were sent and a host of other reasons.

Some collectors went as agents for several dealers, for example, J. E. Warwick was an agent for Herring and Cross, while also collecting giraffes for the Zoological Gardens of London and Surrey in 1844. He proposed to go to catch a hippopotamus in 1847, but the British Consul in Cairo (C. A. Murray) asked for one from Ibrahim Pasha who sent troops to the White Nile. They caught a small male on the island of Obaysch, a name passed on to the animal. Obaysch arrived on a P & O steamship in May 1850, before being put on a train to London. The advent of steam was of enormous benefit to collectors who could get their cargoes home from India and Africa, from the 1840s onwards, in weeks rather than months. Even difficult, large animals like the hippopotamus and rhinoceros could now be shipped and there was less strain for more delicate and highly nervous passengers, such as antelopes. Jamrach built up his large network of collectors around the world and could communicate his requirements to them more speedily while they were in the field after the advent of steam.

Collectors who went on their own account, returning with their live cargo, took enormous financial risks. The results of two years' collecting might be lost from gales and high seas on the way home. Sending the animals on in advance in the care of sea captains, whose first priority they certainly were not, led to many losses. The rewards could be considerable, with hitherto unknown mammals fetching scores of pounds and even birds, ten or more guineas each. Much depended on the condition of the animals when they arrived in port and buyers drove a hard bargain if the animals were not in the best of health.

Menagerie owners preferred to have their animals collected free of charge, but could only achieve this if relatives abroad could be persuaded to assist them. The aristocracy had a network of contacts in the Foreign Office or in Embassies abroad and these were approached to pay natives to collect. Few wanted the enormous trouble involved and only when they were keen animal lovers themselves were they persuaded to cooperate.

Today there are still animal collectors in the field and pet shops around the world. The main improvement for the animals being transported in the 20th century was the reduction in stress by the speed of air transport. Even so, the death rate while being captured and in transit remains high. It is a trade that many would like to see stopped, but the strong desire of many more to experience the thrill of standing close enough to a wild animal to see, smell and hear it, if not touch it, will ensure continuance of this trade for many years to come.

20th CENTURY

Chapter 15

'What shall we do? We'll go to the Zoo'

This suggestion for an entertaining day out appeared in large letters on the sides of London buses in the 1970s. A more appropriate question at that time was 'what kind of Zoo?' There were more collections of animals from which to choose than at any other period, serving different purposes. The word 'Menagerie' was no longer used and the Zoological Gardens, Regent's Park, long ago had been reduced to 'Zoo' after a music hall ditty, *Walking in the Zoo on Sunday,* became a 'hit' in 1867.

'Walking in the Zoo' The cover for the music of a song celebrating the Sunday visitors' day to Regent's Park to see the animals in the Zoological Gardens. It was this song that brought the word 'zoo' into popular usage from 1868.

In the 20th century there was a shift in the way in which the public viewed collections of animals, with some opposition to the idea of keeping animals caged that forced a new appraisal of the justification for doing so. There was also a change in the way owners, both private and institutional, assembled their collections. This was evident in the range of species kept by the last private aristocratic collector, Walter, Lord Rothschild, the Zoological Society of London and later Whipsnade, private zoos for conservation purposes that were open to the public, the safari parks for public entertainment and education and finally the royal attitude to wildlife within their estates. In the 20th century both the full range of purposes for keeping animals in captivity and all man's attitudes to animals, aesthetic, economic, entertainment, and scientific, were clearly evident. These factors were brought into sharp focus by the Second World War that divided the century into two distinct halves for wild animal traders and keepers.

Private Menageries and Avaries

The last private aristocratic menagerie created for the owner's private study, which flourished from the late 19th into the early 20th century, belonged to Lionel Walter, 2nd Baron Rothschild (1868–1937), who inherited the family characteristic of collecting mania, to which he added a fanatical love of animals and a phenomenal photographic memory. He studied birds and butterflies intensively and could remember the scientific names, localities, and habitats of thousands of species by the time he was aged ten.[1]

The family moved to Tring Park in Hertfordshire in 1872–73 and in 1878 Lord Rothschild began collecting for his museum. The museum was his foremost concern throughout his life. He and his curators, Ernst Hartert and Karl Jordan, with the help of well over 400 collectors in the field, during 50 years amassed 300,000 bird skins, 200,000 birds' eggs and two and a quarter million butterflies and moths besides beetles, fleas, sponges and snakes. Most of this museum may still be viewed at Tring, where it now forms part of our national Natural History Museum collections. At the Tring museum descriptions were compiled of new species that ran to some five thousand and over 250 species bear his name as the discoverer or contributor to their first descriptions.

Besides this astonishing accumulation of museum specimens, Lord Rothschild owned living birds and mammals
throughout his life. As a student he took a flock of kiwis up
to Magdalen College, Cambridge. When he returned home
to Tring he had animals roaming freely in the park, including several species of kangaroo, zebras, wild horses and
asses, a tame wolf, emus and rheas, turkeys, marabou stork,
cranes, a dingo with pups, capybara, pangolins, deer, spiny
anteater and giant lizards. This was a different selection of
exotic creatures than formerly inhabited the paddocks of
aristocratic estates. He personally trained three zebras and
a donkey to pull a trap that he drove down Piccadilly and
into the forecourt of Buckingham Palace, where Princess
Alexandra terrified everyone by attempting to pat the leading zebra.

When the Przewalskyi wild horses were discovered in
1881, he obtained a pair for Tring. A policy of procuring
pairs for breeding purposes was followed, rather than single specimens for the sake of ownership, but this could not
always be achieved. Quaggas were always at a premium
and he could only purchase a single specimen. Wallabies
were in greater supply by this date and six went to Tring.
He introduced the fat or edible dormouse to Tring in 1902
and it has since colonised the Chilterns.

Lord Rothschild's deep knowlege of zoology and its
taxonomy made him aware that, to study a given group,
it was essential to see as many individuals of that species
as possible. When he wished to write a monograph on the

Lord Rothschild driving a
zebra 'four in hand'.

cassowaries, a group of birds of which he was particularly fond, he imported a large number and kept them alive (there were eventually 65 transferred as mounted specimens in the museum). These and the emus and rheas lived beyond the ha-ha dividing the house lawn from the park. He allowed as many animals as consistent with safety to roam freely in large paddocks.

He became aware of the plight of giant tortoises in the Galapagos while writing a joint monograph on them with Albert Günther. His intervention to rescue the giant tortoises was well-timed and based on a fear of their extinction. He negotiated to lease various islands in the Indian Ocean, especially Aldabra, where the remaining population could live undisturbed and achieved this in 1900. Unfortunately he had to sell the island in 1908, but over 60 specimens had been sent to Tring where he carefully observed the difference in behaviour between the species.

Lord Rothschild's collection of living animals was first made for the pleasure of owning and studying exotic and beautiful species, but this developed to become the most scientifically based private collection ever put together in this country. Some of the butterflies and moths he bred were added to form long series of specimens of a single species and today scientists go to Tring from all over the world to study this material, for such a collection could not be put together again today.

Lord Rothschild riding on one of his giant tortoises from the Galapagos at Tring.

When Lord Rothschild died in 1937, several years, post-war, elapsed before other aristocratic collections, called Safari Parks, were opened. The first was at Longleat, followed by Windsor, Woburn, Blair Drummond near Stirling, Knowsley and Cameron, Loch Lomond. Safari Park is a clever name, making people feel this is the real thing, the right way, to see animals in natural, mixed groups in wide, open parks.

It is noteworthy that the first ones were all placed within the grounds of families noted for menageries in the 18th and 19th centuries, first Longleat in 1966 in conjunction with the Chipperfield family, who also helped found Woburn in 1970 and Knowsley in 1971, but this time people were enclosed in cars, the animals free within large paddocks. In Scotland a safari park was opened at Blair Drummond in 1970 and another at Cameron, Loch Lomond, two years later with bears a prime attraction. But, however good the landscaping and management, there is no denying that these collections are mainly for entertainment, and rather less for educational purposes. However, the experience gained by the old menagerie keepers for the greater comfort and welfare of their captives provided a source of valuable knowledge for later forms of menageries and zoos.

The idea of going on safari, safely inside one's own vehicle, was an inspiration which had its origins in the television safaris of Michaela and Armand Denis. Television has had a deep and lasting influence on the public perception of wildlife. While Michaela's attitude was sentimental, this has been carefully and skilfully corrected for many years now by the calm, matter of fact programmes fronted by Sir David Attenborough, who lets the animals exhibit themselves naturally, with short explanations of some of the finer points that might escape the attention of the viewer when occurring at speed on the film. The whole tenor of the presentation changed from merely admiring the beauty and 'cuteness' of the animals, to an appreciation of them as part of a wider picture of nature. Latterly, stress was laid on their plight as their habitat has been destroyed and the need for conservation of both species and living space has become acute.

Far more people now go on safari themselves, visiting the African game parks that were set up for conservation purposes post 1945. Having experienced seeing animals behaving naturally within their own habitat, a change in attitude on the part of those people fortunate to have this experience soon became felt. There was a revulsion against caged animals in zoos and zoo owners had to justify their keeping of each species. The names Otter Trust and Ornamental Pheasant Trust (since 1961 Norfolk Wildlife Park and Pheasant Trust) reflect not only the function of these collections, but an awareness that the name must make it obvious. Specialist zoos to breed endangered species were established, such as Gerald Durrell's Jersey Wildlife Preservation Trust. Since its founding in 1963, the successful breeding of Rothschild's mynah (*Leucopsar rothschildi*), the white eared pheasant (*Crossoptilon crossoptilon drouynii*), the thick-billed parrot (*Rhynchopsitta pachyrhyncha*), St Lucia parrot (*Amazona versicolor*) and others has enabled some birds to be distributed and returned to their native homes. Gerald Durrell's career (1925–95) reflected the changes in the 20th century. He trained as a keeper at Whipsnade Zoo before collecting animals for zoos, then he established his own collection of animals in need of conservation.

Sir Peter Scott provided safe refuge for ducks and geese on wetlands at The Wildfowl Trust at Slimbridge in Gloucestershire, Peakirk in Northamptonshire and Welney in Norfolk. The breeding programme at Slimbridge enabled some nénés or Hawaiian geese to be returned to Hawaii and the neighbouring island of Maui. Other repatriations of note are the Arabian oryx to Oman and Jordan, where they are now breeding in the wild. Twenty-two rare Père David deer from the herd at Woburn Abbey were flown to China in 1984, nearly one hundred years after the 11th Duke of Bedford had imported some from the Chinese Imperial Hunting Park of Nan Hia Ze, south of Peking (pp. 223–224).

The late 19th and early 20th century enthusiasm for naturalising wool-bearing and meat species to supplement or improve our own breeds has continued now on llama and ostrich farms. The practice of hybridisation, which often threw up infertile offspring, has now moved on. Artificial insemination and the implantation of an embryo from a rare species into a host common species is speeding up the increase in numbers of endangered species. Rare birds can be induced to re-lay when their first clutch is removed to an incubator, so increasing their numbers faster than in the wild. Man's interference in the breeding of wild animals can be done constructively.

London Zoo, founded in 1826, became increasingly old-fashioned looking, largely because it has always suffered from a lack of finance. Despite this, it has fulfilled the original purpose of its foundation and made a great contribution to the science of zoology. From the beginning there was a dissecting room in the Society's offices and many famous scientists have worked there following Sir Richard Owen, who performed a post mortem on the Zoo's first orang-utan as early as 1829. Vital records of management, diseases and treatments date from the Zoo's inception. One of the outstanding contributions in the 20th century was the enormous strides it made in the veterinary department. Following the appointment of a zoo veterinary surgeon, Oliver Graham-Jones, in 1951, the first animal hospital was built there. Many techniques used by vets around the world were pioneeered at the London Zoo.[2]

Chimpanzees' tea parties were abandoned in 1972, despite being crowd-pullers, because their training humanised them to some degree. It was considered preferable to leave the groups of chimps together, not isolate some for training and then have problems re-integrating them with their own kind. The alternative, presenting their food in a manner which made them search for it within their enclosure, produced natural behaviour, kept the group together and promoted better breeding opportunities. This exemplifies

Young chimpanzees at London Zoo enjoying a teaparty. Photographed by F. W. Bond.

Copyright   NO. 27. YOUNG CHIMPANZEES AT TEA   Photo by F. W. Bond the change of emphasis in zoos, from promoting unnatural, to encouraging natural behaviour.

The London Zoo's biggest crowds in its history gathered round the polar bear enclosure to witness a success in breeding. Brumas, born in 1950, must have been the most famous polar bear in history, certainly the most visited and observed. His fame has been overtaken only by Goldie the golden eagle who delighted Londoners and the media by evading the keepers' attempts to recapture him for ten days in 1965.

The Snowdon Aviary, designed in 1965 to give birds a good deal of space to fly freely and nest in more natural surroundings, was another highlight in the Zoo's history. People can walk through this huge aviary with its cantilevered bridge, cliffs and waterfalls and have the birds singing, nesting, fighting, roosting, flying and feeding all around them. Being in the middle of an exhibit is a far more stimulating experience than being on the edge looking in.

The beginning of the more enlightened attitude to animals at the Zoo can be dated to the appointment of a new Secretary, Sir Peter Chalmers Mitchell (Secretary 1903–35). He was firmly in favour of fresh air and, while providing warmth and shelter for the animals, also allowed them access to the outside world where they surprised everyone by flourishing and improving in health. Lions rolling in snow was amazing, but finally convinced the sceptics that it was unwise to keep animals, even those from tropical climates, permanently indoors. He also favoured panoramic displays for the animals and, in 1913, built the Mappin Terraces. His most important contribution to the health of the zoo animals was the foundation of Whipsnade Park in 1927, where 480 acres of Bedfordshire farmland were turned into the first completely open zoo in the world. Large groups of different species of animals in spacious paddocks browsed peacefully together. When it was opened in 1931 a new era of breeding rare specimens in captivity began, including the Père David deer, some of which were presented to Peking zoo in 1956. The first cheetah cub bred in Britain was born in 1967, followed by many more. The water mammals exhibit, opened in 1972, was then among the finest of its kind in the world.[3]

Credit for much of the good zoo practices in the early 20th century is due to Carl Hagenbeck, who created the

A bison on the hillside at Whipsnade, photographed by F. W. Bond.

Copyright

AMERICAN BISON, WHIPSNADE

Photo by F. W. Bond, F.R.P.S.

imaginative park for wild animals at Stellingen near Hamburg after purchasing a large flat field in 1900. He was a master landscaper and skilfully created suitable habitats for the animals, with ditches instead of fences, canals, moats and hedges instead of walls and iron bars. His influence in England was first evident in Chalmers's Mappin Terraces for bears and sheep and has continued since in the Charles Clore Pavilion for small mammals, with a section for nocturnal animals where day is turned into night, and Michael Sobells Pavilion for Apes and Monkeys, where the animals live in family groups as in the wild, but with private areas to which mothers and infants can retreat.

This is the aim now, to provide a more natural environment to encourage natural behaviour including breeding which is crucial for the long-term survival of a large number of species. Zoos are more than menageries. They are gene pools for collections of species, some of which will become extinct in the wild. They are medical resources, for example, the capybara have compounds in their blood that can combat leukaemia, and we are only just beginning to discover such assets. They are educational sources and may be entertaining at the same time.

Travelling and Commercial Menageries

Travelling menageries, where close confinement of the animals in cages for travelling purposes and training them to behave anthropomorphically, ensured that this type of collection fell out of favour and they dwindled in numbers until they ceased to exist independently in the 20th century.[4]

Although other menagerie owners could not compete with Wombwell and Bostock, nor become as wealthy, they could still make a living in the last quarter of the 19th century. Ernest Henry Bostock entered the field in September 1883 and his number two menagerie began travelling in February 1889 with a third in October 1892 which he had bought from Frank Hall (called Barnham's Menagerie). Bostock also had bought out the small menagerie of John (who died 1888) then William Day in 1891, setting the trend for far fewer travelling menageries in the 20th century. Bostock wrote in 1927, 'all that remains of all these wandering teachers of natural history is my own original menagerie', which had earlier belonged to his great uncle George Wombwell. Another menagerist William Sedgewick was in business in the 1860s but sold up during World War I.

Some menageries camped alongside circuses to benefit from their crowds. Younger family members saw that the future lay in training their animals to perform and they became lion tamers. There was a thin line between menageries, which had Lion tamers and Lion Queens, and circuses. After World War II, the 'menagerie' was really only the circus putting their wild animals on show to the public between performances in the ring.

In 1899 the Purchase family, in the menagerie business since Andrew Purchase (1802–79) started the business, had a good collection of animals in five or six cages, with the additional attraction of three wagons of waxworks. Andrew Purchase the second went into partnership with his brothers in Purchase Brothers' Circus and Menagerie which, with 20 wagons in total, travelled in fourteen countries for eight years. When he died in 1909, his son, Andrew the third, continued to travel with four brothers and a sister. By 1912 this was stated to be only one of two, the other was Sanger's circus, with a combined circus and menagerie on tour in Britain.

John Purchase joined G. B. Chapman's menagerie and circus as general manager for the 1928–29 season. The menagerie could tour from February onwards, but the show did not get on the road until the weather improved. The menagerie wagons were arranged in a square with a ridge pole down the middle and canvas over the top. The menagerie trainers showed off the lions and tigers, monkeys, etc in the animals' living quarters in the wagons. In 1932 Tommy Purchase was mauled by a lion and died. Rosie Chipperfield (née Purchase) carried on the show, which was now a part of the circus. The Chipperfield family continued in the circus business, but was off the road for most of the war. They included animals in their circus when it resumed touring and showed them between performances, as did Billy Smart, who entered the circus business in 1946. These interval side-shows gradually died out, and with them the word 'menagery'. Even the genuine menageries, private collections of animals shown for profit, were re-branded as 'Safari Parks' and those with a more serious scientific purpose called themselves 'zoos'.

Dealers

Importers and traders in animals continued as before in the first half of the 20th century, the largest businesses belonging to William Cross and Jamrach.

William Cross of Liverpool was a menagerist and major importer and dealer for menageries and zoos in Britain. He worked in Liverpool, with a large staff and agents in all parts of the world, during the last quarter of the 19th and into the 20th century. Both William, and his son William Simpson Cross, drove zebras through the Liverpool traffic. In 1903 a trap harnessed to zebras worked all day for one of the MP's, taking people to the polls. William Simpson Cross, who traded for many years at their menagerie in Earl Street, Liverpool, flourished until 1921 at least. The menagerie was still being advertised when at Otterspool House, Aigburth, Liverpool in October 1917. His stock was very varied, as his advertisements in the *Avicultural Magazine* 1911–17 show.

The Jamrach animal trading business was continued into the 20th century by Albert Edward Jamrach (c.1854–1917) who had premises at 180, St George's Road, London. He wrote of trade lessening here because of fierce competition from German traders c.1910. G. B. Chapman bought his business in 1917 and sold up in 1940, when importing wild animals became next to impossible.

After World War II, new dealers entered the market and are still paying collectors for wild captures, but this trade has been severely regulated by law. The Convention on

CROSS'S
MENAGERIE, LIVERPOOL.

PET ANIMALS ALWAYS IN STOCK.

Lemurs, Coati-Mundi, Jackals, Civets, Ocelots, Caracals, Mongoose, Ferrets, Porcupines, Wombats, Gazelles, Deer of kinds, Antelopes, Shetland Ponies, Tortoises, Lizards, Snakes, Crocodiles, &c.

Monkeys, etc. Chimpanzees, Baboons, Apes, Mandrills, Dogfaces, Sooties, Caratrix, Moustaches, Puttynose, Capuchins, Spiders, Squirrel Monkeys, Marmozeets, Hussars, Jews, Rhesus, &c.

Large Animals. Elephants, Yaks, Camels, Emus, Rheas, Ostriches, Canadian Bears, Japanese Bears, Russian Bears, Wolves, Hyenas, Lions, Tigers, Panthers, Wild Asses, Buffaloes.

A million Cowrie, Tridacna, and giant clam shells, also Curios of every description.

Waterfowl, &c. Swans of kind, Marabous, Cranes, Storks, Gallinules, Ibis, Egyptian Geese, Bernicle, Brent, Canadian, Chinese, White-Fronted, Pink-footed, Barheaded, and other geese. Flamingoes, Peligans, Cormorants, Heron.

Ducks. Tree Ducks, Mandarins, Carolinas, Sheldrakes, Roseybills, Pochards, Pintail, Widgeon, Wild Ducks and fancy varieties of Call Ducks, every kind.

Birds. Talking Grey Parrots, Amazon Parrots, Piping Bullfinches, Hartz Mountain Roller Canaries always in stock, Alexandrine Parrots, Bengal Parrakeets, Conures, Lories, Rose Cockatoos, Slenderbill Cockatoos, Lemoncrest Cockatoos, Quaker Parrakeets, Banded Parrakeets, Madagascar, Red-faced and Australian Love Birds, Macaws, &c.

Falcons, trained and untrained.

Miscellaneous. Small Finches, &c., talking Mynahs, Pies, Weavers, Whydahs, Saffron Finches, Black-throated Finches, Java Sparrows, White Doves, Ring Doves, Tambourine and Blood-breasted Pigeons, Australian Crested Pigeons, South American Spotted Pigeons, Californian Quail, Cardinals, Toucans, Peafowls, Japanese long-tailed Fowls, Silky Fowls, Guinea Fowls, Ornamental Pheasants, Typical Poultry of all varieties.

Please enquire for Wants.

Cables and Telegrams : " Cross, Liverpool."

National 'Phone 6491 Central.

Also at

THE WINTER GARDENS, SOUTHPORT.

William Cross of Liverpool was long established as a 'Wild beast, bird and reptile importer' in Liverpool. This is his advertisement in the *Avicultural Magazine*, 1911.

International Trade in Endangered Species initiated an agreement that came into force in 1975, prohibiting any trade in a category of 8,000 highly endangered species and controls on trading in a further 30,000 species. Well over 100 states have signed this agreement. Controls on standards in collections have also been tightened. A conservation and animal rescue organization in the United Kingdom, The Born Free Foundation, was originated by the two actors in the film about Joy Adamson's lioness Elsa, whom she trained for a return to the wild, described in the book and then film entitled, *Born Free*. This was also a campaign against zoos. The Zoo Licensing Act and Dangerous Wild Animal Act impose severe restrictions on zoos involving careful record keeping of the origins of the animals held in captivity and stud books being kept for the safe breeding of species within a country, rather than importing stock from abroad.

Zoos tried to become self-sufficient by breeding, but are far from accomplishing this. The only way they could cut out the trade would be to limit their stock to animals bred in other zoos. Larger groups of the same species where they are gregarious, rather than just one or two individuals of many species, would be the way ahead and provide much more natural exhibits. (This is not possible for all species, especially those where the male and female only come together for a very short period for breeding purposes, requiring space to house them separately for much of the time). This is necessary because, however good the collector, the wastage while in transit between the country of origin and the zoo is still too high to be tolerated. Pet shops, trading mostly in birds and small mammals, state that they are recycling cage-bred birds, so doing no ecological harm, but that is far from the truth as any opportunity to trade encourages smuggling and smugglers will run the high risks and fines for the most valuable animals, the rarest and often most vulnerable. Any modern book about wild animals in Africa still records acts of poaching and smuggling, so that species once abundant such as lions, elephants and gorillas, to name some of the most popular mammal exhibits, are now endangered.

Royal Menageries

The tradition of presenting the monarch with precious species of animals as presents continues, albeit more rarely, nowadays. Most presents go straight into the care of the Zoological Society.[5]

Buckingham Palace Gardens, once the home of the first royal zebra, is now carefully managed as a conservation area for native plants, birds and mammals. The present garden was designed by William Townsend Aiton in 1825, when asked by George IV to create a more natural landscape. He made a three-acre lake with two islands, planted many trees and built a mound densely planted with trees and shrubs. This is now home to thirty bird species. Nesting boxes and heron platforms encourage breeding and wild flowers with their associated insects are encouraged by cutting the grass only twice a year. The walled garden is truly a natural

A Duck with ducklings hatched in Buckingham Palace Gardens crossing the road to St James's Park. Mallard females, normally resident in St James's Park, move to Buckingham Palace gardens to nest in peace and safety. Female mallards introduce their ducklings to water shortly after hatching. These day-old ducklings cannot fly so have to walk back to the park and need a police escort through the traffic swirling round Buckingham Palace. (*Daily Telegraph,* 4 May 1964).

haven in the centre of London.[6] The sight of a policeman holding up traffic while a mallard duck leads her ducklings, hatched in the palace grounds, across the road to St James's Park, has often featured in newspapers in spring. Providing safe, undisturbed natural habitats, whether in large estates or small gardens, is the way forward for all species in the 21st century.

NOTES

Chapter 1

1. A. L. Poole, 1951. William of Malmsebury, *Gesta regnum,* 1847: 433. Matthew Paris, *Chronica majora,* vol. 3: 324, 334. William the Conqueror had chosen as his English residence the Manor of Woodstock. The earliest note of a foreign animal being kept there was when a bear from Woodstock was given away (Rybot, p.47).
2. Pipe roll 22 Henry II: 91. Poole, ibid.
3. Poole, ibid.
4. Stow, 1720:19, said that it was 1233 when Frederick the Emperor sent to Henry III three leopards, 'in token of his royal shield of arms wherein those leopards were pictures'. Poole, ibid. Glover *Rolls of the reign of Henry III,* c.1250 royal coat of arms has leopards.
5. Maitland, 1756, 1: 171 (Liberat. 36 Henry III.m.4, and Alb. Tur. Henry III.m.15.) 13 September and 29 September 1252.
6. Close Rolls, 37 Henry III, 1251–53. Bayley, 1830: 263, Maitland, p.161, the order was dated 30 October, for a white bear sent to the Tower which had been brought to him as a present from Norway. Rot. Liberat. De anno 37 Hen. III m.15.
7. Foster, p.82. Close Rolls 1254–6: 34, 36 and 1256–9: 256, and Pipe Rolls. Poole, ibid. Paris, *Chronica majora,* vol. V: 489 and Paris also mentioned a camel vol. 3:324, 334. Bailey, p. 263.
8. Maitland, 1756, 1: 147–8. The building housed the royal menagerie until 1834 when it was pulled down.
9. Calendar of Close Rolls, Edward II, orders concerning the lions in the Tower on 26 July 1313, 24 June 1314, 3 November 1314, orders concerning the leopard in the Tower 14 March 1315, 23 October 1317 and 7 November 1318, 6 November 1319 and 23 November 1320. Bayley, 1830, repeats information on lions and adds that the office of Keeper of the Lions and other wild beasts in the tower was at later periods granted by letters patent the fee of 12d per diem and 6d every day was also allowed for the maintenance of each of the lions, lionesses and leopards. Maitland, 1756, repeats information on the leopard. Bayley's original source was Rot. Claus 7 Edw II .m.2, 27, 8 Edw II.m.27, 9 Edw II.m.15, 12 Edw II.m.25, 14 Edw II m. 14 and 18.
10. Close Rolls, 1337–39 Edward III. Berengar Caudrer was keeper of the King's lions and leopards 7 January 1337, Peter de Arragon on 9 August 1339, and he was told that he was 'deputed by the King for the custody of his lions in the Tower of London from which he cannot depart'. Bayley, 1830: 264 gives original sources Rot. Claus. 9 Edw III m.19, 11 Edw III pars.1.m.13 etc.
11. Menzies, 1864. Close Rolls Richard II, 4 June 1380. William de Garderoba is Keeper of his Lions, and there is a young lion present. Hone noted that in 1382 Richard II appointed John Evesham, one of his valets, keeper of the lions, and one of the valets-at-arms in the Tower of London during his pleasure. His predecessor was Robert Bowyer.

12. Loisel, 211. The new Lion Tower that it was originally called the Bulwark, but received the former name from its use.
13. Close rolls, Henry VII, 1485–1509. The office of the keeper of the menagerie was added to that of constable of the Tower, for the sake of emolument. Rymer, XII: 276. Bayley, 263–66.
14. Bolton, 1845, 2nd ed, p.vii.
15. Marmosets belonging to Henry VII. Festing, 1988 *Journal of garden history,* (8) 4: 104.
16. Loisel, p.212 Braybrooke, pp. 146–49.
17. Calendar of State papers, Henry VIII, 1509–47. The Calendar of State Papers is a catalogue of all the domestic state papers from 1547 to1704, arranged by reign containing further statements about the animals imported for the pleasure of the kings and added to the menageries. The information in the calendar varies from complete transcripts of the original text to short summaries.
18. Henry VIII's carved menagerie. Rohde, 1932: 84–5. The heraldic beasts were surmounted gables and parapets of Hampton Court palace and also mounted on pedestals throughout the gardens. The pedestals were painted in green and white stripes, the Tudor colours.
19. Thurston, 1974. Larwood quoted state papers of 1572 about the pond keeper. Hentzner toured England in 1598. Platter's travels occurred in 1599.
20. Kent, p.595.
21. Loisel, p. 212.
22. Historical MSS Commission Reports: HATFIELD MSS part XIV: 281. Foster, 1927, chapter V. *Chronica majora* V: 487.

Chapter 2 1603–1660

1. Kent, p. 595.
2. Ibid. Bayley, pp. 263–66.
3. Minney, pp. 179–80.
4. Bayley, ibid
5. Calendar of State Papers 1604, 1605.
6. Ibid, 1635 Charles I.
7. Hollar etched several species that were included in the works of Francis Barlow, such as *Multae et diversae avium species*, 1655 and *Various birds and beasts, drawn from life*, 1660–70. Referred to by Loisel, p. 13.
8. Thurston, p. 36.
9. Egerton MSS, no. 806 in BM (now British Library).
10. Larwood, p. 328. Braybrooke, p. 151 reports Monconys mentioning the live cassowaries that were first brought to Europe in 1597 by Dutch spice traders and Coryat recording them in England in 1611 in his Preface Verses. Thomas Moufet in 1655 said 'There are some which lately brought hither certain chequer'd Hens and Cocks out of New Guinea, spotted white and black like a Barber's apron whose flesh is like to the flesh of Turkies'. So noting the first occurrence of guinea fowl in Britain.
11. Foster, pp. 89–90 St James's Park.

12. Harting, James E. pp. 423–40. Essays on sport and natural history. James gave an order upon the Treasury, a copy of which, with the bill annexed, is in the appendix to Devon's Issues of the Exchequer (temp. Jas. 1.) James also caught fishes with cormorants in a large pool where he kept wildfowl at Theobald's, his hunting lodge in Hertfordshire. Jackson, 1997: 202–03.
13. Foster, p. 83, 84.
14. Braybrooke, p. 150.
15. Pennant, 1766, vol. 1: 11. Raphael Holinshed, (died c.1580) published *The chronicles of England, Scotland and Ireland*, 2 vols, 1577.
16. Willughby and Ray *Ornithology*, 1678: 329–32.
17. Travels of Peter Mundy, vol. II: 120.
18. Larwood, pp. 330–31.
19. Larwood, p. 333
20. Howell, p. 24. Larwood, pp. 330–31.

Chapter 3 1660–1685

1. Evelyn, 6 February 1685 (de Beer edition IV: 410)
2. Larwood, p. 345 noted the pheasant walk, also (p. 342) that a visiting Dutchman saw Charles II frequently swim in the canal. Timbs, p. 591 and Braybrooke, p. 158 and Wheatley, vol. 1, p. 187, wrote of birds in Bird Cage Walk.
3. Monconys, 1663 vol 2: 22–3, 53. Mundy, vol. V: 155–57. Edward Browne in Sir Thomas Browne, *Works*, edited by Wilkins, i: 50 (in 1664).
4. Mundy, vol V: 156–58. Evelyn, 9 February 1665.
5. Walter Charleton *Onomasticon zoicon*, 1668: Aves, 61–117.
6. Foster, pp. 89–90.
7. Mundy, ibid, p.158.
8. Foster, ibid.
9. Mundy, ibid,
10. Foster, p. 92.
11. Foster, p. 94–5.
12. Bayley p. 309 refers to Colley Cibber (1671–1757) who was an actor and dramatist and from 1730 Poet Laureate. Timbs, p.12 confirms this, 'In the 1660s in the park there were flocks of wildfowl breeding about the Decoy, antelopes, an elk, red deer, roebucks, stags, Guinea fowls, Arabian sheep &c; and here Charles II might be seen playing with his dogs and feeding his ducks'.
13. Wheatley, vol. ii: 292.
14. Larwood, p. 350.
15. Uffenbach, 29 June, 1710, p. 79.
16. Ibid, 3 July 1710, p. 91.
17. J G Wood, *Illustrated natural history*, n.d. p.361. Braybrooke, p. 165 said the white raven was seen up to 1695 and not mentioned thereafter. Larwood, p. 370, said it was old and famous.
18. Mundy, 12 Sep. 1660, vol V: 122.
19. Pepys 30 May 1663. Will Stankes looked after his father's land at Brompton. He had brought horses from the country to London for Samuel.

20. Routh, pp.220–21; 224, quoted *Memoirs of Sir John Reresby*, p.201, also BM Add. MSS 19872 f.81. (now British Library).

Chapter 4 1685–1714

1. Narcissus Luttrell, (1657–1732) compiled *A brief historical relation of state affairs from September 1678 to April 1714*, published in 1857 in 6 vols, see 8 February 1686.
2. Larwood, p. 370. Braybrooke, p.165.
3. Celia Fiennes, visit made c.1701, p.305.
4. Uffenbach, p. 12. Zacharias Conrad von Uffenbach, the eldest son of Johann B von Uffenbach a prominent citizen and senator of Frankfurt am Main was born 22 February 1683 and well educated. He began his research journeys in 1702 and travelled extensively, visiting England with his brother, landing on 5 June 1710 and remaining for five months. He purchased books and manuscripts on a large scale, so that by 1711 he owned 12,000 books and in 1720 published an extensive catalogue. He died 6 January 1734.
5. Loisel, p.13, in 1708 there were 11 lions, 2 leopards or tigers, 3 eagles, 2 owls, 2 mountain cats and 1 jackal.
6. Luttrell. Ibid., 6 July 1708.
7. Uffenbach, pp. 38–9.
8. La Roche, p.118. Louise de Kerouille was Charles II's mistress and their natural son was created Duke of Richmond (who also had a menagerie, q.v.)

Chapter 5 1714–1760

1. Saussure, letter dated 17 September 1725, p. 48.
2. Ibid, letter dated 14 January 1726, p. 138.
3. Ibid. letter dated 16 December 1725, p. 50.
4. Jesse, vol.1: 147–48.
5. Delany, Bulstrode 14 September 1756, 8 November 1760, 22 July 1773. Bustrode was the second seat of the Dukes of Portland, their main residence being Welbeck Abbey. Knowing how fond his wife was of birds the duke had aviaries made for her at Bulstrode, their second seat in Buckinghamshire. References to Bulstrode and the Duchess of Portland are numerous in Mrs Delany's letters.
6. Larwood, p. 407.
7. Ibid., 401, 401.
8. Braybrooke, p. 170.
9. Walpole, *Correspondence,* vol XX, 9 feb 1751
10. *Tower of London*, 1830, issued by the Tower.
11. Hone, column 1004 The Lions in the Tower, also column 1035.
12. Ritchie, p. 123.
13. Maitland, vol.1: 172.
14. Ibid.
15. Edwards illustrated a quagga (pl. 223) alongside a male zebra, assuming it to be a female zebra. Pennant (1793, 1: 14–14) correctly separated the quagga from the zebras but did not illustrate it. He said Sir Joseph

Banks had enabled him to clarify the distinction from having seen quaggas alive at the Cape in 1771. George Forster in his translation of Sparrman's *Voyage to the Cape of Good Hope 1783*, published 1785, vol. 1: 223, named 'One of the animals called quagga by the Hottentots and colonists'. *Nature* 11 October 1974: 468/2 noted that the last quagga died in the Amsterdam Zoo in 1883, but it is thought that this one had outlived by several years the wild quagga in South Africa.

Chapter 6 1760–1820

1. La Roche, 1786 p. 253.
2. Bullock, 1819.
3. Collenette, 1937.
4. This cloth for the elephant was the subject of Records of the Lord Chamberlain's Dept. PRO LC 9/310 (130, 'Richard Harris made this cloth for the elephant').
5. Tower of London. *A visit to the Tower*, 1820, Of the Lions and other wild beasts in the Tower, pp. 13–16.
6. Richard Howe (1st Earl, 1726–99) First Lord of the Admiralty, took command of the Channel Fleet when war broke out with France in 1793 and in an engagement with the French off Ushant won a famous naval victory 1 June 1794.
7. Pennant, 1790, p. 391. He saw the black panther in April 1787 and had an engraving of it done for his *History of quadrupeds*, p.283 tab. lv.
8. La Roche, 1786, p. 126.
9. Ibid.
10. Coke, vol. 1: 208.
11. Larwood, p. 369, and Braybrooke, pp. 308–09.
12. Larwood, chapter XXX 'A celebrated aquatic character'. Braybrooke, p.176. Watkins, 1819, vol.1: 184–85.
13. Records of the Lord Steward, LS 10/4, PRO. (Now National Archives).
14. Walpole, Horace on Kew in his journals of visits to country seats, Annual volume number 16, 1927–8: 9–80.
15. Loisel, vol. 1: 38–39 said of the Duke of Cumberland, 'We have heard that his menagerie commenced *c*.1764 when 16 July an Eastindiaman brought home a number of animals for the Duke of Cumberland, including 2 tigers (or cheetahs?). He liked to see his animals fight and several times after receipt of the tiger he went to see these animals chase their prey and had one of the tigers placed in a kind of arena surrounded by fencing, and a deer was put inside. The tiger chased the stag which used its horns to good effect on three separate attacks and the tiger retired beaten. The stag took refuge under the fence but was given no peace, for a herd of deer trapped it in and the stag promptly killed one. The Duke finally decided to give the stag its freedom after placing a large golden collar round its neck'.
16. The 1st Lord Thomas Erskine, (1750–1823) who was 1st Baron Erskine, raised to the peerage in 1806 when he became Lord Chancellor. On the lawn at Oatlands he met a monkey with long white flowing hair, raised his hat, and bowing three times said, 'Sir, I sincerely wish you joy – you wear your wig for life'.

17. Watkins, p.496. Pennant, *Quadrupeds* 1793, 2: 29, plate LXIV, Kangaru. 'In the spring of the present year I had opportunity of observing the manners of one brought to the capital alive. It was full of health, very active, and very mild and good natured'.

Chapter 7 1820–1901

1. Bennett, p. 181
2. Richardson, p. 312. Scherren p. 29 quotes address to the Zoological Club of the Linnean Society in November 1827 describing the giraffe and another description appeared in the *Literary Gazette*, 1 December 1827 stating that R B Davis had many opportunities of closely observing the animal while painting its portrait for George IV and he described its limbs as deformed by the treatment it had experienced at the hands of the Arabs on its overland journey from Sennaar to Cairo, confined on the back of a camel after they had, 'huddled it together for this purpose, they were not nice in the choice of cords or the mode of applying them'.
3. Letters of Queen Victoria, ed. Benson and Esher, vol.1: 15–17, quoted in Richardson, p.313.
4. Richardson, p.304 quoting William Monk *The life of Sir Henry Halford, Bart.* 1895. A royal warrant was dated 19 May 1827. His seat was Wistow Hall, county Leicester.
5. Richardson, p. 304, quoting Letters of George IV, 1812–30, edited by A Aspinall, 1938: 255–56, Letter dated 12 July 1827.
6. While the buildings were being erected by Decimus Burton in Regent's Park, the exotic animals already donated to the Zoological Society were looked after by keepers at the Tower zoo and Exeter 'Change.
7. Scherren, p.44. There were 627 animals in cages in 1829.
8. Ibid, p.201.
9. Mendelssohn, letter to his mother after his return to Germany, quoted in B. Wilfred Blunt, *On wings of song: a biography of Felix Mendelssohn*, 1974, pp. 224–25.
10. Queen Victoria, *Private life of the Queen*, 1897, chapter XIII, The Queen's Pets, pp. 142–52.
11. The Reverend Edmund Saul Dixon of Cringleford was an authority on poultry and the author of *Ornamental and domestic poultry.*
12. Scherren, p.236.
13. Mute swans have a life expectancy of about 21 years.

Chapter 8

1. Strutt, p. 241.
2. Sir Hamon L'Estrange of Hunstanton, Norfolk (1583–1654), BL Sloane MSS, 1839.9.5: 9. Benjamin Harry, 1681, BL Sloane MSS 3668, and quoted in Errol Fuller, *Dodo from extinction to icon*, 2002, p. 69, p. 75.
3. Sparrow, *British sporting prints,* p.33 quotes from Thoresby 22 September 1677. The Verney memoirs, vol. 2:375 also quoted in Foster *John Company*, pp. 84–5.

4. *London Gazette*, 13, 20, 30 October 1684. She remained on exhibition until 4 April 1686, (ibid. 22 March 1686).
5. Evelyn saw the camel in 1661, vol. 3: 27.
6. Wheatley, vol. 1: 4.
7. Wroth, p. 34.
8. Pennant, *Quadrupeds*, 1793: 198, Pl. 198, Lion-tailed baboon Simia veter.
9. Timbs, p.32.
10. McKechnie, p.52.
11. Pepys, 31 August 1661 first visit, 4 September 1663 took his wife.
12. Sarah Spencer, afterwards, Lady Lyttleton, *Correspondence*, 1912.
13. Edwards, *Gleanings*, 1757, Part 1, *Stephanoaetus coronatus* Crowned eagle.
14. Thomas Bewick, 1970, letter to John Bewick, dated 9 January 1788.

Chapter 9

1. *Notes and Queries*, 1808, series 1, IX, 6: 517 Polito. High Wycombe.
2. Frost, pp. 241–42.
3. Spencer *see* Lyttelton *Correspondence*, 1912: 286 Van Amburgh.
4. George IV lion/tiger 'greatest curiosity of the beast world' McKechnie, pp. 211–13.
5. Frost, p. 302, pp. 304–05.
6. McKechnie, p. 220. Hone, vol.1, columns 1175–9. Wombwell had winter quarters in East Anglia and the Ipswich Museum acquired several specimens from Wombwell when his animals died.
7. E. Stirling, *Old Drury Lane*, 1881 pp. 24–5.
8. Hood, *Ode to the Cameleopard*, p. 183.
9. Sir Robert Heron, 1850: 331.
10. *The Times*, 1850: 27 November, 7.f. Obituary of George Wombwell. *Gentleman's Magazine*, 1851: 420 obituary of George Wombwell.
11. Frost, p. 310.
12. Ibid. 363.
13. Ibid. 377.
14. Kilvert, vol. 2, 7 May 1872.
15. *Verses addressed to Mr Wombwell, the great menagerist,* by the author of *The trip to Tipree when exhibiting at Weldon Fair.* 1938.
16. Bostock, 1927, p. 12.
17. *Illustrated London* News 19 January 1850, wood engraving of the Death of the Lion Queen.

Chapter 10

1. Smith, 1845 p. 107
2. *Pictures of London*, 1808 pp. 287–89.
3. Sir Charles Blagden to Banks October 1802, Banks's Letters. Blagden was an Edinburgh physician who sent specimens and copious notes on the birds of the American colonies while acting as physician to British forces there. He was on the Delaware river from 1777–86.
4. Bullock, 1819, Catalogue of the London Museum of Natural History.

5. Bennett, 1829. Jardine, Sir William *The natural history of monkeys*, Naturalist's library series, 1833.
6. M. R. Audubon, *Audubon and his journals*, vol.1: 279–81.
7. Hood, Poems, *Monkey martyr*, p. 147.
8. Byron, 1832, 2: 256.
9. Hood, ibid Remonstratory ode from the elephant at Exeter Change to Mr Mathews at the English Opera House, p.96.
10. Bartlett, 1898.
11. *Zoological magazine*, 1833: 96.
12. Thornbury, vol. VI: 265–66.

Chapter 11

1. Coke, vol 2: 433, 'I looked into the Sydney papers, & found the will of the Duchess of Northumberland who is buried at Chelsea . . . The number of legacies are prodigious: one I must mention. She leaves to the Duchess of Alva her green Parrot, having nothing, she says, more worthy of her. Such a legacy would not be acceptable now, though I dare say it was then'. This refers to the wife of the Duke of Northumberland, Jane, daughter of Sir Edward Guildeford. Northumberland and his son were beheaded in 1553, immediately after the accession of Queen Mary. The duchess died in 1555.
2. Harrison *Historie of England* vol. iii: 17.
3. Letter from Robert Laneham to Master Humphrey Martin, mercer of London, written during Queen Elizabeth 1's visit to Kenilworth Castle, Warwickshire in 1575. Quoted by Rohde, 1932, p. 82.
4. Bacon, 1626.
5. Lovell, 1687. Thévénot's *Travels* ii: 105.
6. Margaret Calderwood, 1756, in Coltness Coll. p. 186.
7. Evelyn diaries Sir Thomas Fowler, 8 May 1654. Eltham 14 July 1664. Ham 27 August 1678. Evelyn's own aviary at Sayes Court, visited by Marquis of Argyle and Lord Lothian, 14 June 1656.
8. Pepys's starling, 22 April 1668. Mynah bird, 25 April 1664, described, but not named. (Lady Mary Coke is credited with first naming this bird in English literature according to the Oxford English Dictionary, in her journal 11 August 1769 (*Journals* vol. 2: 131) but it had been etched earlier by Eleazar Albin (*Natural history of birds*, 1738, 2, pl. 38) and George Edwards (*Natural history of uncommon birds*, vol.1, pl.17 dated 25 September 1740 and called a 'minor bird' by him). Earl of Clarendon 27 August 1667.
9. Pepys, 27 August 1667.
10. Fiennes, p. 173
11. Ibid. pp. 228–29.
12. Ibid. pp. 97–8.
13. *London Gazetteer*, 1685, no. 2077/4.
14. Bogdani, 1691, British Museum, Additional MSS 22950.
15. Baker, 1949, pp. xvi, 39, 45, 64, 127, 185, 270.
16. Festing, 1987, p. 125. The Longleat menagerie was got rid of in 1734, by sending eagles and vultures to the Tower and killing the bear.

17. Jackson, 1985, pp. 88–102.
18. George Edwards, *Gleanings A natural history of uncommon birds.* Otis arabs (1743, pt. 1) 'This bird was kept alive many years by my honoured patron Sir Hans Sloane Bart at his house in London. It was brought from Mocha in Arabia Felix and presented to Sir Hans Sloane by Charles Dubois, treasurer to the India company. Otis arabs. Not yet described'. Spotted Greenland dove or 'black guillemot' (1743, pt. 1). 'Sir Hans Sloane kept it alive some time, given to him by Captain Craycott who brought it directly from Greenland'. Cock Padda or Rice bird was *Padda oryzivorus*, the Java sparrow (1743, pt. 1, pl. 41) 'I saw one of these at Sir Hans Sloane's: they came from China'.
19. Brett-James, *The life of Peter Collinson,* pp. 81–2.
20. Edwards, 1743, pt. 1 Pl. 5 Black parrot from Madagascar, presented by Charles Wager to Duke of Richmond who employed George Edwards to draw it May 1742. 'I believe it has not yet been described'. Triangular spotted pigeons from Guinea, Edwards ibid. pt. 2.
21. March, pp. 138–39. 2nd Duke of Richmond.
22. Lennox, 2nd Duke of Richmond. BM Sloane MSS 1839.5.1 f. 54.
23. March, ibid.
24. Edwards, *Natural history of uncommon birds*, i: xvi.

Chapter 12

1. Rolfe, W.D.I. 1983 William Hunter (1718–83) On Irish 'elk' and Stubbs's 'moose'. *Archives of natural history*, II (2): 263–90
2. Walpole, *Journals*, 1927/8, vol. XVI: 9–80 Visits to country seats.
3. Ibid. vol. 7 (1928) p.53. Walpole *Correspondence*, vol.10: 334. Jackson-Stops, pp. 2–7.
4. Edwards, *Gleanings,* January 1761
5. Edwards, pp. 157, 159.
6. La Roche, Hastings at Beaumont Lodge, pp. 268–70.
7. Clive of India, Walker, 1968, pp. 92–93. He brought porcine deer from Bengal (or hog deer from the thickness of their bodies). Tobacco-stoppers were made from their feet as well as those of musk deer and antelopes.
8. John Byng, Torrington diaries 4 vols covering 1781–94. 14 August 1787
9. Loisell, vol. 2: 16.
10. Longleat, Llanover's Delany letters, from F. Boscawen to Mrs Delany 25 September 1783, vol. VI: 141–42. Burnett, p.103. Lady Weymouth of Longleat was the daughter of the Duchess of Portland.
11. Powys, 1899.
12. Delany, Bulstrode references,October 1754, 14 September 1756, 8 November 1760, 22 July 1773, August 1774, 1777. The Duchess of Portland (who was the Dowager Duchess when Mrs Delany stayed at Bulstrode with her each spring and summer 1768–1785) was the daughter of Edward Harley (1689–1741) the 2nd Earl of Oxford, who had had a small menagerie at Wimpole.

13. Powys, Bulstrode, pp. 120–21.
14. John Hunter (1728–93) was Scottish and the founder of scientific surgery. The animals in his museum and the preparations, including their skeletons, formed the basis of his anatomy lectures and his own museum that he built in 1785 and then, finally, the collection of 10,563 specimens was presented to the Royal College of Surgeons. Two-thirds of the collection was destroyed when a bomb hit the building in 1941.
15. Dobson, 1962, John Hunter's animals, *Journal of history of medicine*, 17: 479-86.
16. Dobson, 1959, John Hunter's artists, *Journal of history of medicine*, 9: 138–49.
17. Middleton, p. 342.
18. Church, unpaginated and illustrations unnumbered. Volume 1 nylghau and orang-utan, vol. 2 leopard.
19. Jackson, 1998: 37–74.
20. Walpole, vol.16: 9–80.
21. Jackson, 1985: 122–35 William Hayes.
22. Powys, 120, the temple owned by Owen T Williams near Marlow, Lady Ailesbury.
23. Walpole *Correspondence*, vol. 35: 282, 286, 289, 293, 320, 335. The Earls of Strafford lived at Wentworth Castle, Yorkshire. Lady Mary Cook's sister Anne, was Countess of Strafford. Coke, vol. 1: xlviii.

Chapter 13

1. Taylor, p. 159
2. Thompson, Francis 1949, *A history of Chatsworth*.
3. Burne-Jones, Edward. 1904, 2 vols. *Memorials of Edward Burne-Jones*, vol.1: 162–63. The first specimens of wombats to reach Britain were donated by the second Governor of the Australian colony from 1795 to 1801, Governor John Hunter (1738–1821), to the Literary and Philosophical Society of Newcastle in 1798 and this animal was figured by Thomas Bewick in his *History of quadrupeds*, 1800.
4. Clemency Fisher, 2002 Papers of the Earls of Derby deposited in Liverpool Public Library and Liverpool Record Office.
5. Stevens, J. C., 1851. *Atheneum*, Knowsley collection sale, November, p. 986.
6. The dealings between the 2nd Earl Fitzwilliam and Robert Heron are referred to in Heron's *Notes*. Wentworth Woodhouse, formerly the seat of Charles Watson Wentworth, Marquis of Rockingham (1730–82) where `Pennant saw a moose in the 18th century', was owned by the senior branch of the Fitzwilliam family in the 19th century.
7. Heron's *Notes* on his menagerie were taken from his journals from 18 November 1812 until December 1851. These contained scattered jottings of his days in parliament as an MP, family details, menageries records and items of news.
8. Hamilton, 1896. *The Pall Mall Magazine* X, September–December: 48–61.

9. Chalmers-Hunt, under 1896.
10. Forbes, 1833, p. 285.
11. Lyttelton, 1912.
12. Pückler-Muskau, 1832: year 1826.
13. Scherren, p. 69. Duke of Bedford to Yarrell.
14. Russell, John Robert, 13th Duke of Bedford 1959, Woburn rare animals, pp. 14, 18–19, 163.

Chapter 14

1. Edwards, *Gleanings,* 1760, vol. 2: 122, under Calandra. Brookes in London Directories 1775, 1791. Advertisement BM (L23 c.3) *circa* 1775.
2. Thomas Pennant, in British Zoology and Quadrupeds refers several times to birds and mammals seen at Mr Brookes', including White eyelid monkey and spider monkeys.
3. William Henry Herring married Ann Flowry in 1813 and had a son William Cross Herring, born 1821. William Henry took over the shop from Brookes and was succeeded there by his son, William Cross Herring who married Mary Gerrish in 1846, so the Mrs Herring whom Agasse painted c.1838 was the wife of William Henry. William Cross Herring, aged 59, was noted in the 1881 census as a 'retired naturalist'. They were registered as dealers in Euston Road up to 1872, but gone in 1881.
4. La Roche, 1786, pp. 96, 133.
5. Coke, pp. 130–31, 137, 135.
6. Faulkner, p. 432. London Directories 1791–1811. Lysons vol.II, pt 1: 148.
7. London Directories. Lord Stanley (13th Earl of Derby) bought extensively from Castang between 1807 and 1814.
8. Heron, *Notes* 1852, entry for 17 June 1815.
9. Jacques-Laurent Agasse, 1989, Tate Gallery, pp. 31, 38, 39, 68.
10. Pidcock's menageries at fairs c.1769. Menagerie at Exeter 'Change 1793–1817 when Cross bought it. Pidcock sold birds from Exeter 'Change address.
11. William Yarrell the naturalist and author of books on British fishes and British birds, referred to in Lord Derby correspondence, 1850, the dealer being Thomas Andrews, 'a cage manufacturer, wire worker, dealer in foreign and British birds, animals &c gold & silver fish, birds and beasts preserver, at 17 Old Compton Street, Soho, & Conservatory, Pantheon, Oxford Street'.
12. International Genealogical Index: Yorkshire. Census of England and Wales, 1841, 1851, Brewer Street, London. London Directories 1760–1852.
13. Personal letter to the author from Herman Reichenbach of Hamburg, 2001.
14. Wheatley and Cunningham, vol II: 366.
15. *Nature,* January 1870: 317.
16. Jones, Harry, *East and west London*, 1875, pp. 127–31.
17. Ibid, p.131
18. Foster, p. 87.

Chapter 15

1. Rothschild, 1983.
2. Oliver Graham-Jones, 2002.
3. Pendar, 1991
4. Cherfas, 1984.
5. The Windsor Safari Park, despite its name, was not a royal menagerie. It was established by the circus family of Smart in 1970 on a site near Windsor Great Park, but was short-lived, being closed in 1992 when all 600 animals were sold.
6. Peter Coats, *Gardens of Buckingham Palace*, 1978.

BIBLIOGRAPHY

Place of publication, London, unless otherwise stated.

Ackerman, R. 1812 *Repository of arts, literature, commerce, manufactures, fashions and politics.*

Agasse, J.-L. 1989 *Tate Gallery exhibition catalogue.*

Allingham, E. G. 1924 *A Romance of the rostrum: being the business life of Henry Stevens and the history of 38 King Street, together with some account of famous sales held there during the last 100 years.* (Sale of Surrey Zoological Gardens menagerie pp. 38–39).

Altick, R. 1978 *The Shows of London.*

Atheneum 1851 Knowsley collection sale, November: 986.

Audubon, M. R. 1897 (reprint 1986) *Audubon and his journals,* 2 vols.

Bacon, F. 1626 *Sylva sylvarum, et Nova Atlantis.* Amstelaedami.

Baker, C. H. C. and Muriel I. 1949 *The Life and circumstances of James Brydges, first duke of Chandos, patron of the liberal arts.* Oxford.

Banks, *Sir* J. 1958 *Banks' letters: a calendar of the manuscript correspondence of Sir Joseph Banks preserved in the British Museum, the British Museum (Natural History) and other collections in Great Britain;* edited by Dawson, W. R.

Barjaud, J. B. B. and Landon, C. P. 1810 *Description de Londre et ses édifices* [in 1802]. Paris.

Bartlett, A. D. 1898 *Wild animals in captivity.*

Bayley, J. 1771 *Tower of London – historical description of the Tower and its curiosities.*

Bayley, J. 1792 *Guide to the Tower of London.*

Bayley, J. 1820 *Tower of London – a visit to the Tower: an account of the birds and beasts.*

Bayley, J. 1830 *History and antiquities of the Tower of London.* (pp. 263–266).

Bedford, J. R. R., 13th Duke of, *see* Russell, J. R., 13th Duke of Bedford.

Bennett, E. T. 1829 *The Tower Menagerie.* Printed for Jennings, R. & sold by Wakeman, W. F.

Bewick, T. [1970] *Thomas Bewick, engraver of Newcastle, 1753–1828: a check-list of his correspondence and other papers.* Newcastle. (Letter to brother John 9 January 1788).

Bewick, T. 1790 *A General history of quadrupeds.* Newcastle.

Bielfeld, *Baron von* 1763 *Lettres,* 2 vols (visit in 1741).

Bolton, J. 1845 *Harmonia ruralis.* 2nd ed (p.viii Henry VII's parrot).

Boreman, T., *pubr. see Curiosities in the Tower of London.*

Borg, A. 1977 Monkey business at the Tower. *Country Life* May 26 pp. 1418–1419.

Bostock, E. H. 1927 *Menageries, circuses and theatres.*

Boutell, C. 1907 *English heraldry.* 10th ed.

Braybrooke, N. P. B. 1959. *London green: the story of Kensington Gardens, Hyde Park, Green Park & St James's.*

British Museum 1681 Additional MSS 19872 f. 81 (Charles II's ostriches, 1681).

British Museum Additional MSS 22950 (Bogdani on his working methods)

British Museum Egerton MSS no. 806 (Receipt for cleaning St James's Park ponds).

British Museum *Sloane MSS* (MS 1839.5.1f54 Dodo; 4078 f.66 2nd Duke of Richmond).

Britton, J. and Brayley, E. W. 1801–15 *The Beauties of England and Wales,*18 vols.

Broderip, W. J. 1847 *Zoological recreations.*

Brookes, J. 1828 *A Catalogue of the anatomical and zoological museum of Joshua Brookes.*

Brookes, J. c.1775 *Joshua Brookes, zoologist and his menagery in the New-Road, Tottenham-Court – buys, sells and exchanges all sorts of foreign birds, quadrupeds etc. MS notes.*

Browne, *Sir* T. 1835–36 *Works*; edited by Wilkins, S., 4 vols.

Buckland, F. T. 1858 *Buckland's curiosities of natural history.*

Bullock, W. c.1816 *Museum catalogue.*

Burke, *Sir* B. and J. 1841 *A Genealogical and heraldic history of the extinct and dormant baronetcies of England.*

Burne-Jones, E. 1904 *Memorials of Edward Burne-Jones.* 2 vols, (covering 1833–67).

Burnet, D. 1978 *Longleat.*

Burney, F. 1842–6 *Diary and letters 1778–1840.* 7 vols edited by her niece Barrett, C.

Burt, N. 1791 *Delineations of curious foreign beasts and birds in their natural colours; which are to be seen alive at the great room over Exeter 'Change and at the Lyceum in the Strand.*

Byng, J. 1954 *Torrington diaries (Tours of Colonel the Hon. J. Byng 1781–1794 later Viscount Torrington).* 4 vols edited by Andrews, G. B.

Byron, G. G., *6th Baron Byron of Rochdale* 1832 *Byron's works*; edited by Fletcher. 2 vols. (vol.2:256).

Calderwood, M. 1884 *Letters & journals from England, Holland and Low Countries, 1756.* In Coltness Collection (Maitland Club).

Calendar of State Papers, Henry VIII, V (p. 329 civet).

Cameron, D. K. 1998 *The English fair.*

Chalmers-Hunt, J. M. 1976 *Natural history auctions 1700–1972; a register of sales in the British Isles.*

Chambers, R. 1863–4 *The Book of days.* 2 vols.

Chambers, *Sir* W. 1763 *Plans, elevations, sections and perspective views of the gardens and buildings at Kew in Surrey, the seat of Her Royal Highness the Princess Dowager of Wales.*

Chancellor, E. Beresford 1920 *The 18th century in London.*

Charleton, W. 1668 *Onomasticon zoicon.*

Child's companion and juvenile instructor 1846 Religious Tract Society.

Cherfas, J. 1984 *Zoo 2000: a look behind the bars.*

Church, J. 1805 *A Cabinet of quadrupeds from drawings by Julius Ibbetson, engraved by J. Tookey; with historical and scientific descriptions by J. Church.* 2 vols.

Church, R. 1956 *The Royal Parks of London.*

Close Rolls 1254–6: 34, 36, and 1256–9: 256.

Coats, P. 1978 *Gardens of Buckingham Palace.*

Coke, *Lady* M. 1889–96 *Letters and journal 1756–74.* 4 vols edited by Home, J. A. Bath, Kingsmead reprint 1977.

Collenette, C. L. 1937 *A History of Richmond Park with an account of its birds and animals.*

Coryat, T. 1611 *Coryat's Crudities.* (List of sights of London, by Peacham, H.).

Cross, E. 1820 *Companion to the Royal Menageries Exeter Change containing concise descriptions, scientific and interesting, of the curious foreign animals . . . derived from actual observation.*

Curiosities in the Tower of London, 1741.

Daily Advertiser Saturday 5 December 1741. Advt of a rhinoceros.

Daily Post 17 February 1732. Michael Bland's advertisement.

Davenport, H., 2000 *Fanny Burney at the court of George III,* Thrupp, Stroud, Gloc.

Delany, *Mrs* M. G. 1861–2 *Life and correspondence;* edited by Lady Llanover. Series 1, 3 vols, Series II, 3 vols.

Delgado, A. 1972 *Victorian entertainment.* (Surrey Zoological Gardens). Newton Abbot.

Dictionary of National Biography, see Oxford Dictionary of National Biography.

Directories of London 1730–1892, advertisements and list of wild animal dealers, pet-shops etc.

Disher, M. W. 1950 *Pleasures of London.*

Dixon, E. S. 1848 *Ornamental and domestic poultry: their history and management.*

Dobson, H. A. 1924 *Side-walk studies.*

Dobson, J. 1962 John Hunter's animals, *Journal of history of medicine,* 17: 479–486.

Dobson, J. 1959 John Hunter's artists, *Journal of medical biology,* 9: 138–149.

Duck, S. 1733 *Poems on several subjects; the beautiful works of S. Duck to which is prefixed some account of his life and writings, by J. Spencer.*

Durrell, G. 1976 *The Stationary ark.*

Edwardes, M. 1976 *Warren Hastings (1732–1818) King of the Nabobs.* (p.157, 159).

Edwards, G. 1743–51 *A Natural history of uncommon birds and some other rare and undescribed animals.* 4 vols.

Edwards, G. 1758–64 *Gleanings of natural history, exhibiting figures of quarupeds, birds, insects, plants. Most of which have not, till now, been either figured or described.* 3 vols.

Edwards, J. 1996 *London Zoo from old photographs 1852–1914.* Privately published. (2nd Edition, 2013.)

Egerton, J. 1976 *George Stubbs; anatomist and animal painter.*

Evelyn, J. 1955 *Diaries;* edited by de Beer, E. S. 6 vols.

Farington, J. 1922–28 *The Farrington diary 1793–1821;* edited by Grieg, J. 6 vols.

Faujas de Saint Fond, B. 1907 *A Journey through England and Scotland to the Hebrides in 1784;* edited by Sir Archibald Geike. 2 vols. Glasgow.

Faulkner, T. 1810 *An historical and topographical description of Chelsea and its environs.* (Pilton p. 432).

Festing, S. 1987 Animal crackers, *Country Life* vol. 181, 124–5.

Festing, S. 1988 Menageries and the landscape garden. *Journal of gardening history,* 8 (4): 104–17.

Fiennes, C. 1947 *Journey of Celia Fiennes* (in 1689); edited by Morris, C.

Fisher, C. 2002 *A Passion for natural history: the life and legacy of the 13th Earl of Derby*. Liverpool.

Forbes, J. 1833 *Hortus Woburnensis*.

Forge, J. L. 1972 *Oatlands House*. Walton and Weybridge Local Historical Society.

Foster, *Sir* W. 1924 *The East India House: its history and associations*. John Lane.

Foster, *Sir* W. 1927 *John Company*.

Frost, T. 1874 *The old showmen and the old London fairs*.

Gentleman's Magazine. George Wombwell, obit. 1851: 420; 13th Earl of Derby obit. 1852, ii: 190, 644.

Gesner, C. 1560 *Icones avium omnium*. Tiguri.

Gesner, C. 1607 *The histories of four-footed beastes . . . collected out of . . . Conradus Gesner and all other writers to this present day*, by Topsell, E.

Glover's Roll c.1250.

Graham, A. 1969 *Andrew Graham's observations on Hudson's Bay 1767– 1791*; with an introduction by Glover, R.

The Graphic 1875, Mr Jamrach's wild beast depot, 24 July: 92.

Gray, J. E. 1846 *Gleanings from the menagerie and aviary at Knowsley Hall*. Knowsley, Prescot.

Hahn, D. 2004 *The Tower Menagerie*. New York.

Hamilton, *Lord* F. 1896 'The Lilford vivaria', *The Pall Mall Magazine* X, September-December: 48–61.

Harris, J. 1970 *Sir William Chambers*. Lists buildings created by Chambers for Princess Augusta at Kew including Menagerie (1760).

Harrison, W. 1577 *The Description of England, 1577, 1587* in Holinshed's Chronicles I: New Shakespeare Soc 1877 3 vols 1877–1908 (Our costlie and curious aviaries 1577 BM see iii ii 17) [reprint *The Description of England* by Folger, W. H. (documents of Tudor & Stuart Civilization) Ithaca NY 1968]

Harwood, T. E. 1929 *Windsor old and new*.

Hawkesworth, J. 1773 *Voyages*, 3 vols.

Hayes, W. 1794–99 *Portraits of rare and curious birds with their descriptions, accurately drawn and beautifully coloured from species in the Menagery of Child the Banker at Osterley Park near London*. 2 vols.

H. J., Gent., 1875 *The Parlour menageries wherein are exhibited the habits of the animal creation*.

Hedley, O. 1975 *Queen Charlotte*.

Henricus de Huntingdon 1897 *Henrici Archidiaconi Huntendunensis historia Anglorum. The history of the English*; edited by Arnold, T.

Hentzner, P. 1757 *A Journey into England in the year 1598*, translated by Bentley, R.; edited by Walpole, H. Strawberry-Hill.

Heron, *Sir* R. 1850 *Notes: printed but not published*. Grantham.

Hibbert, C. 1971 *Tower of London*.

Hone, W. 1830 *The Everyday book and table book: or everlasting calendar of popular amusements, sports, pastimes, ceremonies, manners, customs & events*. 3 vols.

Hood, T. *Poems* Warne. (The Chandos Classics, The Monkey Martyr p.147, Ode to the cameleopard p.183, Address to Mr Cross, Exeter Change, p. 428, Remonstratory Ode from the Elephant at Exeter Change to Mr Mathews at the English Opera House, p.96)

Howell, J. 1657 *Londinopolis.* (Tower menageries p.24)

Illustrated London News. 19 January 1850 (wood engraving of 'Death of the Lion Queen'), 4 October, p. 405, 11 October, p. 449 (Derby sale).

Jackson, C. E. 1985 *Bird etchings: the illustrators and their books, 1655–1855.* (pp. 88–102 Edwards, G.; pp.122–135 Hayes, W.)

Jackson, C. E. 1997 Fishing with cormorants. *Archives of natural history* 24 (2): 189–211.

Jackson, C. E., 1998 *Sarah Stone: natural curiosities from the New World.* (Sir Ashton Lever and his museum, pp.37–74.)

James, N. G. B. 1925 *Life of Peter Collinson.*

Jamieson, D. 1997 *Chipperfield's circus: an illustrated history.* Buntingford, Herts.

Jerdan, W. 1866 *Men I have known.* (Bullock pp 67–82.)

Jesse, E. 1832–35 *Gleanings in natural history* 3 vols. London. (Richmond Park vol.1: 147–148.)

Jones, H. 1875 *East and west London.* (Jamrach pp. 127–131.)

Jones, O. G. 2002 *Zoo tails.*

Jonson, B. 1630 *New Inn.* (v.i.)

Kent, W. R. G. 1970 *An Encyclopaedia of London*; revised edition by Thompson, G.

Kerry, *Earl of* 1922 *King's Bowood Park.*

Kilvert, F. 1870–79 *The diary of Francis Kilvert,* 3 vols. (Vol. 1, 1870–71; vol. 2, 1871–74; vol.3, 1874–79.)

Kingdom's Intelligencer 5 January 1662/3: 13–16 (list of presents to Charles II).

Knight, C. 1829–31 *The Menageries: quadrupeds described and drawn from living subjects.* 3 vols.

Knowsley 1851 catalogue *see* Stevens

Knox, R. 1681 *History of Ceylon in the East Indies.*

Lambton, L. 1986 *Beastly buildings.*

La Roche, S. v. 1933 *Sophie in London 1786; translated and edited by Clare Williams, being the diary of Sophie v. la Roche.*

Larwood, J. 1881 *The Story of the London parks.*

Latham, J. 1821–8 *A General history of birds,* 10 vols.

Lefevre, M. 1977 *The little Queen of Oatlands. Surrey Life.*

Lever, C. 1977 *Naturalised animals of the British Isles.*

Lever, C. 1992 *They dined on eland: the story of acclimatisation societies.*

Lewis, J. F. 1824 *Studies of wild animals.*

Llanover, *Lady see* Delany.

Loisel, G. 1912 *Histoire des ménageries de l'antiquité à nos jours.* 3 vols. Paris.

London, Tower of 1820 *A visit to the Tower being an account of several birds and beasts.*

Lovell, A. 1687 *Thévénot's travels in the Levant. In 3 parts viz into Turkey, Persia, the East Indies. Newly done out of French by A. Lovell.* Vol II: 105.

Low, D. 1842 *The breeds of the domestic animals of the British Isles.*

Luttrell, N.1857 *Brief historical relation of state affairs from September 1678 to April 1714.*

Lysons, D. 1795–6 *Environs of London: being an historical account of the towns, villages and hamlets within 12 miles of the capital,* 4 vols.

Lyttleton, S. S., *Lady,* 1912 *Correspondence, 1787–1870.*

McKechnie, S. 1932 *Popular entertainments through the ages.*

Magalotti, L., *Count* 1821 *Travels of Cosmo the third, Grand Duke of Tuscany, through England during the reign of Charles the Second (1660).*

Maitland, W. 1756 *A History of London from its foundation to the present time.* 2 vols.

Malcolm, J. P. 1810 *Anecdotes of the manners and customs of London from the Roman invasion to the year 1700.* 2nd ed, 2 vols.

March, C. H. G. L., *Earl of* 1911 *A Duke and his friends: the life of the second duke of Richmond.* 2 vols.

Marvell, A. 1697 A collection of poems on the affairs of the state.

Mather, G. R. 1893 *Two great Scotsmen: the brothers William and John Hunter.* Glasgow.

Melville, L. 1926 *Regency ladies.* (Duchess of York chap XIV.)

Menzies, W. 1864 *History of Windsor Great Park and Forest.*

Mercurius Publicus 1662/3, 8 January: 1–4 Charles II's menagery.

Merriman, J. J. 1886 *John Hunter at Earl's Court, Kensington, 1764–93.*

Middlemiss, J. L. 1987 *A Zoo on wheels:Bostock and Wombwell's menagerie.* Burton-on-Trent.

Middleton, J. 1793 *View of the agriculture of Middlesex.*

Millar, *Sir* O. N. 1963 *The Tudor, Stuart and early Georgian pictures in the collection of H. M. the Queen.* 2 vols.

Miller, D. P. 1849 *Life of a showman.*

Minney, R. J. 1970 *The Tower of London.*

Mirror of literature, amusement and instructions, 20 June 1829 'View of Exeter 'Change' and 7 July 1832 'Surrey Zoological Gardens'.

Monconys, B. de 1665–6 *Journal des voyages.* 4 parts in 2 vols.

Moore, T. J. 1891–2 Opening address on the history of living collections at Knowsley. *Transactions of the Biological Society of Liverpool*, vol.V: 3.

Morgan, P. J. and Brennan, M. T. 1977 Lord Edward Smith Stanley, 1775–1851, X111th Earl of Derby: a review of his biological collections and their importance. *Biology Curators' Group newsletter*, 6: 20–28.

Moritz, K. P. 1789 *Travels in England, 1782*, translated from the German by a lady; reprint of the English translation of 1795 with an introduction by Matheson, P. E. 1924.

Morley, H. 1874 *memoirs of Bartholomew Fair: a verbatim reprint of the original edition.*

Moufet, T. 1655 *Health's improvement: or rules comprising and discovering the nature . . . and manner of preparing all sorts of food used in this nation. Corrected and enlarged by C. Bennet.*

Mundy, P. 1914–36 *The Travels of Peter Mundy in Europe and Asia 1608–67*; edited by Temple, R. C. and Anstey, L. M. 6 vols, published for Hakluyt Society.

Nature 1891 Jamrach obit, September p. 450.

New London Magazine July 1762 (image of zebra)

Notes and Queries 1849–1922 series 1, IX, 6 : 517 Polito. High Wycombe.

Oxford dictionary of national biography: from the earliest times to the year 2000; 2004, edited by Matthew, H. C. G. and Harrison, B.

Papendick, G. E. c.1820 *Kew Gardens, a series of 24 drawings on stone.*

Paris, M. 1872–83 *Chronica majora*; edited by Luard, H. R. 7 vols. (vol. 3: 324, 334, Woodstock).

Parnell, G. 2000 *The Royal Menagerie at the Tower of London.* Royal Armouries and National Geographic Society.

Peachey, G. C. 1924 *A Memoir of William and John Hunter*. Plymouth.

Pendar, L. 1991 *Whipsnade, wild animal park, 'My Africa'*.

Pennant, T. 1781 *History of quadrupeds*., and 3rd ed. , 2 vols, 1793.

Pennant, T. 1790 *Some account of London*.

Pepys, S. 1971–95 *The Diary of Samuel Pepys 1660–69*; edited by Latham, R. and Matthews, W. 11 vols.

Pepys, S. 1926 *Everybody's Pepys*.

Petiver, J. 1702–06 *Gazophylacii naturae et artis*.

Phillips, H. 1964 *Mid Georgian London: a topographical and social survey of central and western London about 1750*.

Pictures of London 1808, 'Pidcock's Museum over Exeter 'Change in the Strand', p. 287–289.

Pipe Rolls 22 Henry III: 91 Woodstock menagerie.

Platter, T. 1937 *Thomas Platter's travels in England, 1599*; translated from German by Williams, C.

Plot, R. 1677 *Natural history of Oxfordshire*.

Pollard, W. 1868 *The Stanleys of Knowsley; a history of the whole family including a sketch of the Rt Hon the Earl of Derby and the Rt Hon the Lord Stanley MP*; edited by Howell, E. Liverpool.

Poole, A. L. 1951 From Domesday Book to Magna Carta 1087–1216. *Oxford History of England*.

Pougin, A. 1885 *Dictionnaire historique et pittoresque du théatre et des arts qui s'y rattachent*. Paris.

Powys, *Mrs* P. L. 1899 *Passages from the diaries of Mrs Philip Lybbe Powys of Hardwick House, Oxon A. D. 1756–1808*; edited by Climenson, E. J.

Pückler-Muskau, *Prince* H. L. H. 1832 *Tour in England, Ireland and France in the years 1826, 1827 & 1828, in a series of letters; translated by Austin, S*. 4 vols.

Raikes, T. 1856–7 *A portion of the journal kept by Thomas Raikes Esq from 1831 to 1847*. 4 vols.

Ray, J. and Willughby, F. 1676 *Ornithologia libri tres*.

Records of the Lord Chamberlains Department (PRO. 9/310 (13))

Records of the Lord Stewards Department (PRO 10/4)

Reresby, *Sir* J. 1734 *Memoirs of Sir John Reresby*. (Charles II's ostriches, p.201)

Richardson, J. 1966 *George IV: a portrait*.

Ritvo, H. 1987 *The Animal estate: the English and other creatures in the Victorian age*. Harvard University Press.

Robinson, L. G. editor 1902 *Letters of Dorothea, Princess Lieven, during her residence in London 1812–34*.

Rochefoucauld, F. de la 1933 *A Frenchman in England, 1784*; translated by Roberts, S. C.

Rohde, E. S. 1932 *The story of the garden*.

Rolfe, W. D. I. 1983 William Hunter (1718–83) 'On Irish "elk" and Stubbs's "Moose".' *Archives of natural history*, 11 (2): 263–90.

Rothschild, M. 1983 *Dear Lord Rothschild*.

Routh, E. M. G. 1912 *Tangier: England's lost Atlantic outpost, 1661–1664*. (Moorish Embassy to Charles II & presents p.220/1, 224)

The Royal Menagerie at the Tower of London, 1999.

Russell, J. R., 13th Duke of Bedford 1959 *A Silver-plated spoon*. (Woburn rare animals, pp. 14, 18–19, 163).

Russell, M. 1905 *A Record of the collection of foreign animals kept by the Duke of Bedford in Woburn Park, 1892 to July 1905.* Transcript in Natural History Museum, London, library.

Rybot, D. 1972 *It began before Noah.*

Rymer, T. 1704–35 *Collection of historical materials known as the Foedera.*

Saturday Review 17 May 1879: 611 Jamrach.

Saussure, C. de 1902 *A Foreign view of England in the reigns of George I and George II;* translated and edited by Mme v. Mayden.

Scherren, H. 1905 *The Zoological Society of London: a sketch of its foundation and development.* (Royal menageries pp.1, 44, 57, 201, 236. Knowsley menagerie, pp. 103, 108, 109, 111, 160. Duke of Bedford pp. 201, 236–237.)

Scott, Sir W. 1939–46 *Journals* edited by Tait, J. G. 3 vols.

Serre, P. de la 1638 *Histoire de l'entrée de la Reine Mere dans la Grande Bretagne.* Paris.

Shepherd, T. H. 1829 *London and its environs in the nineteenth century.*

Sherborn, C. D. 1940 *Where is the . . . .collection?: an account of the various natural history collections which have come under the notice of the compiler . . . between 1880 and 1939.* Cambridge.

Skelton, J. 'To Mistress Mgt Hussey in The Garland of Laurel'. *Complete poems 1460–1529;* edited by Henderson, P. 1931.

Smith, A. R. 1854 *The Pottleton legacy.* Illustrated by Phiz. pp. 57–63.

Smith, J. 1882 *History of the Royal Garden, Kew.* (MS in Royal Botanic Gardens Library.)

Smith, J. T. 1845 *A book for a rainy day.*

Smollet, T. G. 1771 *The expedition of Humphrey Clinker.*

Spencer, *Lady* S., *see* Lyttleton, S. S., Lady

Stevens, J. C. 1851 *Catalogue of the menageries and aviary at Knowsley formed by the late Earl of Derby, K. C., which will be sold by auction by Mr J. C. Stevens on 6 October 1851 and many days following.*

Stops, G. J. 1983 *The menagerie, Horton.*

Stow, J. 1720 *A Survey of the Cities of London and Westminster, corrected by Strype, J.* 2 vols (reprinted 1971).

Stresemann, E. 1975 *Ornithology from Aristotle to the present.* Harvard University Press.

Strutt, J. 1801 *The Sports and pastimes of the people of England.* (Firecrest facsimile reprint 1969.)

Strype, J. 1754/5 *A Survey of the cities of London and Westminster (of J. Stow) brought down to the present time by careful hands.* 2 vols.

Stukeley, W. 1724 *Itinerarium Curiosum: or an account of the antiquities and remarkable curiositys . . . observ'd in travels thro' Great Britain.*

Swainson, W. 1838 *Animals in menageries.*

Tallis, John 1854 *Illustrated London; in commemoration of The Great Exhibition of all nations in 1851.* 2 vols.

Tatler 1709, no.20 25 May.

Taylor, G. 1953 *Old London gardens.* (Reprint 1977: 159 Chiswick.)

Thompson, F. 1949 *A History of Chatsworth.*

Thoresby, R. 1830 *The diary of Ralph Thoresby FRS 1677–1724.*

Thornbury, G. W., and Walford, E. 1873–1878 *Old and new London.* 6 vols.

Thurston, H. P. 1974 *Royal parks for the people.*

Timbs, J. 1855 *Curiosities of London, exhibiting the most rare and remarkable objects of interest in the Metropolis; with nearly sixty years' personal recollections.*

The Times 1850, 27 November, 7f. 'George Wombwell, obit'.

Topsell, E. 1607 *Historie of four-footed beastes.* (Greenwich animals pp. 448–51.)

Turberville, A. S. 1938–39 *A History of Welbeck Abbey and its owners.* 2 vols.

Turner, E. S. 1959 *Court of St James's.*

Turner, J. M. 1995 *Victorian arena, the performers: a dictionary of British circus biography.*

Tusser, T. 1573 *Five hundred points of good husbandrie.*

Uffenbach, Z. C. van 1934 *London in 1710, from the travels of Zacharias Conrad van Uffenbach;* edited by Quarrell, W. H. & Mare, M.

Victoria, *Queen. Private life of the Queen* 1897. (Pets pp. 142–152.)

Walker, T. E. C. 1968 *The Clives of Claremont.* Surrey Archaeological Society.

Walpole, H. 1912–28 *Journals of Horace Walpole.* Walpole Society, Annual volume no 16, 1927/8: 9–80 (visits to country seats) Oxford.

Walpole, H. 1820 *The private correspondence of Horace Walpole, Earl of Orford.* 4 vols.

Watkins, J. 1819 *Memoirs of Her Most Excellent Majesty Sophia Charlotte, Queen of Great Britain.* 2 vols.

Watkins, J. 1826 *A Biographical memoir of his late Royal Highness Frederick the Duke of York and Albany.*

Wendt, H. 1959 *Out of Noah's ark: the story of man's discovery of the animal kingdom.*

Wheatley, H. B. and Cunningham, P. 1891 *London past and present.* 3 vols. (Petty 1: 163 11:366 Jamrach).

William of Malmesbury 1847 *Gesta regum, Chronicles of the Kings of England from the earliest period to the reign of King Stephen,* with notes by Giles, J. A. Bohn's Antiquarian Library. (Woodstock and its animals p. 443.)

Wombwell, G. 1838 *To Mr Wombwell the celebrated menagerist.* ('Verses addressed to him by the author of the Trip to Tiptree when exhibited at Weldon Fair, 1838'.)

Wood, J. G. n.d. *The illustrated natural history.*

Woolfall, S. J. 1990 History of the 13th Earl of Derby's menageries and aviary at Knowsley Hall, Liverpool (1806–1851). *Archives of natural history* 17 (1): 1–47.

Wroth, W. W., and Edgar, A. 1896 *London pleasure gardens of the 18th century.*

Performing animals of the 13th century (Arthur Pougin *Dictionnaire du théâtre*, 1885).

NAME INDEX OF SPECIES

Generic terms only are given when it is not possible to determine their species from the slight descriptions of the animals.

Checklists of species:

Ernest P. Walker *Mammals of the world;* revised by Ronald M. Nowak. 2 vols. 6th ed. 1999. John Hopkins University Press, Baltimore & London.

The Howard & Moore complete checklist of the birds of the world; revised and enlarged by Edward C. Dickinson. 3rd ed. 2003. Christopher Helm.

NAME INDEX OF PEOPLE AND PLACES

ACKNOWLEDGEMENTS

The author wishes to thank the following persons and institutions for permissions to reproduce the following illustrations:

Master and Fellows of Corpus Christi College: Paris's drawing of Henry III's elephant and its keeper.

Trustees of the Chatsworth Settlement: Chiswick House volary, plan of the house and grounds at Chatsworth, portrait of the 6th Duke of Devonshire.

The Right Hon. The Earl of Derby: portrait of the 13th Earl.

Yale Center for British Art, Paul Mellon Collection: Stubb's *Zebra*, drawing of Pidcock's shop on the banks of the Thames, Agasse's *Guanaco.*

National Fair Archive: Bostock, Wombwell.

National Portrait Gallery: Ballantyne's painting of Landseer sculpting the lions for Trafalgar Square.

Elmbridge Museum, Weybridge: Duchess of York's menagerie at Oatlands.

Hon. Miriam Rothschild Collection: Lord Rothschild driving using zebras, Lord Rothschild riding on a giant tortoise at Tring.

'PA' News Centre: A duck with ducklings . . . crossing the road to St James's Park. (Daily Telegraph, 4th of May 1964).

The author's thanks are owed, for their assistance in locating prints and advertisements, to the librarians of the Cambridge University Library, the British Library and the county libraries of Hertfordshire, Suffolk and Cambridgeshire. The author also acknowledges the long and continuing interest of friends and colleagues who have given both encouragement and valuable assistance in locating sources. Particular thanks are given to Dr C.T. Fisher, Professor W. Hale, Hermann Reichenbach, Maureen Lambourne, Len Rogers, Ann Datta and, in particular, to her husband Andrew.

The President of the Ray Society, Dr N.J. Evans, would like to acknowledge the help given by the staff of Henry Ling Ltd in the production of this book and, in particular, to Mr Frank Hemmings for his patience and professionalism in dealing with the production of this and previous Ray Society works during his long career.